THE SURREY UNION HUNT
OUR HISTORY UNBUTTONED

Julian Womersley

THE SURREY UNION HUNT LIMITED
2007

Published by The Surrey Union Hunt Limited

PO Box 797

Crawley

West Sussex

RH11 0WD

First published in 2007

For photographic and picture credits, see page 124

Designed and produced by Nick Onslow

A catalogue in publication is available from the British Library

ISBN 978-0-9555002-0-6

Printed and bound in the United Kingdom by

Edgebury Press Ltd

PO Box 797 Crawley West Sussex RH11 0WD

This book is dedicated to all those who fight against bigotry and prejudice
– wherever it may be found.

For each copy sold, a contribution will be made to the Hunt Staff Benefit Society

"Hunting, for me, is about me and my horse being completely as one, standing in the English countryside absorbing all the sights and sounds around us. It is a shared enjoyment. My most memorable moment was when my horse and I met the hunt whilst out on a hack, before we knew anything about hunting, and suddenly a mutual passion was born."

Penny Wilson

Foreword

by
William and Pippa Funnell

It gives us both great pleasure to write this foreword for several reasons.

For a long time it has been recognised that taking competition horses hunting does them a power of good and that they become much bolder and self-confident as a result.

At a family level, it was particularly gratifying to see that proper recognition has been given to the part John Funnell played in the rescue of the Surrey Union Hunt during his time as joint-Master and huntsman in the early 1990s.

Living as we do in the heart of the Surrey Union country, we are fully aware of all the good work that the Hunt does in so many ways, in addition to the practical help that it provides to farmers.

We both hope that you enjoy reading this book and its wealth of fascinating stories just as much as we did.

CONTENTS

PREFACE

Through a glass darkly …

The recurring theme from the start of previously published histories of the Surrey Union Hunt has been "not much is known about John Leech" or, for that matter, Samuel Godschall either. Not an inspiring beginning, especially as it is generally considered that their actions led to the formation of the Union Hunt. But outwardly they were men of substance – they must have left some trace, surely?

Accordingly, much time has been spent blundering around tracing obscure events in the late eighteenth century, following a lead here, finding a clue there. From evidence that is both incomplete and disparate, trying to discover quite what happened to cause things to turn out just the way they did has proved to be rather like that moment when following hounds: that very moment when the Hunt, so substantial and there but an instant ago, has entirely disappeared out of sight and sound. One is left in a suspended state, half way between solidity and illusion.

And so it has also proved for the Surrey Union Hunt history thereafter. Year after year, decade after decade and eventually century after century, the succession of good men and true [with a goodly sprinkling of like-minded women, too] have proved themselves adept at covering their tracks. Happily for us, just occasionally there is a trace of the missing image; once in a while a handful of fragments knit together. Eventually, here and there, a few individual figures begin to detach themselves from the dark and silence to which time has consigned them. As we draw slowly towards them, sometimes they show a glimpse of their shadowy faces.

Plus ça change …

As the research continued, it became ever more clear that some things never change. The ties that bind the Surrey Union community together and the threads that link them to the wider society in the County still pertain. As ever, these connections run far and wide. Our Hunt remains a potent economic force and source of philanthropy, just as it was a hundred years ago. Our predecessors adapted to the pressures of change – the spread of the London conurbation, the coming of the railways in the 1850s and especially their third rail electrification in the late 1930s, slippery tarmac on the roads and even two World Wars.

And so we, too, adapt today. We draw coverts at the end of the Gatwick runway as jumbo jets thunder overhead, we recognise that the M25 motorway has effectively curtailed our Hunt country to the north and, perhaps most impressive of all, we have accommodated the requirements of the pernicious Hunting Act 2004. Indeed, as this book was being compiled, the Surrey Union Hunt now has more country open to it than hitherto in recent memory.

Yet this book is not just about retrospection. It has provided an opportunity to explore how the past shapes the present and to reveal why our Hunt continues to prosper. And that, one hopes, explains the title of the work.

Ultimately though, this is a celebration of the tenacity shown by the Surrey Union Hunt in the face of social and economic change and a tribute to all those who have helped achieve it.

Julian Womersley

Dorking

December 2006

Shellwood

In this part of Surrey, foxhounds have been an enduring image in the landscape for the best part of three centuries. The view from Shellwood has changed over that time – in 1806 there would have been more sheep and fewer trees on the North Downs skyline, in 1906 more smoke and steam issuing from the chalk pits or the South East & Chatham Railway at the foot of the scarp and in autumn 2006, when this photograph was taken, there is generally more wire and woodland. Yet hounds still hunt on.

Box Hill and the Mole gap leading to Leatherhead lie on the far left, where the Downs dip away.

CHAPTER 1

In the beginning …

"Now where are all your sorrows and your cares, ye gloomy souls! Or where your pains and aches, ye complaining ones! One holloo has dispelled them all."

Thoughts Upon Hunting, Peter Beckford 1781

How true! Although our modern world is immeasurably different in so many ways to the England of George III when these words were first written, the sounds of hunting can still stir the soul and create a passionate following. And it is back to the eighteenth century that one must look to understand how the Surrey Union Hunt came into existence.

Against a background of agrarian and industrial scientific discovery and expansion, hunting in eighteenth-century Surrey was flourishing, with noblemen and country squires keeping their own private packs in the County and enjoying the activity over their own and their neighbours' land.

Of these establishments, perhaps the most grand was that maintained by the 2nd Duke of Grafton at Lovell's Grove, the seat of the Lord Onslow. From 1735, this pack hunted the country around the village of Croydon. Bearing in mind that the Duke's principal residence was Euston Hall, amidst his Suffolk estates, and that the Duke of Richmond was induced to leave his own Charlton Hunt [in Sussex] several times to hunt with these hounds, clearly there was something special to be savoured in Surrey.

But the Duke of Grafton was not the only nobleman to recognise the attractions offered by this part of the County. From recently discovered papers, it is apparent that Charles, Lord Bruce, the 4th Earl of Elgin and 3rd Earl of Ailesbury, of Tottenham House on the southern edge of Savernake Forest, Wiltshire, maintained a kennel of foxhounds in Leatherhead in 1722. The documentary evidence is particularly detailed and it shows the various expenses incurred by his Lordship's huntsman, William Foard [also spelt Ford], and other servants during their three-month sojourn in Surrey. A digest of the more pertinent information contained in these accounts, including the names of the earth-stoppers and their charges, the costs of shoeing and *"for odd things wanting in ye kennel"*, including brooms and antimony, is set out in Appendix:1.

Slightly later, around 1750, flourished a Mr Samuel Gobsall [there are other recorded spellings] of Jacob's Island, Bermondsey, who was decidedly towards the other end of hunting's social scale. His hounds were kennelled variously at East Hill and Mr Dudin's Wharf, Bermondsey. The East Hill premises were curious two-storey stables, of a design prevalent in the London of the time and their remnants managed to survive until about 1900. With his pigtail and wearing a low-crowned hat, Mr Gobsall would take his pack to draw the coverts of Forest Hill and Peckham Rye or the rural vastnesses of Sydenham. As his mounted field was largely comprised of commodity brokers and other similar City types who had to be back *"on the 'Change"* by 4pm, Mr Gobsall is reputed not to have drawn for a fox after one o'clock.

There is a tantalizing reference in a letter book used by a writer masquerading under the pseudonym Stephonius [possibly John Mildred, proprietor of The Talbot, a Ripley coaching inn, or one of his family], where the author observes on 1st March 1752: *"As for hunting I have had very little this season – was out last week with Sir John Elwill*

A Southern Hound

This breed of hound was both heavier and slower than the modern foxhound. According to the notes that originally accompanied this engraving, another difference was *"their dwelling upon a scent, as if enjoying the pleasure of inhaling the perfume. These hounds would absolutely sit down and throw their tongues in the most melodious tone for half a minute when they met with a particularly strong scent, and then go off again until they came to another similar full stop, upon which the same occurred again; and, as a natural result, the frequent stoppages, added to the absolute deficiency of speed, made the dog wholly incapable of running down any animal which has a safe retreat like the fox … …".*

Lea – The Seat of John Leech, from an engraving by G F Prosser, dated 1828. The original caption included the following: "*The interior, though not spacious, is neat and convenient in its arrangement. South of the house the ground rises considerably, from which, looking to the north, a pleasing view is obtained; in the middle distance is seen Pepper-harrow* [sic]*, the noble residence of the right. hon. the Lord Viscount Middleton; beyond is the Hog's-back, being part of a range of hills which run direct into Kent.*"

and found at Boxhill and run for near two hours and killed". As Sir John was a Member of Parliament and came from Exeter, the nature of their relationship is not wholly clear. In another letter, the same writer is trying to buy birds for a cockfight between Sir John and Admiral Boscawen, of Hatchlands, West Horsley – so we may draw our own conclusions! But to whom the hounds belonged currently remains a mystery.

A snippet from an article in the *Gentleman's Magazine* of May 1763 describing Dorking and its environs goes some way, perhaps, to explaining the popularity of the area in this regard. It records that the countryside around the town was well stocked with game, including pheasants, partridge, woodcock and other wild fowl, which provided plenty of sport for those who wished to go shooting. As for hunting, "*Hares and foxes could be found in abundance on Box Hill*". The town was also within ready distance of the Royal Palaces and the seats of power in London, all of which could be easily reached by saddle-horse or carriage in the course of a day, with sufficient time to spare for business or pleasure on arrival.

Occupying a social position somewhere between the two extremes set by the Duke of Grafton and Mr Gobsall was the Leech family, owners of the Lea Park estate, near Witley. The family moved to the area when John Leech, a surgeon from Alton in Hampshire, bought the property in 1764. This John Leech died in 1778 and his son, also called John, died in 1786, intestate. This difficulty seems to have been soon overcome and a grandson, again called John, took over the running of the estate. This family also kept a pack of foxhounds and, ultimately, was to play a key role in the history of our Hunt.

The nineteenth-century social commentator, William Cobbett, was born in Farnham in 1763. In his famous publication, *Rural Rides*, he wrote:

> "*There is a little hop-garden in which I used to work when from eight to ten years old; from which I have scores of times run to follow the hounds, leaving the hoe to do the best it could to destroy the weeds;*"

As Lea and Farnham were about seven miles apart as the crow flies [or a straight-necked fox might run], it is not too much to assume that young William was an early foot-follower of Mr Leech's foxhounds during the years 1771 to 1773. As we shall see, this youthful interest was to remain with him for the rest of his life.

In the latter years of the eighteenth century, the brothers John and Edward Leech employed Matthew Archer as their huntsman and John Hyde as a whipper-in. These two hunt servants will also go on to play larger parts in this account.

Whilst the Leech siblings were hunting the far west of the County, the occupants of Weston House, Albury, also kept a pack of foxhounds in an old farmstead, seemingly "*located up a sandy lane at the back of the village that was known for many years thereafter as Dog-kennel Lane*". Weston House had formerly belonged to Sir Robert Godschall and, following his death in 1742, it eventually passed to his grand-daughter, Sarah. She married William Man FRS, who thereafter assumed his wife's surname. It was their son, the Reverend Samuel Man Godschall, a Doctor of Divinity from Oxford, who maintained this establishment.

The Rev. Godschall employed Will Baker as his huntsman and the two of them, wearing blue coats with black velvet collars, would hunt their eight to ten couple of hounds over a country limited only by the capacity of their cobs. It seems that Mr Godschall was described as being "*shrewd, keen and satirical*". Some commentators have inferred from this that he may have been a somewhat tetchy individual and as a consequence perhaps not too popular with his mounted field. A more likely, and certainly more kindly interpretation is that all three attributes were just as vital to success as a Master of Foxhounds in the 1790s as they are today.

The hounds in these various kennels were the old "Southern Hounds", arguably the progenitors of every other foxhound variety subsequently bred in England. They were often black and tan or blue mottled and, in this extract from *"A Midsummer Night's Dream"* [Act 4 Scene 1, c.1594], William Shakespeare provides an indication of how far removed from the modern foxhound they probably were, notwithstanding the classical allusions:

"My hounds are bred out of the Spartan kind,
So flew'd[1], so sanded[2]; and their heads are hung
With ears that sweep away the morning dew;
Crook-knee'd, and dew-lapp'd like Thessalian bulls;
Slow in pursuit, but matched in mouth like bells,
Each under each. A cry more tuneable
Was never holla'd to, nor cheered with horn ... "

Although slightly outside this immediate historical period, no review of early foxhunting in Surrey would be complete without at least a passing reference to Colonel Hylton Jolliffe and the Merstham Hunt. Foxhunting was clearly part of the family tradition: the Colonel's younger brother, the Reverend William Jolliffe, assisted him with the pack and their father, after returning from a day's hunting on 18th February 1802, had unfortunately stepped backwards through the open trap door of his wine cellar and broken his neck. From 1804, the Colonel determinedly led his Hunt on its peripatetic way across the East Surrey landscape until he finally disbanded it in 1832. With his hounds of all shapes and sizes, the Colonel ranged far and wide. For as long as month at a time they could be kennelled at the Sun Inn in the village of Crawley and hunted as far south as Bolney and Cuckfield.

It must have been quite a spectacle: the Master rode an estimated sixteen stone and wore a capacious dressing gown-like red coat and a low-crowned, glazed hat, whilst his huntsman, 'Old Roffey' [standing *"about six foot and turns the scales at fifteen stone"*] and whipper-in, 'Yorkshire Jack', wore blue plush coats, yellow breeches and brown 'tops'[3]. As an indication of how the Hunt was run and perhaps the increasing difficulty of finding suitable horses for Old Roffey, in December 1830 the Colonel tried to buy *Mademoiselle de Jeck*, a she elephant, from her circus owner for his huntsman to ride out hunting. It was perhaps for the best that these negotiations came to nothing!

This extract from Chapter 1 of *Jorrocks's Jaunts and Jollities* by R S Surtees [published in book form in 1838] paints a vivid picture of one of the erstwhile Merstham mounted field:

"Yonder he goes," cries a cock of the old school, who used to hunt with Colonel Jolliffe's hounds, and still sports the long blue surtout lined with orange, yellow-ochre unmentionables[4] and mahogany-coloured knee-caps, with mother-of-pearl buttons. "Yonder he goes among the ship[5], for a thousand! See how the skulking waggabone makes them scamper."

Of course, that is the beauty of Surtees' writing. From an age long before television and film, we are given not only an account of the narrative action, but also a full description of a character's dress and often, as in this example, how they actually sounded when speaking. In this instance, with conspicuously Cockney overtones!

Hunting was a serious business to the Colonel. In 1818, when he discovered that Mr Maberley, the Master of the Old Surrey, had dug out a fox on his Merstham estate, the matter had to be settled by a duel on Alderstead Heath.

Notes

1 *Flews are the large hanging chaps of a hound.*
2 *That is of a sandy colour.*
3 *Top boots. The "mahogany-coloured knee-caps" in the Surtees reference contained in the succeeding paragraph probably describes the colour of the tops of these boots.*
4 *Breeches. The jocular use of this slang expression [or the similar 'inexpressibles'] in this period should not be confused with later Victorian prudery.*
5 *Sheep.*

Drawn Etch.
by Rich.ᵈ Dighton

The HERO of the CHASE.

May 1819

Pub.ᵈ by T. McLean, Haymarket.

[The site of this dramatic encounter is almost certainly now buried under the northern stub of the M23 motorway.] Thankfully both parties fired wide and they retired to The Great House, the Jolliffe family home on the western outskirts of Merstham, for breakfast together!

Before leaving Colonel Jolliffe, one final thought flows from all this. Was he a model for the redoubtable John Jorrocks MFH? Despite the obvious lack of similarity between a Cockney grocer from Coram Street and a retired Colonel of the Coldstream Guards, a close reading of the Surtees novels rather suggests this is a distinct possibility.

But enough of such speculation! There is controversy enough to come in the next part of this history, based on the doings of real-life personalities rather than any character from fiction.

However, before returning to the main element of this chronicle, it is perhaps appropriate to record the parlous state of the nation at the turn of the eighteenth century. The price of wheat rose from 43 shillings a quarter in 1792 to 126 shillings by 1812. In 1797, Great Britain was left with no economic markets or military allies in continental Europe, it had lost 40,000 troops in disastrous campaigns in the West Indies, faced rebellion in Ireland and the Royal Navy had dealt with mutinies at Spithead and the Nore. Perhaps worst of all, the Bank of England had suspended cash payments.

Against such a background, it surprising that hunting managed to continue at all, let alone flourish. But it did, as the *Sporting Magazine* [founded in 1792, as a *"Monthly Calendar of the Transactions of the Turf, the Chase and every other Diversion Interesting to the Man of Pleasure, Enterprise and Spirit"*] bears witness. In its heyday, this publication was a veritable treasure trove of anecdotes, many of which bear directly on our history and thereby provide a first-rate insight into the times that they describe.

Colonel Jolliffe
The original title of this contemporary portrait of Colonel Jolliffe succinctly describes his predilections. Later in life he went on to greater national prominence as an MP. The hat he is wearing is blocked to his own peculiar style and is designed to throw rainwater clear of the face and away from the back of the neck.

CHAPTER 2

The Union

"It is this union of the elegant courtesies and business of life with the energetic sports of the field, that constitutes the charm of Surrey hunting; and who can wonder that smoke-dried cits [6], *pent up all the week, should gladly fly from their shops to enjoy a day's sport on a Saturday?"*

Jorrocks's Jaunts and Jollities, R S Surtees 1838

From the historical records currently available to us, there are disparate versions of how the Union Hunt came into being and how it got its name. So there is no getting away from it, honesty has to be the best policy and full disclosure will allow readers to make up their own minds on this controversial topic.

The orthodox view is that some time during the closing years of the eighteenth century, and 1798 is the generally accepted year, the Union Hunt was formed by the amalgamation of packs belonging to the Leech family and the Rev. Godschall. As Samuel Godschall is believed to have taken over not only the Leech hounds, but their huntsman and whipper-in as well, one might surmise that something happened to the fortunes of the Lea estate that brought about this change. Perhaps unsurprisingly, the name of the new Hunt is supposed to have come from this merger.

A likely cause of the Leech brothers forsaking their hounds was the passing of an Act of Parliament *"for granting to his Majesty certain duties on dogs"* on 19th May 1796. This imposed an annual tax on dog owners and was particularly punishing on those keeping hounds or working dogs. Whilst the yearly payment due for a single cur dog was three shillings, the sum of five shillings was levied *"for each greyhound, hound, pointer, setting dog, spaniel, lurcher or terrier"* when two or more of these breeds were kept. This tax may also explain why Mr Godschall handed over so few hounds when he disbanded his pack in 1802.

The rather more heretical view on the source of the Union name comes from an article written anonymously [but under the initials H.H.] in *The Field, The Country Gentleman's Newspaper* of 8th January 1870. From the context, it is clear that the author was paying a formal visit to Kennels and the then Master, the Hon. Francis Scott, is credited with supplying the historical details that augment this account. The piece reiterates the point about Mr Godschall receiving the Leech hounds [and others] into his pack in the late 1790s and goes on to say:

"They were incorporated into a regular pack somewhere near the beginning of this century, and received their name in commemoration of that other and not less important incorporation inaugurated at the commencement of the same, and which the hounds seem likely to survive, viz, the "union" between Great Britain and Ireland.
A document now before me [7] *– in short the preliminary articles before the Act of Union – shows that the occurrence was in this wise: On the 7th day of March, 1802, a meeting was held at Hatchlands Park, the seat of Col. George Holme Sumner, long MP for the county of Surrey, and father of a subsequent master, the late much-lamented Col. Wm. H Sumner – Mr Samuel Godschall having announced his intention of relinquishing his country, giving up his hounds, and offering them to any neighbouring gentleman who might continue with them by subscription."*

From this we may fairly conclude that Samuel Godschall did hunt a merged pack for a few seasons either side of 1800, the year of the passing of the Act of Union between Great Britain and Ireland. Yet, by 1802 and just like the Leech brothers previously, he was quite prepared to hand over his pack of hounds to anyone who would take them.

Notes

6   *Eighteenth-century argot for indigenous Londoners [often derogatory], an abbreviation of 'citizens'.*
7   *Oh how one wishes it was available today!*

R S Surtees in old age by G Denholm Armour.
The artist was a subscriber to the Surrey Union Hunt - see also page 35.

The crisis meeting [being the first of many in the history of our Hunt!] held at Hatchlands was attended by several local gentlemen disturbed by this turn of events.

Despite the somewhat shaky start provided by the Rev. Godschall, the outcome of this gathering put the Union Hunt on a sound financial footing, a new Master was found and a fresh draft of hounds was delivered to new kennels. How all this came to pass is explained in the next chapter of this saga.

CHAPTER 3

The Union Hunt in the Early Nineteenth Century

"Foxhunting is a very fine thing, and very proper for people to be engaged in ... "

Rural Rides, William Cobbett 1825

It was another Reverend gentleman, Arthur Onslow JP, who stepped in the breach and accepted the duties of Master. Despite his calling, it seems likely that he was wise to the ways of the world, as the nucleus of new subscribers present at Hatchlands Park, the home of Colonel George Holme Sumner MP, in March 1802 resolved that it was:

"a principle essential to the success and continuation of a hunt that one person should have the entire and absolute direction" and *"... they bound themselves, and all subscribers, to abstain from every species of interference, either in purchase of hounds or horses, in management in the kennel, in the field or in distribution of days or coverts for hunting."*

Wise words indeed and, as we shall see, ones to be heeded in more recent times by members of the Hunt.

As far as monetary matters were concerned, the 25 gentlemen at the meeting subscribed a total of 600 guineas. Together with the promise of new kennels to be provided by Colonel Sumner at East Clandon [believed to be what later became Kennel Farm, west of Hatchlands and somewhat to the north of East Clandon], all these changes enabled the Union Hunt to operate on a proper basis.

Matthew Archer was re-engaged to hunt the hounds, with John Hyde as whipper-in once more. To augment the 5½ couple of hounds provided by Mr. Godschall, drafts were received as follows:

– 12 couple from the Goodwood Hunt [the successor to one of the first packs known to hunt the fox, the Duke of Richmond's Charlton Hunt],
– 7 couple from Lord Egremont's kennels at Petworth,
– One [or possibly two] couple from Lord Berkeley, Master of the Berkeley.

The Reverend Onslow proved to be both popular and capable as a Master and the Union Hunt prospered for the next ten seasons, before he eventually went to live in Kent.

In 1812 it is thought that a Captain Boulton [perhaps an officer in the Royal Artillery] of Givons Grove, Leatherhead, took over the Mastership for a short time [possibly for only one season] and it seems probable that the establishment remained unchanged during this period.

Known as 'The Squire', it was John Barnard Hankey of Fetcham Park that succeeded the Captain as Master. This was the start of an association with the Hankey family that was to last for a century. Such a continuous interest and tradition passed on from father to son is of inestimable value to any Hunt, where knowledge of the country and friendship with the landowners, farmers and country people is essential to success.

In 1814, Mr Hankey moved the hounds from the old premises at East Clandon to new kennels built by him at Fetcham Park and where they were to remain for the next seven decades, bar a ten-year period between 1866 and 1876. However it seems that the lure of faster hunting country in Worcestershire was too strong and Mr Hankey's first Mastership perhaps lasted but one season.

An extract from the Bryant Map of Surrey of 1823. The kennels at East Clandon are clearly marked.

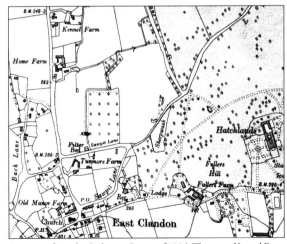

An extract from the Ordnance Survey of 1934. The name Kennel Farm still promotes the association from over 100 years earlier.

When 'The Squire' resigned the Mastership in 1815, Mr Thomas Seawell of Bookham followed him, with Mat Archer and John Hyde still being kept on as the Hunt servants. In view of their long service and because of the other interesting historical details [ranging from social history to medicine] contained therein, it is perhaps appropriate to reproduce this extract describing their exploits from the same article, referred to previously, that appeared in *The Field* of January 1870:

"They were both able and competent men, privileged old favourites, and I fancy both rather preferred the roving habits of hunting of the last century[8] to the more modern system of fixed and stationary kennels. Stories still linger of both of them in the saddle – the deeds of one with the horn, of the other with his whip; with these the villages of Clandon and Fetcham naturally are chiefly redolent. Mat had a quaint, dry way of expressing himself, and no science or knowledge, in his estimation, could be compared with foxhunting. When the Continent was first opened in 1816[9], everybody rushed to Paris, and Mr Seawell, his then master, went there too. On his return Mat said, "Well, sir. How do you find the French? A poor ignorant set, I've always heard; never saw a fox killed in their lives!"

But Mat, too, made his excursions; and once went to see another pack, of which the hounds were said to be very mute, and the master equally noisy and loquacious. One day shortly afterwards, while riding between Clandon and Newlands Corner, he was overtaken by the Earl of Onslow of the day – that lord of four-in-hand and epigrammatic celebrity, of whom it was said or sung:

What can Tommy Onslow do?
He can drive a chaise and two.
Can Tommy Onslow do no more?
Yes – drive a phaeton and four.

"So," my lord said to Mat, "you've been to see Mr R's pack, I hear. Well, how do you like them?"
Mat was rather silent, but my lord who was of an inquiring turn of mind and had a thirst for knowledge, was not to be put off so.
"Come now," said he, "I see there's something wrong; what is the matter?"
"Why, my lord," touching his cap, " there's nothing cheery about them; they've no music, they're all mute, except the master."
"Indeed, and what would be your remedy for that?"
"Why, my lord, I see none, unless you could get them a cross, or vaccinate[10] them with the master, for he has tongue enough for all; and if that don't cure them, I don't know what will."

On another occasion, after a gentleman's horse kicked a hound – a heinous crime in the hunting field, even today – Mat exclaimed in the culprit's hearing, *"If you calls him a man of eddication, be damned to your eddication, say I!"* Strong words indeed from a servant in the late Georgian period – so it seems likely that he must have been respected by the Master for his competence, if perhaps not for his tact.

Matthew Archer was forced to retire from Hunt service through ill health in 1817 and was succeeded by George Hennesey, from Hampshire. He had the nickname "Pop", probably derived from his habit of continually cracking his whip. But perhaps his career in Hunt service did not flourish, as he seems finally to have ended up as a postboy.

Allegedly, Mr Seawell's Mastership came to an end on Derby Day, 1822 and the implication seems to be that a

Notes
8   *That is to say, the 18th century.*
9   *Following the end of the Napoleonic Wars.*
10 *An intervention perfected, in England, by Edward Jenner in 1796.*

disastrous wager was the cause. If this is true, he must have put his money on one of the other 11 runners and not the winner, the Duke of York's Moses at a starting price of 6 to 1, ridden by T Goodisson. As an aside, the value to the winner that year was 1,625 guineas.

In order to gain a feeling for the Hunt country of this period we can turn again to William Cobbett's book, "*Rural Rides*":

CHILWORTH, NEAR GUILDFORD, SURREY Wednesday, Sept. 25th 1822
But my object was, not to see inns and turnpike roads, but to see the country; to see the farmers at home, and to see the labourers in the fields; and to do this you must go either on foot or on horseback. With a gig you cannot get about amongst bye-lanes and across fields, through bridle-ways and hunting-gates; and to tramp it is too slow, leaving the labour out of the question and that is not a trifle.

LEA, NEAR GODALMING, SURREY Thursday, September 26th 1822
. . . went through Godalming, and got to Lea, which lies to the north-east, snugly under Hind-Head, about 11 o'clock . . . We got into free-quarter[11] again at Lea; and there is nothing like free-quarter, as soldiers well know. Lea is situated on the edge of that immense heath which sweeps down from the summit of Hindhead, across to the north over innumerable hills of minor altitude and of an infinite variety of shapes towards Farnham, to the north-east, towards the Hog's Back, leading from Farnham to Guildford, and to the east, or nearly so, towards Godalming. Nevertheless, the enclosed lands at Lea are very good and singularly beautiful. The timber of all sorts grows well; the land is light, and being free from stones, very pleasant to work. If you go southward from Lea about a mile you get down into what is called, in the old Acts of Parliament, the Weald of Surrey.

[From Petersfield] To GODALMING, vîa THURSLEY SURREY 17th or 18th November 1825
. . . These were oak-woods with underwood beneath; and there was a little stream of water . . . . . . We had to cross this brook several times, over bridges that the owner had erected for the convenience of fox-hunters . . . A road through it, made for the foxhunters, was a straight as a line, and of so great a length that, on entering it, the further end appeared not to be a foot wide. Upon seeing this, I asked the man whom these coppices belonged to, and he told me Squire Leech, at Lea. My surprise ceased, but my admiration did not.

From this we can readily construe that Cobbett and the Leech family were not only acquainted, but on good terms. Moreover, although the Leech brothers had given up their hounds, it is also clear that they had not forsaken their interest in venery. In common with other landowners, both then and now, they remained active in keeping their estate open for foxhunting. Equally interesting is Cobbett's view that *"to see the country"* one must *"get about amongst bye-lanes and across fields, through bridle-ways and hunting-gates"*, as many people go hunting today for that very reason. Because of the special and intricate relationship that exists between hunting and farming, those who follow hounds are able to ride through the 'real' countryside in a way that would not be possible otherwise.

Earlier, it was speculated that William Cobbett was an early foot-follower of Mr Leech's hounds and, again from evidence in *Rural Rides*, it seems he went on to become a mounted follower of the Union Hunt. Writing in November 1825, having travelled up through Surrey with his son from Godalming to London, he says:

"But Richard and I have done something else besides ride, and hunt, and of course stare about us during this month. He was eleven years old last March ... He can ride anything of a horse, and over anything that a horse can go over.

William Cobbett addressing a political meeting.
All he needs to go hunting are his spurs, a pair of gloves, a hunting whip and his hat.
The text in the engaving says: *"There is but one man who can extricate the country from its difficulties, why don't you send Him to Parliament."*

Notes
11 *That is, somewhere to stay free of charge.*

So expert at hunting, that his first teacher, Mr Budd, gave the hounds up to his management in the field; but now he begins to talk about nothing but fox-hunting!"

Paternal hyperbole aside, one suspects that many other parents have felt similarly over the last two centuries as their offspring have proved both fearless in their riding and equally impassioned about hunting! He continues:

"When he and I went from home, I had business at Reigate. It was a very wet morning, and we went off long before daylight in a post-chaise, intending to have our horses brought after us. He began to talk in anticipation of the sport that he was going to have, and was very inquisitive as to the probability of our meeting with foxhounds, which gave me the occasion to address him thus: 'Foxhunting is a very fine thing, and very proper for people to be engaged in, and it is very desirable to be able to ride well and to be in at the death; but that is not ALL; that is not everything. Any fool can ride a horse and draw a covert; any groom or any stable-fellow, who is as ignorant as the horse, can do these things; but all gentlemen that go a fox-hunting [I hope God will forgive me for the lie] are scholars, Richard. It is not the riding, nor the scarlet coats, that make them gentlemen; it is their scholarship.'"

[Naturally the author concurs heartily with such an admirable sentiment.]

Following Thomas Seawell's departure from the scene in 1822, it was Captain Richard Boulton [probably the same Capt. Boulton who followed the Rev. Onslow] who took on the responsibilities of Master. From Sir Bellingham Graham's establishment in Worcestershire, "Little Kit" Atkinson was engaged and, having proved to be a capital huntsman, he was to stay in service with the Union Hunt until 1834.

Two letters survive from this period, both written to the same landowner, in which some of the various difficulties facing Richard Boulton are evident. The first mentions his dealings with Col. Jolliffe [see left] and the second, probably written in 1831, is a model of contriteness and expresses a response that may well have been recognised by many Masters over the years [see right].

In the *Sporting Magazine* of July 1830, the Masters of the Union Hunt are listed as being Mr Boulton and Mr Fielding. This presents something of a conundrum, as Mr Fielding is not referred to in any previous history [although a faint hint of a joint-Master may be detected in the letter opposite] and nothing is currently known about him. For example, at the end of that season in April 1831, when it is understood that Captain Boulton resigned the Mastership and was presented with a "*handsome piece of plate*" [bearing the somewhat terse inscription, "*A slight memorial of regard and gratitude to Richard Boulton, for his effective management of the Union Foxhounds*"], of Mr Fielding there is no mention.

This confusion is compounded to some extent by what is effectively a throwaway line buried in an account written towards the end of 1830 by R S Surtees, albeit under the pseudonym Nim South[12]. The piece describes his experiences with the Union Hunt and is composed in his usual acerbic and prolix style. Because it contains a wealth of historical detail, it is reproduced at length here:

"The fixture was Polesden, a few miles south-east [sic] of Leatherhead, whither I set off somewhat early to have a look at the hounds. I found twenty couple of dogs and bitches, accompanied by a sporting-looking huntsman – Kit Atkinson by name – with a somewhat elderly-looking whipper-in stationed at the Lodge leading to a gentleman's house. The hounds are chiefly the Duke of Beaufort's blood, from whom I believe they get a few couple every year. Some of the bitches are uncommonly fine and powerful, more so, I thought, than the dogs. They have one fault, however, and that of no small

Notes

12 *The continuing tradition of hunting correspondents writing under a nom-de-plume started in the 18th century. The most apt alias, Nimrod [see Genesis: 10, verses 9 & 10], was quickly assumed by Charles James Apperley, who went on to write for the Sporting Magazine in 1822. As Frank Sitwell was already writing under the name Nim North when Surtees started submitting work to that publication, it seemed logical to all parties that there should also be a Nim South.*

magnitude – they are the worst gorse-drawers I ever saw in my life. This is the more unpardonable, as I understand they have several very excellent gorse coverts. How Atkinson could let hounds slink though a covert, one after the other, like a flock of geese, as they did, I cannot imagine: I am sure that he did not learnt it of Sir Bellingham Graham, whose whipper-in he formerly was.

On this day we had a good deal of covert and common hunting, the fox running very short, for which he was deservedly killed. I believe we never got far away from Ranmer [sic]Common, a few miles from Dorking, at which latter place was a large assemblage of labourers, to disperse whom a troop of Life Guards had marched through Leatherhead in the morning. During the late fires and disturbances I was frequently in both Kent and Surrey, and had opportunities of conversing with, and ascertaining the sentiments of many of the labouring men, and, from what I saw and heard, I have no hesitation in saying, that though there were some disaffected individuals – as there are in all classes of society – yet that a great majority of the labouring class were well-disposed, and that very many who attended those tumultuous meetings were either acting under the influence of fear or delusion, which decisive measures would have removed. One poor fellow at Dorking refused to leave the street after the Riot Act had been read, and, clinging to a post, swore he had a right to be there. A Life Guardsman remonstrated with him, but to no avail; so bringing one side of his horse to bear upon him, he touched him with the spur on the other, and gave him such a nip between it and the post that he very soon abandoned his right and took to his heels. How much better this was than sabreing the poor man!"

The historical irony of this talk of Ranmore, 'rights' and riot will not be lost on modern followers of our Hunt. [Or, indeed, those of other hunts in Surrey, Sussex and Kent.] He continues:

"But to return to the Union. As I said before, we had not much sport; at least not for foxhounds, though it would have been a pretty day with harriers. The field was not large, but what there were had more the appearance of sportsmen than the other Surrey hunters. In fact, most of the members are, I believe, resident country gentlemen; and the distance of the kennel from London is just sufficient to keep away a great many people who like to hunt and be back in town to answer their letters before the post goes out. Besides this, they keep their fixtures somewhat secret; not that a man going to Leatherhead would have any difficulty in getting them. And then again the want of accommodation for horses keeps others away. The horses in the Union Hunt are also much superior to the rest; and I saw more snaffle-bridle ones with them than with all the others put together. Now a snaffle-bridle horse is a very nice thing, as we all know; but I also know that there is not one real snaffle-bridle horse in fifty; and I am much mistaken if some of the gents I saw riding with them would not have been all the better for a curb.

… The Union hunt three days a week – Mondays, Thursdays and Saturdays: the kennel is at Fetcham, a mile or two from Leatherhead.

I met them again just at the close of November. The fixture was the Blucher, at Effingham, about four miles from Leatherhead in the Guildford direction. We had a much larger field on this day, and, on the whole, better sport. The morning was desperately cold, affording very little hopes of scent: we were, however, agreeably deceived, for it proved a very good scenting day. After drawing some time we found in Great Lea Wood, I believe; but he was a short running beggar again, and kept changing his line every now and then.

I do not know how Atkinson would reconcile the losing of this fox to his mind, but I thought it badly managed. He was evidently beat, and, being a short runner, had laid down before the hounds, who over-run him on a common. Well,

---

The Hon'ble Col. Howard MP[13]
Levens
Milnthorpe
Westmorland

Dear Howard,

Having been moving about I did not receive your letter so soon as I ought to have done, and am quite at a loss to know what to say for myself and Brother Sportsmen in having been guilty of so great an oversight, to say the least, in not having applied to you for leave to draw your coverts. I remember well that you were to have been written to on the subject and thought it had been done, and the only way I can account for the neglect is on account of your going abroad and since your return I can only conclude others must have been impressed with the same idea as myself of its having been done. I now beg leave to return you the thanks of my Brother Sportsmen as well as my own for your kindness to us and to assure you that nothing shall be done by the Union Hounds as far as lays in my power that shall be unpleasant to you.

I remain, Mr Howard,

Yours much obliged,

Rd Boulton

Notes

13 *Probably Colonel Fulk Greville Howard, the 3rd son of Baron Templeton. Born Fulk Greville Upton in 1773, he took his wife's surname on their marriage in 1807 [the second person in this history to do so - see Chapter 1]. They owned much of the land around Ashtead.*

Atkinson tried forward with a short cast without challenge; and, instead of trying back, he made a devil of a flourish round the country without hearing a note from a hound again.

I do not know whether Mr Bolton [sic] or Mr Hankey is the master of these hounds [how remiss not to check such a basic fact, and so impolite!], though, I believe, the former. Mr Ladbrooke is one of their principal men ...

Mr Claggit is the best appointed man in Surrey; and I am only surprised that he does not hunt in a better country. The Hon. Mr Dundas, one of the MPs for York, was out with them on the last day I was, and went, as he does in his own country, like a good one.

As to country, the Union, I should say, have the lion's share both in quantity and quality, the hills in their part being smaller, and the flints fewer[14]. Their kennel is situate almost on the extreme of Col. Jolliffe's Hunt – Box-hill being a covert of his, which is due south of Leatherhead, whence, I believe, he runs down through the Wootton hundred into Sussex; the Union having the whole of the west side of the county up to the borders of Hampshire. The Hunt dress is plain scarlet coat with plain white plated buttons; the men wear caps."

So, alas, no lasting clarity over the detail of Captain Boulton's Mastership and absolutely no mention of primrose yellow collars during this period.

CHAPTER 4
The Return of John Barnard Hankey

"On the whole, not a bad day for Surrey."

Hunting Diary 1831-32, Lannoy Coussmaker

At the start of the 1831-32 season, "The Squire", John Barnard Hankey, took up his second stint as Master of the Union Hunt. Although Hunt kennels were still at Fetcham Park in what is now known as Kennel Lane, Fetcham, the establishment would undergo some radical changes during his tenure.

One only need read this piece by R S Surtees from the *Sporting Magazine* of July 1831 [which subsequently became Chapter 2 of *Jorrocks's Jaunts and Jollities*, when published in book form in 1838] to gain a graphic picture of how much Saturday hunting in Surrey was available from Croydon to the clamouring crowds of sportsmen from the Metropolis during the early nineteenth century. After a calamitous hack from Covent Garden through a pea-souper fog, the eponymous hero finally arrives in the "*Melton of the South*", where:

> "... on the hunting bill of fare were Mr Jolliffe's fox-hounds, Mr Meager's harriers, the Derby stag-hounds, the Sanderstead harriers, the Union fox-hounds, the Surrey fox-hounds, rabbit beagles on Epsom Downs, and dwarf fox-hounds on Woolwich Common."

With hunting being so popular with cockney sportsmen, one can sympathise with Mr Hankey's initial attempts to try to limit the size of his mounted fields by insisting that subscriptions be set at a minimum of £100 and open to only to those resident in the Hunt country. Other Hunts on the metropolitan fringe are also believed to have adopted similar tactics [eg the West Kent], but Mr Hankey had set too high a tariff and the subscription level was reduced to £35 before long.

One of the Union Hunt subscribers of the time was Lannoy Coussmaker of Westwood Place, near Wanborough. His hunting diary for the early part of the season 1831-32 survives, providing us with an unaffected and equally revealing insight into the hunting of this period. The parts of this journal referring to the Union Hunt are transcribed from his neat handwriting in full, as follows:

A portrait of Lannoy Arthur Coussmaker [1810-1880]. The original hangs in the vestry of St Martin's church, Wyke.

FRIDAY 16 SEPT 1831. Morning wet, but cleared up about 11, though showery the rest of the day. The Union at Looseley [sic] at 9, drew it, & several other covers blank, found about 11 at a withy bed near Eashing, run thro' Lord Middleton's Park [Peper Harow], & came to a check, recovered it in about ½ an hour, ran him again pretty well but at last could make nothing of it, tried the covers near Looseley again, but in vain, left about 2, lunched at Looseley, & returned home to dinner – Rode Harlequin did not like him, very hot & a bad fencer, resolved to part with him. Austin out, staging at Shalford. The hounds looking well, but as usual plenty of music, but no choice fox or hare equally the same.
MONDAY SEPT 26. Union at Colliers Hanger at 9. A drisling [sic] rain in the morning & more or less the whole day. Drew the Hanger & round St Martha's, the other side of which we found at 10. No scent. Run him round St Martha's & at last got him to face the open & run him with much better scent over the downs by the race course & killed him under the wall of the new warren tried to jump it but failed the hounds close to him. 3 qtrs of an hour from the time we found, the last 20 minutes fast & very pretty & killed in style a fine cub, tho' only the third this year. Drew then the Netherns[15] found just at the further end of it – run at 12 – run him pretty well to Honey Suckle Bottom up to

Notes

15 *Netherns + land has become corrupted into (The) Netherlands, a covert across the main road from the New Warren, from whence, until 2005, foxes still ran to Honeysuckle Bottom.*

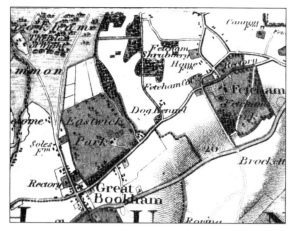

An extract from the Bryant Map of Surrey of 1823. The kennels at Fetcham Park are clearly marked.

An extract from the Ordnance Survey of 1934. The names Kennel Lane, Kennel Shaw and Kennel Covert maintain the association with the site of the Surrey Union Hunt kennels during the Masterships of the Hankey family.

Notes

16 *qv Surtees' similar opinion in Chapter 3 above.*
17 *A covert of some antiquity. Now mistakenly shown on maps as Catherine Frith!*

Mr Lomax's Park paling, went into the Park but must have got upon a stale scent & could make nothing of it, tho' we kept drawing on till 2 when I left – Rode Bugle, like him very fast & a good fencer tho' not in very good wind – on the whole, not a bad day for Surrey.

MONDAY OCT 3. Went to meet the Union at Henley Park but some mistake about the day as they never came. Rode Battle so only gave him a little bit of a gallop.

THURSDAY OCT 6. The Union at Black Heath at 9. Raining hard & continued so till near 2. Found our first fox about 10 in a cover near – but did nothing – found a brace of foxes at Sparkes Furze near Lord Grantley – got one away in about ½ an hour – ran him round Chinthurst Hill & back to cover again – got away again – and again round the hill going back to cover again – a man headed him & went to ground at the bottom of the hill. Hounds very slack and would not face the furze at all.[16] Rode Rattler and went very well – once restive at a leap but made him go. Only Hankey, Sparkes with whom we afterwards lunched & one or two more out – got home about 4 having been wet and dry again about five times.

SATURDAY OCT 8. Sir J. Cope at Kew Hills 2 miles on Farnham & London Road. Found about 10 – ran him in cover for about ½ an hour – got away over the common, gave him 20 minutes pretty sharp & ran into him in the open. Pretty thing but a good deal of doubling about over the heath. Raining hard the whole time though till 10 it had been fine. Tried for another fox but did not find – the rain continuing – left off about 12 about 4 miles from where we met. Rode My Lady- could scarcely hold her – a better hack than hunter. J Molyneux breakfasted and hunted with me. Rode Tom Thumb. Very good hounds.

MONDAY OCT 10. Union at Henley Park. Rode Rattler to covert. Drew Whipley Coppice blank – found near the pond about 11 – went away over the ridges for Holliers But turned to the right for Henley and then back for Pirbright and into cover again – lost him. About 20 minutes over the heath – very pretty & fast. Rode Sportsman, rather hot – Wanted his head but over the bogs and ruts of the heath I was afraid to give him. Tried then Newlands Firs – blank. Hounds went to Catherine Thrift[17] and Albert and myself into lunch at Westwood. Scarcely began before the hounds found – turned out – mounted Bugle & caught them up at Wanborough – back again thro' my covers Catherine Thrift, Newlands Hills over the peat moors and lost him by Henley Park. Gave him up about 3. A large field (& four finished) for Surrey out but fox always a long way ahead.

The remainder of the diary then goes on to record hunting days from Brighton and Leamington Spa. From the latter, Lannoy Coussmaker was able to enjoy at least one day's hunting with 'Squire' Osbaldeston, Master of the Pytchley.

Throughout the period so far reviewed, the overall approach to hunting had undergone a fundamental transformation. Instead of hunting a drag [a line taken by a fox, perhaps some hours earlier] and working slowly up to their quarry, hounds were now in direct pursuit of the fox and, as a consequence, the whole process was conducted at a much faster pace. It was now fashionable to gallop into jumps and many young bloods in the mounted fields of the fashionable packs were decidedly hunting to ride, rather than riding to hunt. Hounds were being bred for pace in the 'shires'; none more so than those of 'Squire' Osbaldeston. By using the progeny of his famous black and white stallion hound *Furrier* [1819], 'Squire' Osbaldeston had, by 1829, bred a pack that would fairly steam along. They were generally regarded as "*the most renowned the World has ever seen*" and when the Osbaldeston pack was eventually sold in 1846, it fetched the unheard of price of £6440 for 63½ couple.

In 1834, the outgoing Master of the Old Berkeley Hunt, Mr Harvey Coombe of Cobham Court, offered Mr Hankey a batch of hounds, known colloquially as "*the Osbaldeston lot*", on condition that John Jennings was taken on as huntsman. This Mr Hankey did. So, with Dick Simpson and John Fairman whipping in to him, Jennings carried the horn throughout the remainder of Mr Hankey's Mastership. 'Little Kitt' Atkinson went back to Worcestershire.

Although the hounds presented by Mr Coombe had been purchased for but 25 guineas a couple, they had nevertheless been bred for speed and dash: both eminent qualities that suited the open 'galloping' grass country of the Midlands. But the topography of Surrey produced a very different type of hunting – and still does. Even though the common lands were rapidly being enclosed, just as they were in the Pytchley country, in contrast many small, rather than large, cultivated fields were being formed amongst the numerous woodlands of our County. From the Coussmaker diary and the technical details in the "Swell and the Surrey" chapter of *Jorrocks's Jaunts and Jollities*, it also seems probable that the new [and patently ridiculous!] fashion of galloping at one's fences had not yet penetrated south of the Thames and many of the field were still happy to follow hounds all day steadily, taking what obstacles came their way calmly, or avoiding them altogether. That way, one horse was able to last the day and still get the rider home again.

Against such a background, it will come as no surprise to learn that "*the Osbaldeston lot*" did not come up to expectations, being found "*too fleet and not low scented enough*". It is also thought that they were sometimes inclined to run mute. That said, these tallies for the period make interesting reading:

Season	Commenced	Finished	Killed (brace)	To Ground (brace)	Blank	Days Hunting
1831-32	20th August	20th April	13	11½	7	not known
1832-33	not known	23rd March Stopped by snow	20	11½	2	101
1833-34	2nd September	22nd March	11	9½	4	103
1834-35	8th November	10th April	18½	6½	6	82

Overall, bearing in mind the fox population of the time, a rather more creditable performance than might be supposed and the Osbaldeston hounds seem to be, at the very least, comparable with their predecessors in terms of effectiveness.

According to *The Times* newspaper of Tuesday, January 14th 1834, the Union hounds found rather more than they were expecting one hunting morning. The grisly story is reproduced on the right.

Plainly there are aspects of this published story that are not wholly consonant with evidence from elsewhere. On the information currently available, it is impossible to determine if this piece is merely sloppy reportage or an accurate statement of previously undiscovered facts. However, this event was of sufficiently local notoriety to cause a local brick-maker, called Fairs, to compose a ballad describing this event, the words and music of which are set out in Appendix: 2.

THE TIMES

SUPPOSED MURDER: While the Surrey Union Fox Hounds (which are under the direction of H. Combe Esq) were out hunting on Saturday last, on Leatherhead Common, a most extraordinary and horrid circumstance occurred, which at present is involved in great mystery. About 12 o'clock in the day, as the huntsman (Kitt) was beating about for a fox, the hounds suddenly made a dead set at a clump of bushes on the common. As no fox made his appearance, the huntsman whipped the hounds off, but they still returned to the bushes, and smelling all round, would not leave. Supposing there was a fox that would not break cover, the huntsman &c beat the bushes, and in so doing, to their astonishment and horror, they discovered the body of a woman in a state of decomposition, so much so, that on attempting to remove it, it was found to be impracticable. A person was placed to watch the remains, and information was sent to Dr Evans, of Leatherhead, who promptly attended. On examining the head, a severe wound was found, and from the general appearance of the body it is supposed to have lain there several months. It was placed in a shell[18] and removed to the Royal Oak, on the common, where a coroner's Inquest is summoned to assemble this day (Monday) [sic]. *Various rumours are afloat, some stating the unfortunate woman was the wife of a travelling tinker.*

Notes

18 *A rough type of coffin.*

In the mid 1870s, the Hon. Francis Scott had *Comrade*, one of his favourite hounds, painted by Edwin Douglas RA, who lived at Lawbrook House, Westcott, and was a Surrey Union subscriber. Unusually, the portrait was on zinc and for many years it was hung on a gatepost and used as a holder for meet cards.

The meet card in *Comrade's* mouth dates from John Barnard Hankey's time as Master and is annotated with the wording, "Two days only on account of the state of the ground."

The meet card is from the last season of Mr Scott's Mastership and is dated February 1876. The encouragement to subscribe to the Hunt Servants' Benefit Society should be noted.

A pen and water-colour drawing of Col. William Holme Sumner by Richard Deighton.

CHAPTER 5
The Hankey Dynasty Continues

In 1842 John Barnard Hankey resigned in favour of his son-in-law, Colonel William Holme Sumner, and who was also the son of the Colonel Sumner who had provided the first Union Hunt kennels at Hatchlands Park in 1802. He remained Master for 17 years and during this long tenure employed several huntsmen. John Jennings was kept on initially, but he soon retired and went to live in Bookham. Oswald Lister, who eventually went to Colonel Calvert in the Crawley & Horsham country, succeeded Jennings. Then came John Dale, with Philip Tocock as first whipper-in. It is said that Dale's son had the good fortune to be allowed to act as second whipper-in when he was but twelve years old. If this is true, it may well explain Will Dale's future eminent career at the Burton, the Brocklesby and with the Duke of Beaufort's.

During the last year of his Mastership, Col. Holme Sumner is believed to have spent some time away in Ireland with his Regiment, the 1st Surrey Militia, and his brother-in-law, Captain Frederick Barnard Hankey RN [also the son of "Squire" John Barnard Hankey] of Fetcham, may have managed hounds during this absence.

It will be recalled that Surtees made the point in 1830 that the Union Hunt "*keep their fixtures somewhat secret*". So, in the 1850s, how did a hunting gent [or lady] find out where the most promising meets might be for the forthcoming week? The answer lay in the sporting section of the *News of the World* newspaper [yes, the very same!] on each Sunday during the season. So, for example, on Sunday 2nd March 1851, one could discover from the top right-hand corner of the front page that, "*the Surrey Union hounds will meet on Monday at Polesden, on Thursday at Albury Heath, and on Saturday at Leatherhead Downs – at half past ten*". In contrast, the Crawley & Horsham were to meet "*on Monday at Star, on Horsham Common, and on Thursday at Newdigate – at quarter to eleven*". Despite it being with a rival, that day in the Weald on Thursday is likely to have proved particularly tempting!

A meeting of subscribers to the Union Hunt held at the Swan Inn, Leatherhead, on 3rd March 1858 learnt from Colonel Sumner that, after all bills and expenses had been paid, there would be a "*deficiency to the amount of £200.*" It was proposed, and agreed, that the Members of the Hunt should liquidate this deficiency, but as we shall see shortly, this was not the end of this particular matter. At this same meeting it is also recorded that: "*A vote of thanks to Colonel Sumner for his good & efficient management of the Surrey Union Hounds ... ... the duties of which he has so long and so zealously performed was proposed by Mr Evelyn and carried unanimously*".

This passage is particularly significant, as it is believed to be the earliest reference to the Surrey Union in the formal records of our Hunt [although the description Surrey[19] Union Hunt was used by the press as early as 1834 – see Chapter 4]. The two names were used almost interchangeably for several years thereafter, often with both appearing in the minutes of the same meeting. However by 1863 the transition was practically complete, at least as far as the minute books of the Hunt were concerned, although formal invitations [to annual meetings of subscribers, for example] continued to use the old name into the 1880s. Happily, the spirit of the Union Hunt still lives on in our Hunt buttons – which continue to bear the initials 𝔘𝔥 [UH = Union Hunt].

Reading between the lines, finding a replacement Master following the resignation of Colonel Sumner may not have been entirely straightforward. A special committee, formed of Col. Sumner, Messrs Hankey, Evelyn, Coombe,

Notes

19 *One suspects that this usage was adjectival - perhaps to help distinguish the Union Hunt from the Essex Union Hunt, which was formed rather later.*

THE SURREY UNION FOXHOUNDS
TO THE EDITOR OF THE SURREY ADVERTISER

Sir,

All lovers of hunting in Guildford, and more so in the whole county, must have heard that Captain Hankey intends giving up the pack after this season with much regret. Though Captain Hankey's position has never been an enviable one, yet still it cannot be denied that he has discharged his arduous duties with fervent ardour, and his continual presence in the field has maintained the ancient prestige of the pack – in days of yore one of the best packs in England. But lately everybody who has hunted with these hounds must have observed that generally some slight contretemps occurred on every occasion of a meet, and there can be no doubt that the gallant captain would never have dreamt of giving up hunting the county unless there was some very good reason. One cannot say with truth that the Surrey Union have had good sport this year, for they decidedly have not. They have obtained several runs, but have rarely killed, particularly in this neighbourhood. How can this be answered? Your readers – I mean your sporting readers - best know that themselves. But with whom does the fault lie? There again we come to a full stop, and are likely to remain at one. Insert this or not as you think proper.

I am, sir, yours respectfully,

NIMROD

Guildford, Thursday

A very cross subscriber, bearing a grudge, seems to have been responsible for this letter and one wonders at such vitriol being expressed so publicly. Why was the grievance, real or imaginary, not raised at the annual meeting? It also serves to illustrate that internecine strife is nothing new in our Hunt or, indeed, any other. Managing the expectations of members and subscribers is a very important part of running a Hunt – an aspect ignored by Masters and the Hunt committee at their peril, as our history has shown more than once.

The use of the pseudonym "Nimrod" might demonstrate a familiarity with the Bible [see footnote 12 on page 10], or it may be a simple plagiarism. However, it should not be assumed that Charles James Apperley, the first user of this soubriquet, wrote this letter. He died of peritonitis on 17th May 1843.

Currie, Elkins & Cockran [Chairman] and Captain Stringer [Treasurer] met at Mr Currie's home, West Horsley Place, at 11 o'clock on 12th March 1858, and several times thereafter, to resolve this seemingly thorny issue.

The outcome was that Captain Frederick Hankey consented to become the new Master, but there were conditions: he should be held free from all expense and that two horses should be provided and kept for his own use at the kennels. To show intent to comply with the first condition, Captain Stringer sent a circular to all subscribers requesting that their subscriptions should in future be paid into Messrs Fuller's Bank during the month of May.

At the end of his first season, Captain Hankey was able to report a balance of income [£1430] over expenditure [£1289-6s-3d] of £140-13s-9d. This balance was carried over to the credit of the Hunt. However he also pointed out *"that there was a debt of £125 due by the Hunt when he took the management"*. As a solution, the subscribers resolved, *"that this debt should at once be liquidated by borrowing the money."* At the next annual meeting, in 1861, the impracticality of this convoluted financial manœuvre became apparent when Mr Henry Currie indicated that he wanted his money back! The debt was finally liquidated by the imposition of a surcharge on those who subscribed during the last year of Col. Sumner's Mastership – this being on top of the extra money that they had already stumped up in 1858.

Finances were not Captain Hankey's only difficulties. He was faced with the almost insoluble problem of keeping his vast country fairly hunted with his four day a week establishment. Hobson's Foxhunting Atlas of 1850 shows the Surrey Union country stretching from the River Thames between London and Staines in the North down to Charlwood, Rudgwick and Godalming in the south; from Sutton, Reigate and Horley in the east to Farnham and Bagshot in the west. An unknown contemporary writer provides this gloomy picture:

"the country which runs off to the north into those heathy wilds beyond Woking, where successive lines of concealed ruts, stonepits, treacherous incipient watercourses and morasses, form an effective barrier against invasion from the fastnesses on Mr. Garth's boundary … The district is not much affected by the generality of horsemen."

Perhaps unsurprisingly, by 1859 the Henley Park side of the Surrey Union country had been handed over to Mr. Garth on loan and to reduce costs, hunting was restricted to two days a week in the season 1862-63, although this was increased to three days the next season. Whilst a request by Mr. Birkbeck of the Burstow Hunt for the loan of the country *"lying east of Brockham, Lye [sic], Rusper & Newdigate"* was refused in 1863, it appears that the country was not being hunted sufficiently. In 1865 the Hunt secretary, the same Mr Currie, received a letter from a *"Mr Thurlow and various other Gentlemen residing in the lower part of the County requesting the loan of some of the Surrey Union country to Mr Sadler"*. It was decided to lend Mr. Sadler, of the Chiddingfold Hunt, *"the country between Ellen's Green and Cranley [changed to Cranleigh in 1867, to avoid confusion at the Post Office with the village of Crawley], in addition to what had already been lent."* So, it seems clear that Captain Hankey had a most difficult country to hunt: still, it is recorded that he carried out his duties *"with a degree of temper and courtesy which will long be gratefully remembered"*. But that temper must have been severely tested at times, if the letter published in the *Surrey Advertiser* on 17th February 1866 is anything to go by – see left.

Under Captain Hankey, Philip Tocock was promoted to huntsman, until he went to Lord Yarborough in 1860. Richard Ford from the West Kent succeeded him, with Bartelot as whipper-in, until 1865, when George Summers was appointed.

CHAPTER 6

Enter the Honourable Francis Scott

In November 1865, Captain Hankey intimated that he intended giving up his Mastership at the close of the season, but no immediate successor was forthcoming. As a stop-gap, with the assistance of Col. Sumner and Mr Helme [a long-serving member of the Hunt committee], Captain Hankey agreed to carry on until 1st August 1866.

Some previous commentators have suggested that the prospects for the continuance of the Hunt were doubtful at this time, not only because of the continuing financial stringency and the difficulties caused by the size of the Hunt country already described, but also on account of the increasing pressures from shooting interests. The Hunt Chairman, the ubiquitous Mr Currie, is reported to have declared that:

"The Bishops may be turned out of the Lords; the Peers abolished; or even the Queen dethroned; but foxhunting as an institution can never cease in England!"

Stirring words indeed. But be that as it may, the record in the minutes book is rather more sanguine. On 23rd February 1866 the subscribers *"unanimously resolved that the hounds should be continued"* and on 4th May, at a meeting held at the Manor House, Little Bookham, and attended by Captain Hankey and Messrs Helme and Currie, *"Mr Scott consented to be the Master of the Surrey Union Hounds with the same Committee – on his being guaranteed £1500 per annum"*. On the face of it, perhaps not such a great crisis after all.

Son of the 6th Baron Polwarth, Chief of the clan of Scott, the Honourable Francis Scott had come down from Scotland to join the English Bar and was married to the niece and sole heiress of the last Earl of Egremont. After twenty years representing Roxburgh and Berwick in the House of Commons, he retired to Surrey in 1858 and enjoyed the life of a country gentleman. Having hunted a pack of beagles in 1848 and, in 1862, taken on the Ripley and Knaphill Harriers to save them from being disbanded [apparently showing excellent sport for the next four seasons in the process], he was 60 years old when he took over the Mastership of the Surrey Union Hunt. It is recounted that when Mr Scott informed a friend that he intended to hunt hounds himself, he was asked if the subscribers knew of the plan. On being told that they did not, the response was, *"Then you are a very sensible fellow, as you would not have obtained half the subscriptions"*!

According to an agèd and disappointed local pedant of the time, the establishment was moved to Burnt Common, near West Clandon, after a period of 52 years and 17 days in Fetcham. As the new Master lived at nearby Sendhurst Grange, the need for this removal becomes much more understandable, despite a cost of £375 for the construction of kennels and other necessary alterations. A press report of the Opening Meet is reproduced on the right.

At the subscribers' meeting held at the Swan Inn, Leatherhead, on 6th July 1868, a vote of thanks was given to Captain Hankey *"for his kindness and attention during Mr Scott's unavoidable absence a great part of the season 67/68"*. Although the precise circumstances giving rise to this entry remain uncertain, it is thought that Mr Scott periodically suffered from chronic bronchitis and, as his father died in 1867, there may also have been family reasons. At this same meeting, an interesting, and continuing, facet of Hunt life was touched upon, when:

"Mr Scott was to take what steps he thought best, to remunerate those who took puppies to walk, either by prizes or gratuities in money."

FIRST MEET OF THE SURREY UNION HOUNDS

Monday was an auspicious day for the first meet of the season for these hounds. The sun shone too bright to give much promise of sport, but shed a gleam on the meeting at Sendhurst Grange. The Hon. Francis Scott sent invitations to breakfast to all the subscribers to the fox hounds, and likewise to the harriers, of which he lately resigned the mastership, and several yeomen and farmers who also love the sport. Accordingly, there was a goodly concourse of sportsmen, together with several ladies; and full justice was done to the ample repast which was provided for them. When this was over the healths of the late and present master, and success to the hounds, was drunk in champagne; and we were glad to observe that a very proper tribute of respect and gratitude was paid to J.G. Hankey, Esq., of Fetcham-park, to the memory of the late Colonel H Sumner, and to Captain Hankey, to whom all willingly contributed subscriptions for a suitable testimonial. We have no doubt that others will gladly add their contributions. The scene upon the lawn before the house, where gentlemen in scarlet and ladies were grouped around the hounds, was pleasing and enlivening. The cavalcade proceeded along the road to Ripley; and, having drawn Old-Lands Copse blank, proceeded to Brambleside, where a stout old dog-fox was viewed away, and rattled with a good scent to Hatchlands across Clandon Common, and having made a wide ring was pursued most perseveringly by the hounds, and pulled down after an hour and a half's run, to the great satisfaction of a numerous field.

We hope that this beginning augurs well for the sport of the season: and we congratulate the lovers of sport around Guildford, on the kennels being brought within four miles of their town. At the same time, we regret to hear that all the coverts about Wonersh have been drawn blank, and a fox has been found dead in the heart of the country by no fair means. We hope also that it is untrue that any foxes have been dug out, and sent to the country of an adjoining hunt. These proceedings are most unfair and disheartening to any gentleman, who, like Mr. Scott, is using his utmost endeavours to show sport and to afford satisfaction.

Surrey Advertiser 3rd November 1866

By the spring of 1869, there were reportedly 20 to 25 couple of puppies at walk. To modern readers this may seem a very large number indeed, but it needs to be borne in mind that distemper was capable of eradicating a puppy population at a stroke during this period. A near contemporary veterinary manual records that the disease could be particularly virulent in foxhound kennels, notwithstanding scrupulous attention to hygiene.

At the start of the 1869 season there were 50 couple of hounds in kennel under the care of George Summers, hunting four days a week. The majority of these were drafts from Lord Fitzharding's pack, which were "*noted alike for their rich music and good noses*". There were also hounds drafted from Mr Scratton's [the Essex Union] and Lord Leconfield's packs. They were reported to be a "*fine looking pack containing some of the best blood in England and show very good sport.*" Although the policy was clearly to rely heavily on such drafts, Mr Scott did eventually breed some of his own hounds from this very promising material. Lines descended from *Whalebone*, a dark coloured hound of uncertain temper, and *Countess*, a tan coloured bitch, were to remain in the Surrey Union kennel for at least 40 seasons after this period. [See also Appendix 3.]

With the discontinuance of the Chiddingfold Hunt following the retirement of the Sadler brothers in 1872 and the return of the Surrey Union country loaned to them, Mr. Scott found himself responsible for hunting practically the whole of the County of Surrey lying west of the Reigate-Crawley road.

A meeting in Guildford on 6th April 1872, "*of Gentlemen interested the hunting of that district*", chaired by John Ramsden [soon to become the Surrey Union Hunt Chairman] passed a resolution "*requesting the resumption of the hunting of that part of the country, giving assurance of the support of the landowners and occupiers of the district & of their determination to use their best endeavours towards securing the preservation of foxes & also of a certain subscription towards the maintenance of the Surrey Union Hounds*". Just over a fortnight later, the annual Surrey Union subscribers' meeting was told that " *... on the above undertaking such district be hunted fairly and equitably to the satisfaction of the Gentlemen in such district – without prejudice to or any diminution of the advantages enjoyed by the subscribers hunting in the other districts*". Even now, one can recognise the diplomacy represented by this wording and the magnitude of the task that the assurance implies. A great deal of organisation and a need to continue hunting four days a week were the inevitable outcomes. The extract from a meet card [left] for one week in February 1876 is probably typical.

As we have seen from the 1870 kennel visit, George Summers was employed as kennel huntsman whilst Mr Scott carried the horn during the early years of his Mastership. In the latter part of Mr Scott's tenure, Summers was to hunt hounds on the increasing occasions when the Master was unable to do so. On one such day, hounds found in Reigate Park and ran vîa Leigh, Newdigate and Rusper, to catch their fox at Holmbush on the outskirts of St. Leonard's Forest – a point of some 12 miles.

Between times, Mr Scott recognised that the lot of Hunt servants after retirement was not always a happy one. Out of his concern for Summers' future, he was instrumental in the formation of the Hunt Servants' Benefit Society in 1872. Its purpose was neatly described by Charles Dickens, Junior, in the section on Friendly and Benevolent Societies of his 1879 *Dickens's Dictionary of London* thus:

Hunt Servants' Benefit Society, Messrs. Tattersalls, Albert Gate-Subscription: Honorary members, for life, £5 or upwards; annually, £1 or upwards; benefit members according to age and benefits subscribed for. Object: To provide for huntsmen, and whippers-in of fox or stag-hounds, sickness pay, annuities at 60 or 65 years of age, and provision for their widows and orphans.

Meet Card February 1876

Monday   14th   *Ripley Green*

Wednesday   16th   *Baynard's Park Gate, Cranleigh*

Thursday   17th   *Lawbrook House, Shere*

Saturday   19th   *Fetcham Kennels*

This Society is still flourishing today, under the guise of the Hunt Staff Benefit Society – a name adopted in 2004, as befits our politically correct age.

During his ten years as Master, Mr Scott clearly worked hard – a point perhaps not universally appreciated at the time. This extract from a newspaper report of a meeting at the White Hart in Guildford on 1st May 1875 provides an insight into some of his tribulations and the trenchant response he made to his critics:

"Mr Scott remarked that he had heard that considerable dissatisfaction existed in certain quarters because he had not sufficiently drawn some coverts. He begged gentlemen who complained to bear in mind that hounds were very much interrupted by frost. In this county he had always endeavoured in each week to distribute the meets in different directions in the several districts, but in consequence of these interruptions, and of the desire of some to keep hounds away from coverts at times, it became impossible always to comply with the wishes of owners of coverts at the moment they expected their coverts drawn. The hounds were stopped for six weeks, comprising in all no less than twenty-two days, and as hounds only hunted seventy-two days last season, it might well be imagined how serious these interruptions had been, and that the management of the hounds was not alone to blame for these deficiencies. He would also mention that the loudest complaint came from a quarter where no less than seven or eight fixtures out of the entire number were made during the season. It had been hinted that he should hunt fewer days, but that would have made the complaints more numerous, for it was impossible to hunt the extent of the country with fewer than four days a week, and the finances had enabled that to be done without deficiency upon a minimum subscription as compared with others, for he doubted if any pack in England hunted an equal number of hounds for so small an amount, and none in Great Britain hunted four days a week with so small a pack as forty-six and a half couples. It reflected great credit on the huntsman that though the country was extensive, the hounds never travelled in [a] van, and rarely slept out, yet they had never been the worse for work, and were in better condition at the end than at any time during the season."

Such unthinking criticism often cuts deep [and is still capable of doing so today – so please think both long and hard before being disparaging about a Master!] and it probably had a dispiriting effect on Mr Scott. Indeed, in a letter written a week earlier indicating his intention to retire at the end of the 1875-76 season, he said, *"There are increasing reasons why I should at that time surrender their* [the Surrey Union hounds] *management into other and younger hands"*. Given the circumstances he described, it is perhaps hardly surprising.

It was suitably fitting, then, that in his valedictory speech he was able to declare, *"It is to me one of the greatest satisfactions to feel that I leave behind me a capital pack of full fifty couple of good working hounds. I don't believe that you could find a pack of hounds more suited for this country than those with which we have been lately hunting it. I only wish that some of you had been out yesterday and seen what they did. For an hour and fifty minutes they ran without a check and without assistance, and ran into the fox. Gentlemen, I am afraid I am becoming garrulous as man often does in the seventy-first year of his age …"*. Some say that that not only was he hunting hounds himself that day [Summers having broken his collar bone], but also it was his birthday and the full tally was a brace on top, with one to ground!

In June 1876 a testimonial fund was closed at 470 guineas and it was decided to commission a portrait of Mr Scott on *"horseback with hounds"* from one S. Pearce, an artist of the mid-Victorian period noted for his depictions of the great and the good.

The Surrey Union Hounds in Mr Bennett's time. The original caption to this photograph merely says, "The Surrey Union Hounds, with portrait of the Master, Mr T W Bennett". However, from other evidence it is clear that the huntsman is William Whiten and the photograph was probably taken during the season 1888-89. The coloured collars on the coats of the Hunt servants should be noted.

CHAPTER 7

Another Hankey: The Third Generation

The retirement of Mr Scott made plain the sheer enormity of the responsibilities that he had borne as Master. At the heart of this burden was the size of the Hunt country and clearly something needed to be done to make this more manageable. Delicate negotiations were held throughout the spring of 1876 and their outcome was as follows:

> *"1. Having conferred with Mr J B Hankey and Mr C Hammond respectively, they recommend that the coverts called Hammond and other coverts hitherto held on loan by the Burstow Hunt, be resumed by the Surrey Union Hunt.*
>
> 2. *That the boundary line between the Surrey Union Hunt and the Chiddingfold Hunt be as follows: From Ellen's Green on the Horsham-road through Cranleigh, to the lane across Smithwood Common: thence leaving the Helmet copse [up on Winterfold] to the east by Farley Green, to the South-Eastern railway at Brook, thence following the South-Eastern railway to Guildford.*
>
> 3. *That portion of the country included by the above-mentioned boundary and the Guildford and Cranleigh road as far as Smithwood Common, be offered on loan to Mr C Godman [Master of the Chiddingfold Hunt], with an understanding that if such portion should be resumed an equal extent of country will be offered in substitution.*
>
> 4. *That the portion of the country lying W. and N.W. of the Woking and Guildford Railway and Hog's Back, together with that lying W. of a line drawn generally from Puttenham to Haslemere, be offered on loan to Mr R Combe [thought to be Master of the Hambledon], subject to agreement with Mr C Godman."*

Captain Hankey had once told Mr Scott that the country north of the London to Woking railway could never be properly hunted, as the number of old women with ducks and geese meant the poultry bills would exceed all the subscriptions he might receive. As the outgoing Master still considered Tom Garth to be an excellent fellow for poultry bills and old women, this part of the Surrey Union country remained on loan to him!

Following these boundary changes, Thomas Helme, the Hunt secretary, was able to announce at a meeting held in the Swan Inn, Leatherhead, on Saturday, 6th May 1876, that: *"The Committee for the Surrey Union Hounds have the satisfaction of informing you that they have made arrangements with Jno. Barnard Hankey Esq., to take the Mastership from the 1st of last April"*.[20] Being the grandson of Captain Frederick Hankey, Mr John Barnard Hankey was thus the third member of the family to hold the Mastership.

Also at this meeting, it was further decided that the new Master should write to Mr Arthur Sumner, thanking him for the use of his field and premises during Mr Scott's Mastership and to say when the hounds would be able to leave Clandon. Owing to dilapidations, it was not possible for Mr Hankey to move straight back into the former Hunt kennels at Fetcham Park. To help remedy this problem, the Hunt committee undertook to deposit a sum of £150 at Messrs Fullers, the bankers, to enable Mr Hankey to pay for the necessary repairs. Reading between the lines of Mr Hankey's memo book, one gets the impression that this money was perhaps slow in coming from the subscribers, but Walker, the builder, was eventually paid off in two tranches in 1876, on 23rd October [£100] and 15th December [£50].

To square up the Hunt boundary to the south-east, the country loaned to the Burstow was taken back in 1878. Lest this now much larger country should prove too much for Mr Hankey to hunt, a resolution was suitably passed that

Mr Hankey's poultry bill account for the 1881-82 season. It is interesting to see how much of his Hunt country is still open to us today.

Notes

20 *As the hunting year starts on 1st May, the knowledgeable may well wonder at this starting date, but the printed circular bearing this news is quite explicit and no other contemporary explanation is available. Also, when with but one extra letter the name could be reproduced in full, quite why the printers of the period used the abbreviation Jno. remains another mystery! That said, it was a form that Mr Hankey himself adopted in his minute book.*

The cheque made out by John Barnard Hankey for £195-7s-8d to set up the Surrey Union Hunt Reserve Fund. It is dated June 5th 1883 and drawn on an account held at the bank of Messrs Fuller Banbury Nix & Mathieson, 77 Lombard Street, London.

empowered him to "*make any arrangement that he may think proper with Mr Godman as to a portion of the Surrey Union country being lent to Mr Godman on the usual terms viz a request to the Committee of the Surrey Union thro Mr Hankey for a continuance of the loan on the 1st April each year.*"

With Summers remaining as his huntsman, Mr Hankey was able to hunt the country for several seasons on £1500 per annum. But at the end of the 1879-80 season, a combination of factors threw the financial stability of the Hunt into disarray. Several members had left the district and Mr William Farnell-Watson JP "*one of the oldest and most liberal of subscribers*" had died in November 1879. This was an accurate description indeed, for at a time when most subscriptions were around £10 to £25, the Farnell-Watsons, father and son, had regularly contributed £100, or more, each season. This financial crisis was soon overcome by the simple expedient of transferring the capital sum of £261-10s-0d in the Hunt '*horse fund*' into the annual income general funds for the season 1880-81 to offset the deficit. As it turned out, this was not quite the sure route to penury that it could well have been. Happily, these fiscal strictures were of temporary duration and Mr Hankey was able to return some £195-7s-8d of the subscription monies from his last season as Master, which were transferred into a reserve fund managed by trustees, to be used at the discretion of the Hunt committee.

As an illustration of the frustrations that could beset a Master [and, one suspects, still do], in response to a complaint from the Earl Lovelace that the meets in the 1880-81 season had been unequally distributed throughout the country and that his particular district had been hardly hunted, the Hunt committee resolved that " *... the Master should remind his Lordship that that in compliance with his directions last year his coverts were left undrawn till January...*". This is clearly yet another example of not being able to please all of the people of all the time, despite every effort being made to take the Earl's shooting interests into account!

The "*very large attendance*" of members and subscribers at the Annual Meeting on 20th March 1882 was told that Mr Hankey "*must resign the Mastership of the Union Hounds at the end of this season on the 1st May 1882 in consequence of his failing health*". However, in the end, he was to maintain his active interest in the Hunt well into the next century, very nearly 100 years after his grandfather had first accepted the Mastership.

CHAPTER 8

Two Short Masterships

It also became clear at this March 1882 meeting that the Hunt secretary, Thomas Helme, had been busy obtaining *"the valuable assistance & guidance of Gentlemen interested in the continuance of the Union Hunt – and he is happy to be able to report that a most successful result has been obtained, by Mr Farnell-Watson's acceptance of the Mastership of the Union Hunt – if it met with the approbation of the meeting"*. This was unanimously approved by all present and Mr Hankey graciously placed the Fetcham Park kennels at the service of the new Master.

Mr William Farnell-Watson had inherited from his father the family's brewery interests in Isleworth and their country residence, Henfold House, Beare Green. He was previously the Master of the Warnham staghounds and virtually his first task on taking on his new role was to arrange for a dinner to be given to the keepers of fox coverts in the Hunt country.

At the end of his first season, Mr Farnell-Watson *"expressed himself quite satisfied with the support given by the subscribers"* and, in return, thanks were *"tendered to him for the spirited manner in which he had hunted the country"*. Reading the minute book, one might be forgiven for thinking that all was set fair, but clearly there was more going on behind the scenes than has been recorded – another recurring theme over the years!

It will come as no surprise then, that on 26th March 1884 the local newspaper reported that Mr Rickards [the hon. treasurer] *"... was sorry to announce Mr Farnell-Watson's resignation of the Mastership ..."*, going on to explain that *"... it was a consolation to know that his retirement was not due to any want on the part of the subscribers, who had completely fulfilled the expectations held out to Mr Watson before he took office"*. Does this sound a mite defensive?

In contrast, Mr Helme is recorded as saying: *"That this meeting tenders cordial thanks to Mr W. Farnell-Watson for his liberal, energetic, and successful Mastership of the Union Foxhounds, and accepts his resignation of office with much regret"*. This resolution *"was seconded by Mr Budd and carried by acclamation"*. A further hint of trouble at this time comes from a minute made two years later [on 20th March 1886] that refers to the succeeding Master *"undertaking the Hounds in a time of difficulty in 1884"*. Sadly, we shall probably never learn the full story as, perhaps significantly, there are no other records for the 1883-84 season extant in the Hunt archive.

The same press report goes on to say: *"... the recent inquiries made with a view to obtain a new Master had been successful, and that Colonel George Pilkington Blake, of Worcester-park, had declared himself ready to come forward if invited. Colonel Blake was known to many of them as a fine horseman and a good sportsman, and he was willing to take the country on the terms of hunting it at least two days a week, and be prepared to give up his whole time to the interests of the hunt"*.

The Colonel clearly possessed the right credentials and in his acceptance speech made some telling points that are equally valid today: *"A pack of foxhounds demanded the attention of the Master almost as much during the summer as in the hunting season, and he hoped to be able before the next season commenced to make himself acquainted with every landowner and farmer and every covert from one end of the country to another ..."*. As may be imagined, this was no small undertaking, particularly as he also intended to hunt hounds himself.

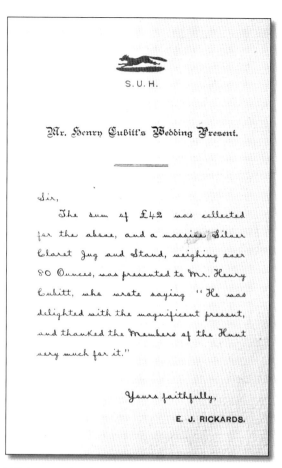

S.U.H.

Mr. Henry Cubitt's Wedding Present.

Sir,

The sum of £42 was collected for the above, and a massive Silver Claret Jug and Stand, weighing over 80 Ounces, was presented to Mr. Henry Cubitt, who wrote saying "He was delighted with the magnificent present, and thanked the Members of the Hunt very much for it."

Yours faithfully,

E. J. RICKARDS.

This letter was found pasted into the Hunt Minute Book, entirely without any additional comment. For an explanation and a wholly unexpected connection, please see the page opposite..

This latter desire rendered the long-serving huntsman George Summers redundant [and it seems that he was still seeking a post in hunt service some two seasons later], although William Whiten was retained as the first whipper-in, having come from the Atherstone in 1880.

At the end of his first season, Colonel Blake acknowledged *"the hearty encouragement he had received"* and stated an intention to move the establishment to a more central position in the country. In reality, the old kennels at Fetcham Park were given up and new ones built at Worcester Park, convenient only in that they were always under the Master's eye. Coupled with a press cutting from 1888, saying *"Colonel Blake worked hard to win the popularity his sportsmanlike qualities merited, but he did not quite get touch of farmers and covert-owners, upon whose support foxhunting is everywhere dependent"*, this evidence points to pious words not always matching the deed – another peril to which even Masters today can be prone!

At a subscribers' meeting, the Colonel provided the following statistics for the 1884-85 season, up to 7th March 1885:

40 days hunting   18 foxes killed [21]

14 run to ground   7 blank days

4 days stopped by frost

The Colonel also expressed a desire to hunt the country three days a week, providing his guarantee was raised from £1250 to £1500. The subscribers were not wholly enamoured with this idea, despite 22 new ones having come forward that season. Accordingly, the Master accepted the promise of £1250 again for 1885-86, whilst endeavouring to provide a bye-day once a fortnight. As Mr Rickards, the Hon Treasurer, said somewhat prophetically at the time: *"Hunting three days a week was simply a matter of money"*.

However, things were not destined to work out. By February 1886 it was apparent that there was going to be a serious shortfall in subscriptions and that the pressures of shooting interests were making hunting very difficult indeed. Against such a background, it is understandable that, on 6th March, Colonel Blake gave notice of his resignation at the end of the season. But the committee that had been assembled to resolve this crisis was remarkably swift in its actions; by 10th March 1886 it had identified Mr Thomas Bennett as a replacement.

Notes

21 *It is not clear if this is 18 or 18 brace etc, as all the figures in this table come from an unattributed press cutting.*

CHAPTER 9

The Establishment Moves Again

So, in May 1886, Mr Thomas Bennett, of Cobham Court, took over 24 couple of hounds from Colonel Pilkington Blake and his Hunt committee [under the chairmanship of Lord Foley, it comprised Sir Robert Hawthorn Collins KCB, Messrs J B Hankey, B Jenkins, T Mashiter, F C Bryant and the Colonels Hornby-Buller and Pott] ensured that the outstanding financial issues were quickly resolved by adopting the well-tried expedient of raiding the Hunt Horse Fund.

From their remote corner in Worcester Park, kennels were moved to Cobham Park. If anything, this was even more convenient than Fetcham, with any part of the then hunt country being accessible without wearisome journeys. This must have pleased Whiten, who was now hunting hounds. [See also Appendix 4.]

As seems to be the way after a crisis, financial stability eventually returned to the Hunt. Subscription income started to increase and, by May 1887, it was agreed "*certain portions of the Cranleigh country lent to General Marshall* [of the Chiddingfold] *should be resumed*" – almost certainly a product of both the sensible location of Kennels and new-found prosperity. An attempt by General Marshall to take up the loan again the following season was firmly, but politely, rebuffed. An innovation also introduced at this time was the Poultry Fund, initially administered by Mr Arthur Moon. This fund was used to compensate poultry owners for the depredations caused to their flocks by the resident fox population – see also Chapter 27 – Tales from the Hunt Poultry Fund. Previously, these payments had been the personal responsibility of the Master [see Poultry Bills season 1881-82 on page 23], but by this action Mr Bennett was now clearly attempting to shift this burden onto the subscribers, thereby reducing his outgoings.

In May 1889, the Master reported that 15 brace of foxes had been killed, with a further 10 brace run to ground, and that the issue of meet cards was 288.

It was also made explicit that gentlemen subscribing annually £10 and upwards were to be regarded as members of the Hunt. This gave the automatic privilege of being able to wear the Hunt button without more ado. Prior to this announcement, it is probably fair to assume that this right was only accorded following the express invitation of the Master – just as it is today. Continuing this sartorial theme, in 1891, the Master "*requested more Members to ride in pink*". This gives us a valuable insight into both the hunting argot of the times and how Thomas Bennett clearly viewed the look of the mounted field to be important in public relations, especially with landowners with shooting interests and the farmers. There is an old adage along the lines that a red coat may be forgiven most indiscretions in the hunting field, but a black coat may not! However, nowadays, use of the term "*pink*" [as in pink coat, to hunt in pink, etc] is, as Nancy Mitford might have said, decidedly non-U! The current description is most definitely[22] a 'red' coat and today they are generally only worn in our Hunt by the joint-Masters, the Hunt staff or members of very long-standing [and who have worn one for very many seasons]. To conclude this clothing review, a portrait is known to exist of Thomas Bennett wearing his full hunting kit as, complete with primrose yellow collar on his coat. Adoption of the yellow collar has been the subject of fashion, as can be seen in the photographs, and is a topic that will recur later in this history.

Mr Henry Cubitt's Wedding Present: The Explanation

Henry Cubitt and Maud Marianne Calvert were married in Ockley Church on 21ˢᵗ August 1890.

Maud Calvert, the daughter of Colonel Archibald Motteux Calvert and Constance Peters, was born in 1865 in Charlton, Sussex.

Henry Cubitt was born on 14ᵗʰ March 1867 and educated at Eton College, graduating as a Master of Arts from Trinity College, Cambridge in 1891. Between 1892 and 1906 he was the Conservative MP for South East Surrey. He was also Colonel of the Surrey Volunteer Regiment; Honorary Colonel in the service of the 4th Battalion, The Queen's Royal Regiment and Lieutenant-Colonel and Honorary Colonel of the Surrey Yeomanry between 1901 and 1912. Between 1905 and 1939 he was both Lord-Lieutenant and Custos Rotulorum of Surrey. He received the Territorial Decoration and was invested as a Companion, Order of the Bath.

He succeeded to the title of 2ⁿᵈ Baron Ashcombe, of Dorking, Surrey and of Bodiam Castle, Sussex on 26ᵗʰ February 1917.

Henry and Maud had six sons, three of whom were killed in the First World War. Their fourth son, Roland, became the third Baron on Henry's death in 1947. They were also great-grandparents of the present Duchess of Cornwall.

Henry Cubitt – Maud Marianne Calvert

Roland Calvert Cubitt – Sonia Rosemary Kepple

Bruce Shand – Rosalind Cubitt

Camilla, Duchess of Cornwall

Notes

22 *The supporters of the adjective scarlet would argue otherwise. This debate has gone on for decades!*

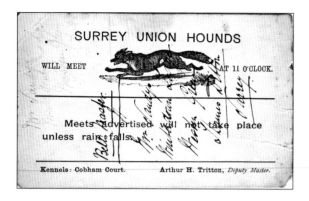

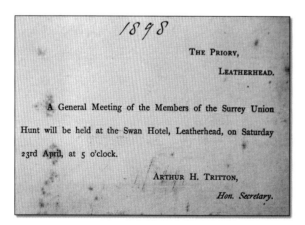

The statistics for the 1890-91 season were:

Hounds went out 58 times without a single blank day and killed 19 brace on top and running 11½ brace to ground. 23 days were lost to frost.

For the next four seasons matters seem to have run their course without undue concern, with hounds commonly out four days a week. With members of the royal family in the mounted field, including HRH Edward, Duke of Clarence; the Duke and Duchess of Teck and the Princess of Wales [later to become Queen Mary], the Surrey Union Hunt carried a social cachet at this time that it has never *quite* equalled since.

But, yet again, financial storm clouds were starting to gather. On 2nd November 1895, a general meeting at the Swan Hotel in Leatherhead learnt from Mr Tritton, the Hunt secretary, that *"the meeting had been convened to consider the matter of the Hunt finances which were in an unsatisfactory condition"* and the Master was called on *"to explain how the account stands"*. Mr Bennett reported that the subscriptions and the poultry fund had not been sufficient to meet expenditure and that the deficit for the 1894-95 season was £105. The solution adopted to resolve this problem would, today, be described as 'name and shame'! It was proposed that a statement of accounts be drawn up in the form of a circular, giving a list of subscribers, the amounts subscribed and the deficit. This was then sent to *"all interested in the well being of the Hunt"*. A copy of this circular survives and its contents, including the names of 147 subscribers, make interesting reading – see opposite.

This expedient seems to have worked, as the minute book for the next two seasons is entirely silent, except for recording the combined subscription and poultry fund incomes received, the respective totals being £1752-4s-0d and £2019-8s-0d.

At a general meeting held on 9th October 1897, a motion was proposed by Mr Hue Williams, seconded by Mr Horace Avery QC, that neatly combined sympathy with practicality in its wording. It said:

"That this Meeting of Members of the Surrey Union Hunt has heard with sorrow of the distressing illness of the Master, Mr T H Bennett, and hoping that the same may be of temporary character, hereby empower the Hon. Sec, Mr A H Tritton, to act as Deputy Master and draw cheques on the Hunt Account."

Unfortunately, Mr Bennett did not recover sufficiently from these complications following a bad fall and, in this regard, it may be significant that it was his brother, Mr T J Bennett, who submitted a letter of resignation on his behalf in February 1898. A committee was immediately constituted to select a new Master, there already being two applications, from a Mr A B Worthington and Mr A Labouchere. Mr Tritton was not able to continue carrying the burdens of Mastership single-handedly and the kennels were, he averred, too far from his home in Leatherhead.

—◆—

Three examples of Hunt notices from the season 1897-98. The top one indicates that drought conditions are nothing new and was issued by Arthur Tritton whilst he was acting as Deputy Master. It seems to have been used as an aide memoir of a name and address at a later date.
The one in the middle is a calling notice for a meeting of members, landowners and farmers on what is clearly a hunting morning, whereas the bottom one is for a General Meeting in the early evening.

Statement of Accounts, List of Subscribers etc. Season 1894-95

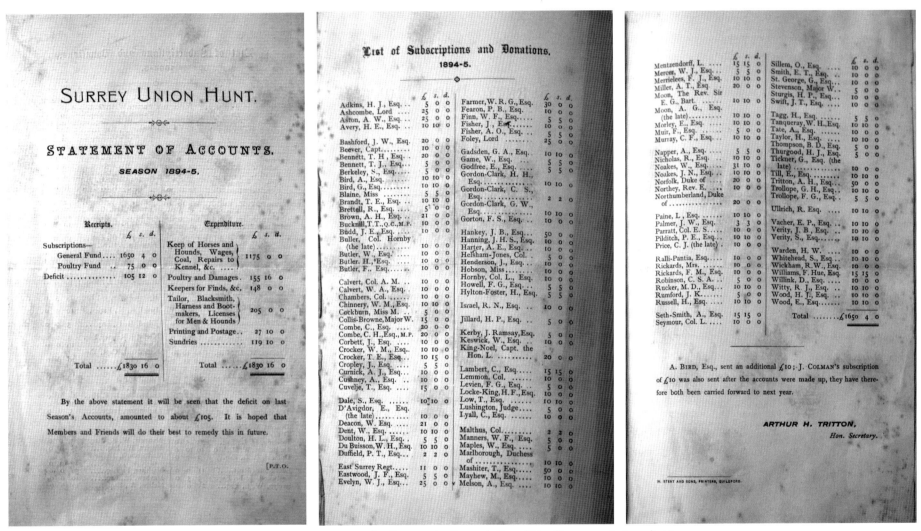

SURREY UNION HUNT.

STATEMENT OF ACCOUNTS.

SEASON 1894-5.

Receipts.	£	s.	d.	Expenditure.	£	s.	d.
Subscriptions—				Keep of Horses and Hounds, Wages, Coal, Repairs to Kennel, &c.	1175	0	0
General Fund	1650	4	0				
Poultry Fund	75	0	0	Poultry and Damages	155	16	0
Deficit	105	12	0	Keepers for Finds, &c.	148	0	0
				Tailor, Blacksmith, Harness and Bootmakers, Licenses for Men & Hounds	205	0	0
				Printing and Postage	27	10	0
				Sundries	119	10	0
Total	£1830	16	0	Total	£1830	16	0

By the above statement it will be seen that the deficit on last Season's Accounts, amounted to about £105. It is hoped that Members and Friends will do their best to remedy this in future.

[P.T.O.

List of Subscriptions and Donations.
1894-5.

	£	s.	d.		£	s.	d.
Adkins, H. J., Esq.	5	0	0	Farmer, W. R. G., Esq.	30	0	0
Ashcombe, Lord	25	0	0	Fearon, P. B., Esq.	10	0	0
Aston, A. W., Esq.	25	0	0	Finn, W. F., Esq.	5	5	0
Avery, H. E., Esq.	10	10	0	Fisher, J., Esq.	10	0	0
				Fisher, A. O., Esq.	5	5	0
Bashford, J. W., Esq.	20	0	0	Foley, Lord	25	0	0
Beever, Capt.	10	0	0				
Bennett, T. H., Esq.	5	0	0	Gadsden, G. A., Esq.	10	10	0
Bennett, T. J., Esq.	5	0	0	Game, W., Esq.	5	5	0
Berkeley, S., Esq.	10	10	0	Godfree, E., Esq.	5	5	0
Bird, A., Esq.	10	10	0	Gordon-Clark, H. H., Esq.	10	10	0
Bird, G., Esq.	5	5	0	Gordon-Clark, C. S., Esq.	2	2	0
Blaine, Miss				Gordon-Clark, G. W., Esq.	10	0	0
Brandt, T. E., Esq.	10	10	0	Gorton, F. S., Esq.	10	0	0
Brettell, R., Esq.	5	0	0				
Brown, A. H., Esq.	21	0	0	Hankey, J. B., Esq.	50	0	0
Bucknill, T. T., Q.C., M.P.	10	0	0	Hanning, J. H. S., Esq.	10	0	0
Budd, J. E., Esq.	10	0	0	Harter, A. E., Esq.	10	0	0
Buller, Col. Hornby (the late)	10	0	0	Helsham-Jones, Col.	5	0	0
Butler, W., Esq.	10	0	0	Henderson, J., Esq.	10	0	0
Butler, H., Esq.	10	0	0	Hobson, Miss	10	0	0
Butler, F., Esq.	10	0	0	Hornby, Col. L., Esq.	10	0	0
				Howell, F. G., Esq.	5	5	0
Calvert, Col. A. M.	10	0	0	Hylton-Foster, H., Esq.	5	5	0
Calvert, W. A., Esq.	10	0	0				
Chambers, Col.	10	0	0	Israel, R. N., Esq.	10	0	0
Chinnery, W. M., Esq.	10	10	0				
Cockburn, Miss M.	5	0	0	Jillard, H. P., Esq.	5	0	0
Collis-Browne, Major W.	15	0	0				
Combe, C., Esq.	20	0	0	Kerby, J. Ramsay, Esq.	5	0	0
Combe, C. H., Esq., M.P.	20	0	0	Keswick, W., Esq.	10	0	0
Corbett, J., Esq.	10	0	0	King-Noel, Capt. the Hon. L.	20	0	0
Crocker, W. M., Esq.	10	0	0				
Crocker, T. E., Esq.	10	15	0	Lambert, C., Esq.	15	15	0
Cropley, J., Esq.	5	5	0	Lemmon, Col.	10	0	0
Curnick, A. J., Esq.	10	0	0	Levien, F. G., Esq.	5	0	0
Cushney, A., Esq.	10	0	0	Locke-King, H. F., Esq.	10	0	0
Cuvelje, T., Esq.	15	0	0	Low, T., Esq.	10	10	0
				Lushington, Judge	5	0	0
Dale, S., Esq.	10	10	0	Lyall, C., Esq.	10	0	0
D'Avigdor, E., Esq. (the late)	10	0	0				
Deacon, W., Esq.	21	0	0	Malthus, Col.	2	2	0
Dent, W., Esq.	10	10	0	Manners, W. F., Esq.	5	0	0
Doulton, H. L., Esq.	5	5	0	Maples, W., Esq.	5	0	0
Du Buisson, W. H., Esq.	10	10	0	Marlborough, Duchess of	10	0	0
Duffield, P. T., Esq.	2	2	0	Mashiter, T., Esq.	50	0	0
East Surrey Regt.	11	0	0	Mayhew, M., Esq.	10	0	0
Eastwood, J. F., Esq.	5	5	0	Melson, A., Esq.	10	0	0
Evelyn, W. J., Esq.	25	0	0				

	£	s.	d.		£	s.	d.
Mentzendorff, L.	15	15	0	Sillem, O., Esq.	10	0	0
Mercer, W. J., Esq.	5	5	0	Smith, E. T., Esq.	10	0	0
Merrielees, F. J., Esq.	10	10	0	St. George, G., Esq.	10	0	0
Miller, A. T., Esq.	20	0	0	Stevenson, Major W.	5	0	0
Moon, The Rev. Sir E. G., Bart.	10	10	0	Sturgis, H. P., Esq.	10	0	0
Moon, A. G., Esq. (the late)	10	10	0	Swift, J. T., Esq.	10	0	0
Morley, E., Esq.	10	10	0	Tagg, H., Esq.	5	5	0
Muir, F., Esq.	5	0	0	Tanqueray, W. H., Esq.	10	10	0
Murray, C. F., Esq.	10	10	0	Tate, A., Esq.	10	10	0
				Taylor, H., Esq.	10	0	0
				Thompson, B. D., Esq.	5	0	0
Napper, A., Esq.	5	5	0	Thurgood, H. J., Esq.	5	0	0
Nicholas, R., Esq.	10	10	0	Tickner, G., Esq. (the late)	10	0	0
Noakes, W., Esq.	31	10	0				
Noakes, J. N., Esq.	10	10	0	Till, E., Esq.	10	10	0
Norfolk, Duke of	20	0	0	Tritton, A. H., Esq.	50	0	0
Northey, Rev. E.	10	0	0	Trollope, G. H., Esq.	10	10	0
Northumberland, Duke of	20	0	0	Trollope, F. G., Esq.	5	5	0
Paine, L., Esq.	10	10	0	Ullrich, R., Esq.	10	10	0
Palmer, J. W., Esq.	3	3	0	Vacher, E. P., Esq.	10	10	0
Parratt, Col. E. S.	10	0	0	Verity, J. B., Esq.	10	10	0
Pilditch, P. E., Esq.	10	10	0	Verity, S., Esq.	10	0	0
Price, C. J. (the late)	10	0	0				
				Warden, H. W.	10	0	0
Ralli-Pantia, Esq.	10	0	0	Whitehead, S., Esq.	10	10	0
Rickards, Mrs.	10	0	0	Wickham, R. W., Esq.	10	0	0
Rickards, F. M., Esq.	10	0	0	Williams, F. Hue, Esq.	15	15	0
Robinson, C. S. A.	5	0	0	Willink, D., Esq.	10	0	0
Rucker, M. D., Esq.	10	10	0	Witty, R. J., Esq.	10	10	0
Rumford, J. K.	5	0	0	Wood, H. J., Esq.	10	10	0
Russell, H., Esq.	10	10	0	Wood, E., Esq.	10	10	0
Seth-Smith, A., Esq.	15	15	0	Total	£1650	4	0
Seymour, Col. L.	10	0	0				

A. BIRD, Esq., sent an additional £10; J. COLMAN'S subscription of £10 was also sent after the accounts were made up, they have therefore both been carried forward to next year.

ARTHUR H. TRITTON,
Hon. Secretary.

W. STENT AND SONS, PRINTERS, GUILDFORD.

For comparison purposes, a list of current subscribers to the Surrey Union Hunt appears in Appendix 12.

Wotton Hatch.

W.J.ROSE
WESTCOTT

A commercially produced postcard of a meet at the Wotton Hatch, circa 1900-05. The whole entourage has been grouped around the Master [on foot in the group at the centre of the composition, to the left of his mounted huntsman] in the middle of the main Dorking to Guildford road. Close examination reveals several ladies riding side-saddle and a collection of mounted grooms and second horsemen at the rear of the left-hand group. Walter Rose was a well known local photographer from Westcott, whose business flourished during the first two decades of the 20th century.

CHAPTER 10

Two Even Shorter Masterships

In March 1898 the Hunt committee accepted Mr Arthur Labouchere as Master on the following terms:

> " *1. That the Hounds (which are the property of the Hunt) shall be kept up to their present strength and efficiency.*
> *2. That he is to provide suitable kennels in a central position at his own expense.*
> *3. That he is to provide horses for the Hunt Servants at his own expense."*

Furthermore, Mr Godman, now Master of the Crawley & Horsham, took back country his Hunt had lent and, as a consequence, the Surrey Union had to take back country that had been lent to the Burstow Hunt. But if these changes were not enough, Mr Labouchere would also have to replace a Hunt secretary of longstanding: one who knew the ropes very well indeed [see press cutting, right]. Alas, the seeds of future difficulty were already sown.

Mr Labouchere, born in London on 20th October 1842, was an old Harrovian and a member of his father's banking firm, Williams Deacon & Co. Described as being of a restless, irascible and outdoor nature, he was an excellent horseman and would frequently spend more energy trying to drive a four-in-hand to the bank premises than to understand the workings of the firm once he had arrived. Perhaps unsurprisingly then, he was asked to withdraw from the bank in 1876. After hunting a pack of hounds in Pau, France, he had previously been Master of the Warnham Staghounds.

A Mr J W Board was invited to become his new Hunt secretary, provided that "*he come to live & hunt in the County*". This lack of continuity and Mr Board's likely inexperience of 'how things were done' in the Surrey Union Hunt country would only further compound the obstacles facing Mr Labouchere.

Towards the end of the 1898-99 season, it was clear that nothing had been done about providing alternative kennels and initially the Hunt committee resolved to alter and improve the Fetcham premises. This required £500 to be raised from the subscribers and Mr Hankey also agreed to lend the sum of £1000 at 4% interest for this work. He would charge rent of £140 per annum for use of these improved kennels. There were a series of committee meetings in early March 1899 that discussed this proposition, together with the prospects of Mr Labouchere continuing as Master, but nothing was finalised until the members eventually ratified those proposals on 11th March. But by the end of April all these good intentions lay in ruins.

This cutting from an unidentified newspaper, dated 12th April 1899, tells the tale:

Surrey Union Hunt Point-to-Point Races – A Disappointment

This annual meeting was to have been brought off yesterday afternoon at the well-known course over Mr Martin D. Rucker's estate, at Slyfield, Cobham, but owing to an unfortunate slip on the part of the Master of the Hunt, Mr Labouchere, who failed to give sufficient time for the meeting to be registered, no racing took place. The worse blunder was that the postponement of the meeting was not made known, even in the village of Cobham, until yesterday morning, and consequently a large number of hunting men, sportsmen, bookmakers and Pressmen journeyed to Cobham by road or rail, only to find that they had been deprived of their afternoon's sport. This was even more unfortunate as the entries for the various events were exceptionally numerous and the afternoon being fine, some interesting racing would have been seen. A great deal of dissatisfaction was expressed by those who had made the journey in vain.

THE SURREY UNION HUNT.

An important meeting of the members of this hunt was held on Saturday at the Swan Hotel, when the new master, Mr Labouchere, the successor of Mr T. H. Bennett, who had to resign on account of illness, was introduced to the members. Mr J. B. Hankey occupied the chair. The resignation of Mr A. H. Tritton, as secretary, was accepted with much regret, and a magnificent silver loving cup and set of fruit dishes, which had been subscribed for by the members, was presented to him by Mr Aston.— Mr Tritton sincerely thanked every one for the handsome present, and said he hoped long to hunt with the union. He spoke of the doings of the hunt during the past season and of the very valuable assistance he had received in the secretarial work from Miss Rickards, whose family had so long been connected with the hunt. Mr Tritton, as deputy-master and secretary, then presented a purse of £100, which had been collected by Mr F. Hue Williams and Mr A. Aston from the members, as a parting gift to Will Holloway, who has been huntsman for 11 years.

SURREY UNION HOUNDS

WILL MEET ON

Saturday, Nov. 5th ...... Norbury Park, at 10-30 (Breakfast).

Opening Meet.

Arthur Labouchere, Cobham.

Even in 1898 the Hunt breakfast was a long-established tradition, and it remains so to this day.

SURREY UNION HOUNDS

WILL MEET   AT 11 o'Clock.

Tuesday, Mar. 7th	......	*Effingham.*
Thursday, „ 9th	......	*Punch Bowl, Dorking,* **11-15.**
Saturday, „ 11th	......	*Bagden Farm.*
Tuesday, „ 14th	......	*Black Horse,* **Gomshall,**
Thursday, „ 16th	......	*Holmwood Station,* **11-15.**
Saturday, „ 18th	......	*Mickleham.*
Tuesday, „ 21st	......	*East Clandon.*
Thursday, „ 23rd	......	*Betchworth Village,* **11-30.**
Saturday, „ 25th	......	*West Horsley Station.*

Arthur Labouchere, *Cobham.*

Naturally, Mr Labouchere did the decent thing and offered to relinquish the Mastership. However, his letter of resignation, itself a dignified essay in self-control, hints that all was not well to a much wider degree within the Hunt. Dated, 17th April, it said:

Gentlemen,

At a meeting of the SUH Committee a letter was handed in from me, & read, stating on what terms I would take on the Mastership of the Surrey Union Hounds.

The terms briefly were that suitable & approved kennels and accommodation involving an expenditure of between 15 & £1600 should be found by the hunt, at a fair rental. This money has not been found, & it is now within a fortnight of the end of the season, which leaves me barely any time to make my own arrangements.

Taking also into consideration my view on the mismanagement of the Pt - Pt, the arrangements of which I was practically ignorant of, not having been consulted on the point, also the small differences among the Committee, I beg to tender my resignation.

I shall be ready to deliver over the hounds on 1st May.

I am, Gentlemen, Yours truly
Arthur Labouchere

The Hunt committee met the very next day and unanimously accepted this offer to resign. They also instructed the Hunt secretary to write to Major Goulburn, Mr G H Longman and Mr A H Tritton, asking "*them whether they would take the Hounds, if they were elected as Master*". At yet another committee meeting four days later, on 22nd April, a vote of thanks, proposed by Lord William Beresford VC, was accorded to Mr Labouchere "*for having hunted the country this season*". Lord William also proposed that Major Goulburn be invited to undertake the Mastership, subject to the approval of a sub-committee. The Hunt committee ratified this appointment on 29th April 1899.

As a postscript to this whole affair, the Hunt undertook to pay the outstanding bills resulting from the point-to-point fiasco, whilst the remaining accounts between Mr Labouchere and anyone else were his personal affair. Mr Board resigned as Hunt secretary shortly afterwards.

So, from 1st May 1899, Major Henry Goulburn became the new Master. He undertook to hunt two days a week before Christmas, increasing to three days after, and promised to buy forage for the Hunt horses from farmers in the Hunt country. This note, with a newspaper cutting pasted upon it, sets the scene for the start of the Major's tenure as Master.

Born in 1858, Henry Goulburn had served for twenty years in the Grenadier Guards and was present at the battle of Omdurman. He served under Lord Kitchener in the Khartoum campaign of 1898, gaining the Egyptian and Queen's Medals, and had retired from military service to Betchworth House the same year.

Special Premium given by A. LABOUCHERE, Esq., Master of the Surrey Union Hunt.

CLASS 31. For the best Five Acres of SWEDES, grown by Tenant Farmers only, in the district of the Surrey Union Hunt.

A Premium of   ...   £5 0 0

The inset, right, is a replica of a postcard found in the Hunt archive, upon which is pasted a newspaper cutting and annotated in manuscript. H T W Blakeney, a doctor, had settled in Dorking in 1875 and became a renowned Surrey 'stagger'. One of his hunters, *Tommy*, was so bad tempered as a youngster that many times he failed even to get to the meet. Happily, the horse did eventually come to hand and went on to carry his owner for eighteen seasons.

9th June 1899
Lonsdale House Dorking

Daily Telegraph June 9th 1899
The vacancy in the Mastership of the Surrey Union Foxhounds, caused by the retirement of Mr Arthur Labouchere, has been filled up, great satisfaction having been expressed at the appointment of Major Goulburn, who is well known in the Shires as a hard man to hounds, and may be confidently trusted to uphold in his new office the best traditions of the Surrey Union.

I fully endorse the above remarks and wish you the best of luck - Hugh Blakeney

Lord William Beresford

FOR VALOUR

Lord William Leslie de la Poer Beresford was the son of John de la Poer Beresford, 4th Marquess of Waterford and Christiana Leslie. He was born in Mullaghbrach, County Armargh, on 20th July 1847. After Eton and time in Bonn being tutored in French and German, he went to a military crammer and was commissioned as a cornet in the 9th Lancers (The Queen's Royal) in 1867.

When his regiment was posted to India, Lord William was attached to the Viceroy's staff. On hearing of the British Army's defeat at Isandhlwana, he was "just mad" to fight in the Zulu Wars and was granted six month's special leave to do so. On 3rd July 1879, a Sergeant John Fitzmaurice, of the 1st Battalion, 24th Regiment Foot, was unseated from his horse when surprised by the Zulus near the White Umfolosi River during an advance towards the Zulu capital of Ulundi. Badly wounded, he would have been killed had not Lord William Beresford and Sergeant Edmund O'Toole, of the Frontier Light Horse, ridden back to save him. When the trio finally returned to their own lines it was far from clear quite who the wounded party was, Fitzmaurice having lost so much blood. For his gallantry and being an officer, Captain Beresford was immediately cited for the Victoria Cross. To his lasting credit, Lord William pointed out that Sergeant O'Toole was equally worthy of the award and that either both should receive it, or neither. Accordingly, both were later decorated with the Victoria Cross for their bravery.

Back in India, 'Fighting Bill' served three successive Viceroys as Military Secretary and gained the rank of full Colonel. He was well known as a polo player, steeplechaser, a whip [both trotting and with a team] and was, according to Lord Baden-Powell, "a great man after a pig". Whilst in the Simla hill station during 'the hot weather', he saved the Gaiety Theatre from financial ruin and launched an ambitious improvement scheme to the Annadale sports facilities that provided a new cricket pavilion and expanded polo grounds.

His racehorses were prodigiously successful, inter alia, winning the Viceroy's Cup six times [thrice with Myall King in 1887, 1888 and 1890]. He was invested as a Knight Commander, Order of the Indian Empire [KCIE]. Whilst in India, Lord William also became interested in spiritualism.

He married Lily, the dowager Duchess of Marlborough, on 30th April 1895. Born Lillian Warren Price, the daughter of Commodore Cicero Price USN of Mobile, Alabama, the Dowager Duchess was just as much a character as Lord William. She had married, firstly, Louis Hammersley in the USA. Widowed, she married, secondly, George Charles Spencer-Churchill, 8th Duke of Marlborough, on 29th June 1888 in City Hall, New York City. Although now a Duchess, she was again a widow when her marriage to Lord William took place. Lily is recorded as saying that she married first for money; second for social position and third for love. The couple made their home at Deepdene, Dorking. Whilst horses and hunting remained key elements in Lord William's life, he was also well known locally, together with his wife, for charitable works. His horse Sibola won the 1000 Guineas in 1899 and had Lord William lived but six months longer, he would have won the Derby with Volodyovski. A son, Billy, was born to the Beresfords on 4th February 1897.

Sadly, Lord William died from peritonitis on 28th December 1900 at Deepdene. He was buried on 3rd January 1901 in Clonagam, Curraghmore, County Limerick, Eire.

Lily died from heart failure at Deepdene on 11th January 1909.

This colourful newspaper account of a run in 1900 serves to show modern readers that at meet at Betchworth House was just as much a precursor to a fine day's hunting then as it is now:

"On Boxing Day the meet of this pack was at the seat of the popular Master, Major Goulburn, at Betchworth House. There were from 70 to 80 horsemen present and a large number of pedestrians. After a sumptuous breakfast, the coverts near at hand were tried without success. A move was then made to Rice Bridge copse and here Reynard was at home. He made off at a rattling pace through the Furze Field, then between Constable's Farm [Little Abbotts] and Leigh and on by Gadbrook to Brockham Park and into the rough. Here another fox bolted, but Kennett kept the hounds to the old 'un's track, who doubled, made his way back through Flint's[23] coverts and The Wilderness to the starting place. He was, however, soon compelled to quit, and off he went to Leigh, to a well-known drain on Mr Wells' farm. This found he stopped, and the fox now went by Burys Court, Little Flanchford, Bures Manor and on to Sidlow. There he once more doubled and made his way back again to Rice Bridge with the hounds close to his heels. Finding no resting place he made his exit for the third time, went by Santon and on to a field close to the residence of the late Mr St. Barbe on Reigate Heath, He was killed after a run of a little over two hours. The brush was presented to Miss M. DuBuisson, second daughter of Mr T DuBuissson of Snower Hill House. The plucky fox had crossed and re-crossed the River Mole five times."

It is opportune that most of the papers and ephemera associated with running the Hunt under the Goulburn Mastership survive and are sufficient to produce a book in their own right. But perhaps the contents of a single letter [see left], are indicative of his regime and provide a tantalizing glimpse into rural life as it was lived. Much more will be heard of Mr Heath in later chapters. Interestingly though, it was Mrs Cuthbert Heath that was recorded as having subscribed £5-0s-0d for the 1899-1900 season!

Despite having once retired from the Army, fresh military duties forced the Major to resign after only one season as Master. It was the Boer War that caused him to be recalled to the colours and become second-in-command of the Guards Reserve. In his final report to the Hunt committee, the Major stated that hounds had had eight blank days and killed 7½ brace. Regrettably then, it seems that the gloom of William Holdaway, the huntsman, had not been lifted.[24]

Since its foundation in July 1841, the magazine, *Punch*, had developed a reputation for the cartoon-and-caption style of humour and, by the end of the 19th century, this was a well-established art form. The equestrian scene in general, and hunting in particular, was too rich in comic possibilities to be ignored and often as many as three hunting cartoons would be published in a week. One of the more prolific, and famous, of this new breed of satirists was G Denholm Armour – at this time a Surrey Union subscriber. Two of his cartoons are reproduced opposite, with further details of his life and times.

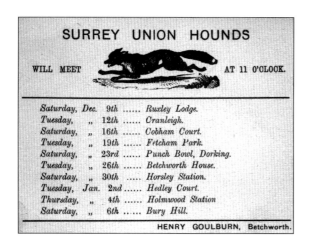

SURREY UNION HOUNDS

WILL MEET   AT 11 O'CLOCK.

Saturday,	Dec. 9th	Ruxley Lodge.
Tuesday,	" 12th	Cranleigh.
Saturday,	" 16th	Cobham Court.
Tuesday,	" 19th	Fetcham Park.
Saturday,	" 23rd	Punch Bowl, Dorking.
Tuesday,	" 26th	Betchworth House.
Saturday,	" 30th	Horsley Station.
Tuesday,	Jan. 2nd	Hedley Court.
Thursday,	" 4th	Holmwood Station.
Saturday,	" 6th	Bury Hill.

HENRY GOULBURN, Betchworth.

Notes

23 *Charles Flint, gamekeeper for the Betchworth House estate for over 60 years, died in 1902, aged 84.*
24 *See Appendix: 5.*

G.D. Armour

For at least two seasons [1899-1901], George Denholm Armour was a member of the Surrey Union Hunt. Born in Lanarkshire on 30th January 1864, he was the son of a cotton broker. After attending St Andrews University, he studied at the Edinburgh School of Art and the Royal Scottish Academy. In 1885 he visited Morocco, to paint and to buy cheap horses, only returning when his money ran out. On a subsequent expedition to Tangiers he met Joseph Crawhall, who remained a great friend until the latter's untimely death in 1913. Both hunting mad, the two friends ran a stud together at Wheathampstead, Hertfordshire. The household only broke up when Armour married, with Crawhall standing as his best man.

Armour's work first appeared in *The Graphic* [1890] and, subsequently, *The Sporting & Dramatic News*, *Country Life*, & *The Tatler*. He also illustrated a wealth of sporting publications and painted equestrian portraits of society figures. He contributed cartoons to *Punch* for 35 years. When hunting he always carried a sketchbook, and it is this immediacy which lends so many of his animal portrayals their power and flowing movement.

During the First World War, he commanded a cavalry squadron and rose to the rank of lieutenant-colonel with the British Salonika Force. He was appointed OBE in 1919, following his command of the army's remount depot in Salonika. He died in 1949.

Cartoon humour does not always travel too well through time. However, these two examples of Armour's work have a resonance with modern experience and readily show how the verities of the hunting and equestrian world endure.

G Denholm Armour on a favourite hunter.

Small Boy. "I THINK THEY'VE KILLED A FOX."
Purist. "CUB, MY BOY, CUB; FOX ONLY AFTER THE END OF OCTOBER."
Small Boy. "MY! FANCY THREE MORE DAYS MAKING ALL THAT DIFFERENCE."

DEALER (*to youth in search of Christmas present*) : "Buy 'im, sir, and the lady'll 'ave the best-lookin' 'ack in London."
CLIENT : "Oh, his looks are all right : it's his thoughts that worry me."

Hounds moving off from a meet at the White Horse Hotel in Dorking High Street. There is no date given for this photograph, but the evidence of the clothing worn by the bystanders, particularly the hats of the ladies, the design of the three motor cars and the coloured collars of the two mounted followers wearing top hats [to the left of the garage & stables entrance] suggests a date after 1905. Prominent in the centre of the photograph, mounted on a horse with a white star and short blaze, is a gentleman closely resembling Edward Murray [see page 49]. If it is him, it points to the photograph being taken either during his joint-Mastership in 1907-08 or after becoming sole Master in 1910.

The Surrey Union Hunt Puppy Show 2005

Straw hats are always worn at a Puppy Show, as demonstrated [left to right] by SUH subscriber Rose Williams, an unknown *Felix the Fox* manqué and a visitor from the Tywi & Cothi Hunt, Miss Rachel Evans MFH.

Alison West receives her trophies [she walked the overall champion, the bitch *Lapwing* - by Crawley & Horsham *Landlord* '02, out of SUH *Matchbox* '00] from Mrs Meller MFH and is applauded by Lulu Hutley and her daughters, Iona [left] and Isabella.

Ian Shakespeare demonstrates the art of showing, whilst Miss Pat Sutton [Staff College & RMA Sandhurst Draghounds] and Mark Bycroft [huntsman, Old Surrey Burstow & West Kent] cast a critical eye as judges. Also taking a keen interest are professionals from other Hunts, in their de rigueur dark suits and bowler hats.

The Puppy Show appeals to all ages, although some might take a more ardent interest than others! From left, Neil Scott, Linda Scutt, Tracy Scutt, Mark Welsh and Darren Scutt [holding his daughter].

On Boxing Day 2005, Nick Prior demonstrates that an ability to jump hedges is still a prerequisite for a 1st whipper-in at the Surrey Union.

The field pause and take a refreshment break. Prominent in his red coat is former joint-Master Freddie Ford. Also readily recognisable is the broad back of Edward Hutley [second from left], a major landowner and great friend to our Hunt.

"Come behind". Hound control and woodland hunting at its best.

A timeless winter scene, with the Surrey Union Hunt spread out in all its glory.

40

The Joint Masters 2006-07

Mark Sprake MFH	Ian Gilchrist MFH	
		Mrs Katharine Meller MFH
Jeremy Gumbley MFH	Edmund O'Reilly-Hyland MFH	

42

The Secretaries 2006-07

Geraldine Firth pops a set of rails in fine style.

Judeth Chamberlain busy collecting caps and field money..

Jane Williams. She did catch her horse soon afterwards.

Rachel Brooker on *Cobra*.

Penny Wilson. Cheerful as ever and happy to be hunting.

43

Ian Shakespeare acknowledges the cheers and applause as he moves off from the Meet at Kennels on 17th February 2005, the day before the Hunting Act 2004 came into force. A multitude was standing behind the camera.

CHAPTER 11

A New Century – New Masters – A New Establishment

So it came to pass that, though still a sick man, Thomas Bennett offered his services again, as joint-Master with Mr. G. H. Longman for the season 1900-01. However this was conditional on there being a guarantee of £300 beyond the subscriptions actually received, up to £2,000. Additionally, the subscription for all hunting Members [not being land or covert owners, or farmers] was raised to 15 guineas.

Sadly, Mr. Bennett died in September 1900, leaving Mr. Longman to carry on alone. George Henry Longman lived at West Hill House, Epsom. He was born on 3rd August 1852 and educated at Eton. At school he was a keen cricketer and also Master of the Beagles 1870-71. After Trinity College, Cambridge, where he was University cricket captain, he played [as a gentleman, naturally] for Hampshire in 27 matches and in the 1920s was President of Surrey County Cricket Club. He was a member of the publishing firm Longmans, Green & Co.

Wisely, Mr Longman agreed terms with the representatives of Mr Bennett's estate to hold over at the Cobham kennels for the ensuing season. Clearly a longer-term solution was needed and Lord Ashcombe offered to build new kennels at Bookham, to be leased to the Hunt at a ground rent of £50 per annum and 6% upon the amount of the outlay. However, an estimated building cost of £5,700 [later revised to £3,200 for the kennels and £800 for cottages] was too steep, as was the rate of return. The Hunt committee suggested 4%, which Lord Ashcombe turned down, but he would consent to cheaper buildings. Consequently tenders were sought from Messrs Humphrey; the Portable Buildings Cº and Boulton & Paul, it being the latter who won the contract. Also the site of the works was moved nearer to the road to lessen cost of access and drainage. These new kennels[25] were eventually ready for use in time for opening meet of the 1902-03 season.

Despite these modern facilities being a huge improvement on those at Cobham Court, life in the new kennels was still hard. From the memoirs of Jack Molyneux, the 2nd whipper-in during this period, it is possible to learn just how harsh conditions really were and to gain an insight into the life of a Hunt servant in the early 1900s. His account of life in the service of the Surrey Union Hunt is set out in Appendix: 6.

At the 1901 general meeting, Mr F M Rickards resigned as honorary secretary and was replaced by Frederick Hue Williams [of Uplands, Leatherhead, and a keen point-to-point rider, with wins as a heavyweight in 1906 and 1907]. Also a Mr Beresford Heaton *"intimated a wish on behalf of the residents in the south of the country, that occasional meets should be held on Saturdays 'below the hills'"*. With hounds going out on Tuesday and Saturday before Christmas, and on Tuesday, Thursday and Saturday after Christmas, the reason for this plea becomes apparent when it is understood that at this time the New Year Tuesday country centred on Bookham, Fetcham, Norbury Park, Box Hill and the southern side of Epsom; the Thursday country was the Weald and hills lying between Holmwood and Guildford and the Saturday country was the Oxshott, Cobham and Byfleet districts to the north-west.

Several times during Mr Longman's Mastership, the Hunt committee was asked to help him *"on all occasions to help to protect crops and hedges and property from reckless riders"* and *"to see that fences were not ridden over recklessly & that all gates used in a run should be left properly & securely closed"*. Whether the cause of these requests was merely

The newly constructed kennels at Great Bookham were of sufficient local interest to appear on a contemporary postcard. The horseman is standing in what is now called Dorking Road, the lane that leads to Polesden Lacy. The premises now form the core of Kenilworth Riding Stables and the dwellings, in particular, are still recognisable. The unusual proximity of the buildings to the road remains very noticeable.

Notes

25 *See Appendix: 9 for a description.*

preventative or in response to actual unruly behaviour is unclear, but this corporate approach to Field mastering seems to have been most effective, as the extract from the *Victoria History* indicates [see left].

It was during this time that the bitter controversy over which hunt had the right to draw 'Glovers' at Charlwood was finally settled between the Surrey Union and the Burstow. This is a large covert of nearly 200 acres and was highly prized as a sure find, although deep ghylls and the Dolby Brook made getting away from it with hounds rather difficult.[26] In 1900, the Master of the Burstow, Mr Lambert, formally renounced his Hunt's claims on Glovers, in return for which he was allowed to draw it during December, February & April and not more than twice in any of those months. In 1906, the covert was taken back absolutely by the Surrey Union.

There were other issues concerning the Hunt country that also needed to be addressed. At a general meeting held in the schoolroom adjoining the Master's residence in Epsom at 10 o'clock on Saturday, 8th November 1902 [ie before hunting], Mr Longman *"intimated that owing to the fact that the country on the western boundary of the hunt lying between Cranleigh & Guildford not having been properly hunted by the Chiddingfold, to whom it was* <u>lent</u> [27] *in 1876, it was thought desirable to reinclude the same in the Union Hunt"*. The revised boundary eventually ratified at that time ran from Ellen's Green and followed *"the main turnpike road through Cranleigh, Gaston Gate, Shamley Green & Wonersh to Guildford"*.

Mr Longman did not breed his own hounds, preferring each season to buy unentered drafts from the Duke of Buccleuch. He kept only bitches and hunted the big bitch pack himself whilst Will Kennett hunted the small bitches, with Jim Hackett as first whipper-in. According to Jack Molyneux, the same horses that used to draw Mr. Longman's brougham, incredibly, also carried him out hunting. He also records that Mr Longman rode purely by balance, without any grip, and rode at a fast trot into his fences. So it will come as no surprise that he took any number of falls as a consequence, but apparently this did not diminish his bravery across country. With this in mind, having *"intimated that he would be unable to continue the mastership after the present season"* in January 1904, is it coincidence that on 12th February Mr Longman was too ill to attend the meeting to select his successor?

Fortunately, Mr Longman recovered and remained a Member of the Hunt for several years, eventually moving to Bearehurst, Holmwood, presumably to be nearer the centre of the action.

Notes

26 *Several Hunt bridges were built after the Great War to reduce these hazards.*

27 *The underlining is in the original text and is clearly there to make a point.*

CHAPTER 12

As Keen as Mustard? The Colman Years

Being a member of the famous starch and mustard milling firm from Norfolk, [although he, himself, worked in their London head office at 108, Cannon Street], Frederick Gordon Dalziel Colman of Nork Park, Epsom Downs, was well-chosen when asked to became Master in 1904, at the age of 23 [having been born in March 1881]. An old Etonian, he had gained his experience with the Worcester Park Beagles, the Brookside Harriers, the West Surrey Staghounds and the Southdown Foxhounds. He was a good judge of a horse and was always superbly mounted and well turned-out.

During Mr Colman's Mastership some dog hounds were added to the pack, which numbered about 50 couple, and they hunted four days a week. Will Kennett retired and Jim Hackett was put on as huntsman in his place. Initially, A Smethurst and S Dunn assisted him as 1st and 2nd whippers-in respectively, but in 1905 Joe Overton came with a good character from Mr Lee-Steere's Warnham Staghounds as 1st whipper-in. But Overton did not stay [he went to the Surrey Staghounds] and in 1906 Dunn was promoted in his stead, and B Jones was employed as 2nd whipper-in. Jones did not last either and was replaced by W Stickland in 1907. At the start of the 1908-09 season it was nearly all change again, with R Lawrence as huntsman, E Cross as 1st whipper-in and Strickland staying on as 2nd whipper-in. In 1909-10, Mr Colman's last season as Master, Strickland was replaced by J Smith [late of the West Kent]. Such a rapid turnover of staff points to a general level of dissatisfaction and an indication that things had not significantly improved for the Hunt servants since Jack Molyneux's time in the early years of the decade.

Towards the end of his first season as Master, Mr Colman invited all members of the Hunt *"wearing pink"* [qv comments on this phraseology in Chapter 9] to wear the Hunt yellow collar and this request usually helps to date turn of the century photographs of uncertain provenance. It is interesting to note that his portrait photograph when he took on the Mastership plainly does not show this feature and it seems that this usage did not last – a theme to which we will return. As will become clear, if one is privileged enough to be invited to wear the Hunt button today, it is an indication that the Master also expects that the primrose yellow collar of the Surrey Union Hunt should adorn a hunting coat, be it red, black or navy blue.

Intriguingly, there was a whiff of scandal in summer of 1906. *"The Master (Mr Colman) informed the committee of a libellous article which appeared in the Daily News of July 4th respecting himself and offered to resign the Mastership, but on the motion of Mr Wells [from Leigh], 2nd Mr Land [from Horsley], the committee unanimously expressed their utmost confidence in Mr Colman & refused to accept his resignation on such an untruthful statement"*.

The offending piece was written as an adjunct to a report about the forthcoming debate in the House of Commons about the Land Tenure Bill and was introduced, after a preamble, as follows:

"Let it be remembered that this case is simply an example of what is going on through the length and breadth of England. The peasant is being dislodged by the pheasant. The country is becoming a solitude in order to provide shooting for wealthy idlers. Here we touch on the very heart of the whole evil of modern England".

However the real damage was done in the main body of the article. Under the headline *"Aceldama*[28] *– The Story of a Landlord, His Tenant, and Some Rabbits"*, the journalist, Fred Horne, described Mr Colman's allegedly nefarious

When this photograph was taken in at the start of the 1904-05 season it was thought that Mr Frederick Gordon Colman was the youngest Master of Foxhounds in Britain. This studio portrait shows him wearing completely new kit, ready for the opening meet at Norbury Park. He must have cut quite a dash in his double-breasted swallowtail coat, but his new hunting whip looks to be something of a handful.

Notes

28 *Aramaic, 'a field of blood'. It refers to the field outside Jerusalem supposedly bought with the blood money of Jesus.*

estate management practices, including the implied use of his wealth and the existing law to dispossess a virtuous tenant and his implied responsibility for the suicide of an itinerant worker. It is all provocative stuff and, at best, smacked of emergent socialism and, at worst, provided a repugnant example of the politics of envy.

In at a meeting called for the purpose at Uplands, Leatherhead, on Wednesday 30th October 1907, Mr Colman announced that, "*he had to go abroad to Egypt for most of the season*". Accordingly, Mr Edward Murray of Mickleham [born in 1869, he was another old Etonian and a previous Master of the Surrey Staghounds] was asked to step into the breach as joint-Master for the 1907-08 season. There were some 106 subscribers that season, who contributed £1624 to the Hunt funds, with 29 donors providing a further £39-7s-0d. For the start of the next season, 1908-09, the annual subscription was raised to 20 guineas, plus 5 guineas for an extra horse. It was also resolved that the Master be allowed to cap, which rather points to people coming out hunting on a regular basis, but without paying a subscription.

In 1908 a famous run took place from Charlwood. Apocryphally, it has been recorded as a run of 1 hour and 35 minutes duration, with a ten-mile point. However, if the run is traced on a map, a more objective assessment makes it perhaps no more than a seven-mile point. Yet cartography soon makes it evident that this disparity may well be the confusion of 'a point' [the distance between the two farthest-apart points of a run (not the start and the finish), measured 'as the crows flies', ie in a straight line] with 'the distance hounds ran' [literally that, including every twist and turn]. Even so, there can be no doubt that this was still an exceptional day. Initially, the field had had a good 50 minutes with a fox from the recently reclaimed Glovers. Hounds then drew the Lyons [29] and got away close to their fox, running with a breast-high scent to Lowfield Heath, where they checked. No sooner was the pack at fault than the fox was viewed crossing the Brighton road, close by the White Hart crossroads [30]. Hounds then ran past Lovell House, over the main line of the London, Brighton & South Coast Railway between Horley and Three Bridges and through Worth Park by way of Copthorne. Turning right-handed, they crossed the railway branch line near Rowfant station and bowled their fox over in the open at Miswell Farm, near Turners Hill. This was a fast hunt all the way, with very few at the finish. Amongst that small number was Mr Murray and he considered it to be one of the best hunts in which he had ever participated. Modern map-readers will soon recognise that this run took place in a time long before Gatwick airport, Crawley New Town, the electrification of the railway, Dr Beeching and the M23 motorway!

In October 1909 Mr Colman announced his intention to resign at the end of the season and it was proposed by Mr Longman, seconded by Mr J Bernard Hankey [ie two previous Masters] and carried unanimously that "*a vote of gratitude be accorded to Mr Colman for the excellent manner in which he has hunted the country during the past six* [sic] *years of his Mastership: & that a record be made that the Hunt has never been in a more perfect state than at present*". A month later, a general meeting of the Hunt was held at the Red Lion in Dorking and, after 29 members had spoken to the motion, it was resolved "*that this meeting of subscribers, land & covert owners & farmers desires to place on record its very highest appreciation of the services rendered by Mr F G Colman to all departments of the Hunt during his five years Mastership – & also to express its regret that* [he?] *has found it necessary to resign that position*".

Clearly Mr Colman was going to be a very hard act to follow.

Notes

29 *Thought to have been one of Mr George Stonor's coverts, down Spencer's Lane, lying between Telvet Copse and Rainbow Wood.*
30 *If St Michael's church is a fixed point, probably near to where the current Old Brighton Road South now joins the airport's Perimeter Road South.*

CHAPTER 13
Hard Times, But Saved by Guarantors

As we have seen, Mr Edward Murray, now of Beare Green, Holmwood, had already had experience as a joint-Master for a season in 1907-08 and he agreed to carry on alone, expecting to stay as Master for no more than three years. The year 1910 also saw a complete change at the kennels, too. Albert Povey was put on as huntsman, with Sam Kilbourn as first whipper-in.

Hound breeding was also re-introduced. The new Master used bloodlines from the North Shropshire and Lord Middleton's to good effect, with sufficient success to warrant taking his hounds to the Reigate Hound Show. Though now a long-forgotten event, the Reigate & Redhill Horse and Hound Show was founded in 1900 and soon became an established part of the hunting calendar. Held six weeks before the Royal Hound Show at Peterborough, it provided a trial ground for packs in the south of the Kingdom to test their mettle on the flags. To quote from a contemporary record, *"Three well-appointed covered-in rings stand in the middle of a square of temporary kennels, the judging of foxhounds, harriers and beagles proceeding simultaneously, the music of the various breeds mingling in pleasant harmony"* [31]. Amongst those on the committee of the show in 1913 were the erstwhile Master, Mr F G Colman, and Mr H C Lee-Steere [of whom there will be more to say, presently], whilst Mr Murray was a steward. As a further illustration that there is rarely anything new under the sun, the Duke of Beaufort's huntsman, George Walters, *"had a blue or red ribbon in every button-hole of his green coat, winning three firsts, one second and two reserves"* that year. [See also Appendix: 7.]

As is becoming despairingly predictable in this account, a period of economic stability can soon change to one of distress. In the 1910-11 season there were considerable shortfalls of income against expenditure and these financial difficulties were only overcome by Sir Frederick Mirrielees [32] and Mr Cuthbert Heath [33] each contributing sums of £500 to the funds. This stringency carried forward into the next season, when hounds were restricted to only two day's hunting a week until after Christmas. Yet capping and the advertising of meets were both abolished at the same time, which rather suggests that, once again, a lot of people wanted to go hunting, but were not prepared to pay a full subscription.

By the end of the 1911-12 season things had not improved and the Hunt was still costing more under Mr Murray's Mastership than the guarantors had anticipated. Some drastic action was called for.

The Hunt secretary was instructed to send a circular to Hunt members and subscribers *"intimating that part of the pack would be sold and the hounds only hunted two days a week in future – unless a sufficiently large increase in subscriptions to warrant a continuation of the whole is manifest before March 30th"*. Such a manifestation did not occur and it was agreed to sell to 25 couple of hounds and to hunt only two days a week, with occasional bye-days when possible. On 19th December 1912 the Hunt committee met at the Swan Hotel in Leatherhead to consider the position. The minutes speak for themselves:

"A letter was read from the Master, Mr Murray, intimating that the three years for which he accepted the Mastership wd. end after this season & that he was not prepared to go on unless he could do so as 'hunting Master' with a practically guaranteed sub.

This photograph of Mr Edward Murray is in marked contrast to that of Mr Colman on page 47. Here is a man who is clearly used to hunting in all weathers, as the practical cut of his coat demonstrates. His general demeanour is that of a man about to go hunting and his heavily used boots, with their sensible mahogany tops, indicate he has done so many times before.

Notes

31 *Hound show habitués might question this curious remark. As the writer also went on to state that Reigate was forty miles from London and in Lord Leconfield's country, one wonders if he may have spent rather too much time in the luncheon tent.*

32 *A wealthy businessman from Dorking, married to an heiress of the Union Castle shipping line.*

33 *As mentioned earlier, from Holmwood and a most successful insurance underwriter at Lloyd's.*

After much discussion it was agreed to advertise the fact that a Master would be required after this season.
Mr Tritton agreed to keep the Hunt going as Master for one season or part of a season until a suitable Master is found."

A crisis, indeed. At the general meeting of the Hunt held at the Burford Bridge Hotel at 10.30 on Saturday 8th February 1913 [another hunting morning], the chairman referred to the resignation of Mr Murray *"and stated that the committee had advertised without much success – but that they had received an offer to accept the Mastership for next season from Mr A H Tritton on condition that he should be allowed to appoint Viscount Malden as Huntsman & deputy Master under certain circumstances. He did not ask for a guarantee"*. This offer was accepted, albeit somewhat reluctantly.

The essential cause of this difficulty was neatly summed up by Mr H H Gordon Clark JP [from Mickleham], who *"drew attention to the fact that subscribers should be more generous in their subscriptions – as all things connected with hunting are so much more expensive"*. Just so.

CHAPTER 14

The Great War

From this distance, it does not seem that Arthur Tritton's offer was taken up with much enthusiasm and quite why this should be so remains a puzzle. He had a history of stepping into the breach when needed, as his work in 1897 during the illness of Mr Bennett shows, and he was a contender for the Mastership in 1899. Yet despite knowing that he was willing to take on the job again, the Hunt committee still persisted in advertising the vacancy. Were they singularly aware of his capabilities and possible lack of focus [34] or, bearing in mind past glories, merely hoping innocently for someone to appear even better experienced and, perhaps, with a still deeper pocket?

But whatever may have been on the minds of the committee, Mr Tritton's first season as a Master in his own right seems to have passed off reasonably successfully. However, before accepting the Mastership for the 1914-15 season, he wished to give up that part of the Hunt country between Rusper and Faygate, as Viscount Malden was of the view that it was *"too rough and devoid of foxes"*. He also required reassurance about the Hunt finances.

At a committee meeting on 22nd May 1914, the Master reported that expense for the past season had been £2549-15s-5d, whereas the receipts only amounted to £2047-9s-0d: a deficit of some £500. Mr Tritton attributed the root cause of the problem to the increase in prices, particularly labour and provender. Fortunately, Mr Heath again offered to share any future deficit with the Master and this allowed hunting to continue as before. But things were about to get even worse.

The war against Germany was declared on 4th August 1914. In *Memoirs of a Foxhunting Man*, Siegfried Sassoon gives a graphic description of how speedily both countrymen volunteered for, and horses of all types were requisitioned into, the rapidly mobilising army. Many fine animals became military property almost overnight – especially hunters, as they were considered to make ideal officers' chargers. With the country at war on a scale never before experienced, it was a time of dreadful apprehension. So, when the Hunt committee met at the Priory, Leatherhead, on 14th August, it was perhaps more an act of faith rather than certainty when they agreed *"that notwithstanding the war, an effort should be made to keep the Hunt in existence. All present undertaking to renew their subscriptions & the Hon. Sec. was instructed to write to Mr Heath to this effect – & also issue a circular to all the subscribers of the Hunt, asking them if, under the circumstances, they would subscribe as usual"*. A month later it was decided to limit expenditure for the season to £1,400, with Mr Tritton and Mr Heath each contributing £200 to this amount. Following a review of the position in January 1915, it was decided to carry on hunting until the end of the season.

As the Viscount Malden had ceased hunting hounds, having presumably gone away to war, for the season 1915-16 Mr Tritton promoted Kilbourn to be his huntsman and D Grant [from the Ledbury] was put on as 1st whipper-in. Despite a repetition of the financial underpinning by the Master and Mr Heath, the rent payable on the Bookham kennel accommodation was a large drain on the Hunt's depleted resources and application was made for an amelioration of the terms. As a result, the landlord waived any claim to dilapidations and the tenancy was downgraded to an annual agreement. Midway through the season, greatly increased prices resulted in the budget having to be drastically reconsidered. It was clearly very tough indeed to make ends meet, but a valiant effort by all concerned managed to achieve it.

Notes

34 *He did have a wide range of sporting and other interests - he was the first chairman of Leatherhead Urban District Council, a County Councillor from 1904 until the end of the Great War and also enjoyed sailing, polo, cricket and shooting.*

In December 1915, the War Office sent a letter to the Hunt secretary *"expressing the desire that the Hunt should, if possible, be continued"* [see left] One can understand the morale boost that hunting would provide to those on leave from the fighting, but why would the War Office seek to make the continuation of hunting official policy? The answer seems to have been as simple as it was cynical. There was still a need for officers' chargers or other troop horses. Hunting ensured that such horses were still being bred and Hunts were able to make them just as effectively as the remount sections could, but at no cost to the military authorities.

From the Hunt's perspective, the season 1916-17 was essentially a repetition of the privations of the previous one, the only change of particular note being the reduction in rent of the kennels to £150 per annum for the duration of the war. At the end of the next season, in April 1918, Mr Tritton had clearly had enough of struggling with such hand to mouth survival and resigned the Mastership. Predictably, there was no-one immediately willing to take on the role and the Hunt secretary, Mr F Hue Williams, of Uplands, near Leatherhead, was *"requested and empowered to overlook and carry on matters with the staff and kennels until Sept 1st"*. Quite who *"the staff"* were is unclear, particularly as it is thought that Kilbourn had been conscripted somewhat earlier in the war. More alarmingly, the committee also made arrangements *"to inspect the hounds and to kill off any that are considered ... to be useless"*.

The reason for this drastic action was a direct consequence of the German U-boat blockade of this country in the last year of the Great War. It is not widely realised quite how effective this tactic was nor how close the nation came to being starved into surrender – the upshot being that any foodstuffs that were available went towards fighting the war and maintaining the civilian population, not feeding foxhounds. The letter [below], drafted by Mr Hue Williams in August 1918, reveals the stark realities of the position.

At a committee meeting held at the Red Lion Hotel in Dorking on 7th August 1918, Mr Henry Lee-Steere proposed that:

"The grateful thanks of the committee and the members of the Hunt be tendered to the late Master, Mr A H Tritton, for his energy & exertions during the whole time of his Mastership & especially for such during the trying time that we have been at war. Also to him & to Mr Heath for the great financial assistance they have given & are giving to the Hunt".

Never have truer words been spoken. Quite properly and justifiably, this proposition was carried unanimously.

At this same meeting, it was agreed that Mr Lee-Steere should become the Master for the season 1918-19 *"and Sir B Brodie, Major Henry Goulburn and Arthur Tritton undertook to help him on all possible occasions (perhaps month by month)"*.

Only by the skin of its teeth had the Surrey Union Hunt survived the Great War.

CHAPTER 15

The Post War Recovery

Henry Charles Lee-Steere of Jayes Park, Ockley, had previously been the Master of the Warnham Staghounds and his grandfather was the original Master of the Crawley and Horsham in 1836. Recognising the parlous position that the Hunt had placed itself in regarding kennels, in January 1919 he asked Lord Ashcombe if the Hunt could hold over for another year.

From the start of the season 1919-20, Mr Cuthbert Eden Heath OBE, now of Anstie Grange, Holmwood, became joint-Master with Mr Lee-Steere. Mr Heath had been made OBE for equipping and allowing his home to be used during the Great War as an officers' hospital. Nearly 700 patients were treated, most arriving straight from the Front by special trains from Dover and Southampton to Holmwood Station. During the hostilities he had also drawn up a scheme by which the Government could insure the public against losses caused by Zeppelins and other enemy aircraft. Before the War, he had famously cemented Lloyd's reputation in the United States by ensuring payment of all claims in relation to the 1906 San Francisco earthquake and fire, irrespective of policy wordings.

Meanwhile, the Warnham Staghounds establishment was being wound up, thereby rendering their kennels, which were owned by Mr Lee-Steere, vacant. So it will come as no surprise that on 17th January 1920 Mr Lee-Steere, "*in a short speech explained the position re kennels & the advisability of moving same further south & offering, if no suitable could be found, his old Warnham kennels at Oakwood Hill*".

Accordingly, the establishment did indeed move south to Oakwood Hill, where it remains to this day. Once the Bookham kennels were vacated, Lord Ashcombe sold the entire holding in June 1920. The auction particulars from this disposal survive and are reproduced as Appendix: 9.

At that same general meeting in January 1920, the vital "*question of the Hunt uniform*" was also considered. Now readers of this account would be forgiven for thinking that, bearing in mind all that has gone before, that this would be confirmed as being a primrose yellow collar and the UH Hunt buttons on a coat. But, no. After discussion "*it was left that the uniform was & is scarlett* [sic] *coat yellow waistcoat*". The sartorial confusion deepens when it is realised that this is neither a description of our evening dress nor a coat for the hunting field as worn by a member of the Surrey Union Hunt in the years prior to the Great War. It is true the former has no yellow collar, but it does have white silk facings [of which there is no mention], whilst the latter clearly did, and does, have the yellow collar! This pronouncement seems inexplicable, so readers are encouraged to debate the point amongst themselves during winter evenings spent in convivial company before a roaring log fire, after a tremendous day's hunting. [There is yet more still to be said on this topic in a later chapter.]

Two spectacular poultry claims were made in 1921. A cheque was sent to a Mrs Humphrey for £8-5s-0d [representing 33 chickens at 5/- each]. In contrast, a claim by Mrs Greville [the fabulously wealthy society hostess and chatelaine of Polesden Lacey] required a visit from the Master and the Hunt secretary was required to write to Messrs Clutton, her land agents, informing them of that fact.

Shortly before Christmas that year, the secretary also wrote to landowners "*north of the Guildford-Leatherhead L.&S. W.Rly informing them that the Hunt found it impossible to hunt that part of the country regularly this season, but to do the best it could to hunt it next season"*. This was clearly a result of logistical difficulties following the move south to Oakwood Hill and several times up to the outbreak of Word War II approaches were made by third parties to hunt this part of the country on an irregular basis.

On 9th March 1922, the Hunt committee met at the White Horse Hotel in Dorking to discuss in somewhat haphazard detail the arrangements for the point-to-point races to be held the next month at Shellwood Manor Farm: *"It was decided to give the catering for the Farmers' Lunches to Mr Fabis (late Kearleys) of 31 Bell Street Reigate. 6/- per head including mineral water, English meats & 1 tent for dressing & weighing room. One enclosure to be reserved for subscribers' carriages, non-subscribers to be admitted to same charge 21/-. Another enclosure for parking carriages at a charge of 5/-per carriage. Details of the race programme & cards as per forms attached. The holding of the Pt-to-Pt was subject to getting sufficient entries"*. As it turned out, entries were not sufficient and the meeting was cancelled. Unfortunately, there was worse to follow.

The point has already been made that one should not criticise the Mastership of a Hunt without exceedingly good grounds and a complete understanding of the facts. Unfortunately, a hapless Captain Hudson failed to appreciate this nicety[35], as the minutes of a committee meeting held at the Holly & Laurel public house in Holmwood on 25th March show:

"The Sec. then read a letter from Capt. B. Hudson expressing dissatisfaction at the way the Hunt was being carried on, & stated that other Members were also dissatisfied. Mr Heath expressed his views & said that under the circumstances he tendered his resignation as Master, but that he should continue his support to the Hunt as before. Mr Lee-Steere also tendered his resignation & expressed the same views as Mr Heath. The committee accepted the resignations with deep regret ...".

Significantly, the next section of this minute is scratched out, but it went on to say: *" ... & asked the Masters to reconsider the position. This they could not see their way to do"*.

A general meeting of the members of the Hunt was speedily called for March 31st at the White Horse Hotel in Dorking. In a desperate bid to defuse the situation, the chairman of the meeting, Sir Benjamin Brodie, *" ... brought forward the resignations of the Masters & Sec. He pointed out what a great loss to the country it would be if they could not get the Masters to withdraw their resignations, & he also pointed out what a great deal they had done for the Hunt. Certain suggestions were then put before the meeting with the idea of improving sport in the future. It was pointed out that these were mainly questions for the Masters & the committee & it was left at that. Proposed by Mr Humphrey & seconded by Mr Berry that the Masters & also the Sec. be asked to withdraw their resignations – carried unanimously"*.

The committee present at the meeting then all resigned. However a fresh committee was promptly re-elected and it was resolved to make such an election annual, with one third of their number to retire, in alphabetical order, each year.

On the 10th April, the new committee were informed that as a result of the recent meetings, the Masters and the Hunt secretary had all withdrawn their resignations. To help repair the damage done, the Hunt committee held a dinner for the Masters and the Hunt secretary, Mr M B Bovill, on 20th April. Thus was all peace and harmony again. And the moral of this particular tale? Criticism of a Mastership can lead to dire consequences, particularly in the absence of a viable change management strategy!

Notes

35 *Although to be fair to the Captain, his views do seem to have been well founded and widely shared by the field. See Appendix: 11 - Extracts from J C " Jack" Calvert's diary.*

Equally constructively, the same meeting arranged to take back the country loaned to the Burstow in 1906 and for a circular to be sent to members and subscribers, "*asking for their support & help financially*" to purchase hounds. As a start, the following amounts were immediately promised in the room:

Major Hanloke	£100	Mr J Humphrey	£100	Mr E Bell	£100
Lt. Col. Barclay	£100*	Mr H H Gordon Clark	£10	Sir B V S Brodie	£10
Mr S J Hack	£5	Mr M B Bovill	£5		

*Spread over 4 years, later altered to £50 down

There are records showing that Mr Lee-Steere paid 355 guineas for 9½ couple at various sales around the country and the most he paid was 184 guineas for 2½ couple from the Eglington. He also registered 16½ couple of home bred hounds in the Stud Book, so clearly the depredations of the Surrey Union pack caused by the Great War were still being felt. Indeed, this replacement policy was carried on each season throughout the 1920s.

The year 1922 was a time of change for the Hunt servants, too. A testimonial collection of £171-4s-0d was raised for the retiring huntsman, J Dawson. He was replaced by Will Farmer [previously 2nd whipper-in at the Chiddingfold, although before that he hunted the Grafton hounds], with W Windley and A Farnington put on as whippers-in. The terrier man was a chap called Greenfield. When his wife sadly died, the funeral expenses were heavy and some £6 was collected for him at the general meeting in December.

The kennel premises needed repair, adaptation and extension and a new fund was set up to help finance these alterations and the building of new hound lodges and yard and improvements to the barn stable. These are still visible and in use today.

At the start of the 1922-23 season, the Surrey Union took on loan from the Crawley & Horsham a tract of country "*East of the road from Newdigate to Rusper and North & East of the road from Rusper to Ifield, & from Ifield to Crawley, & from Crawley to Three Bridges station & East of the LB&SC Rly from Three Bridges station to Balcombe*".

An attempt to resume hunting three days a week was made in the season 1923-24. Following the precedents of earlier seasons, initially this was achieved by two days a week plus bye days when possible, with three days proper after Christmas. But in February 1924 this was reduced to five days a fortnight "*on account of accidents to hounds*". Overall though, these extra days can be considered a success, as there was a credit balance of £7-18s-8d on the Hunt Account at the end of the season. Recurring ill health finally forced Mr Lee-Steere to resign in 1927. However, in January of that year, a run was recorded with a point of nine miles, but some 24 miles as hounds ran. A report of this run, published in *Horse & Hound*, is shown on the right.

THE SURREY UNION FOXHOUNDS

These hounds met at Oakwood Hill on Saturday last*. After a short draw near The Kennels, a brace of foxes were soon found at Farm Place, and a wonderful run ensued. Going away to Great House Farm, and then by Ware [sic] Street Lane to Holbrook's, they came back to Great House and just south of Ockley Village. Going across Standon to Leith Vale, and then to the left by Chapel Copse to Oakwood Hill, and by Ruckmans to Northlands, Stone Farm Gill, Oakdale, and Wattlehurst. Crossing the Horsham main road by Shiremark and Kingsfold Place, they went over the railway to Stammerhew Farm, by the Nunnery Gill to Rusper, then to the left by Chaffolds to The Jordans, and on to Newdigate Place. Going across to Cudworth, we had a check of five minutes here, but Will Farmer hit it off and on we went to Green's Farm, through The Views to Henfold and Brexells [sic], and over the railway just north of Holmwood Station (where a good engine-driver pulled up his train) to Holmwood Park. Hounds ran nearly the whole length of the Common, and then turned to the right by Black Brook, over the railway near Brockhamhurst to High Ridges Wood, and across Shellwood Manor to Ewood Farm, when hounds were stopped at dark, with their fox just in front of them, after a five hours' run, Those up at the end were the Hunt servants, Mrs. Gregson, Mr. John Humphery and Mr. Ward. The point was nine miles, but hounds must have run over quite 24 miles of country. The pack hunted splendidly and too much praise cannot be given to Will Farmer, who was always there on the very few occasions that they wanted any help. I have hunted with these hounds for many years, but this is undoubtedly the best run I have ever known.

SENEX

HORSE & HOUND February 5th, 1927

* 29th January 1927

According to the caption accompanying this photograph taken at a meet in the late 1920s, Frederick Crow, a Hunt committee member who lived at Shellwood Manor near Leigh, has his hand on the shoulder of the land agent to the Duke of Norfolk, Captain Mostyn. Mr Cuthbert Heath MFH is in hunting kit to the left and his daughter, Genista [later Lady Claude Hamilton] stands with whip and gloves in hand on the far right. The contrast in hunt coats is particularly noteworthy – Captain Mostyn wears a "body" coat, whilst Mr Heath's longer style dates from an earlier age and neither has a coloured collar. All the gentlemen's hunting boots carry a parade ground gloss and their "champagne" tops must have taken some cleaning after a day in the Weald. The lady to the immediate right of Mr Heath seems to be exhibiting all the signs of a broken collarbone – a classic hunting injury.

CHAPTER 16

Further Joint-Masters with Mr Heath

From the start of the 1927-28 season, Major F C G Naumann MC of Redhurst, Cranleigh, joined Mr Heath. The new joint-Master was a county-standard cricketer in his younger days, having captained his school XI at Malvern and going on to play for Oxford University and Surrey.[36] At his suggestion, a wire fund was set up [which was also later spent on hunt gates, bridges and ride clearance], into which members were expected to pay 2 guineas. He also gave horses to the Hunt, which helped reduce the debit balance for the season to £725-19s-3d. Inevitably the Hunt secretary asked for more support from the subscribers, but it was Mr Heath who still picked up the tab – as he continued to do, as the need arose, for season after successive season.

Financially, the next season was slightly less catastrophic, the debit balance being £576-2s-2d. At a committee meeting on 15th July 1929, Mr Heath handed over cheque for £500 and agreed to pay off the balance when the accounts were made up. Probably somewhat over-awed by this generosity, the Hunt committee then immediately made up the difference from those attending in the room. Also of moment was the desire of the Crawley & Horsham to take back their country from loan at the end of the 1929-30 season. Accordingly, the Hunt secretary was instructed to write a letter, which was drafted as follows:

"The question of your Hunt taking back at the end of this season the country so kindly lent us was considered. The Committee came to the conclusion that deprived of the whole country in question, it would be impossible for them to carry on the Hunt. But if your Committee could see their way to our hunting in future that part of the country which lies north of the Surrey & Sussex boundary, we should be able to continue. My Com^tee also understands that your Hunt might want to hunt four days a week this season. Should this be the case, much as my Com^tee would regret the loss of the Sussex country for this reason, they would be willing that the Sy and Sx boundary line should come into force say Nov 1st 1929 if your Com^tee desires. Hoping that this can be arranged, & with best thanks for the use of the country loaned to us for so many years." [There is no further mention of this matter until 1938.]

At the end of the season, in 1930, Major Neumann resigned as joint-Master *"on account of business reasons"*. From 1st May 1930, Major H D Roberts of Beare Green became the new joint-Master with Mr Heath and took over control in the field. From the North Hereford, Harry Ashley came to replace Farmer as huntsman and Leslie Amess[37] came as 1st whipper-in. Ashley had a motor car of his own, although quite how he managed to afford it is uncertain, and in 1933 he was paid £10 per year for its use on Hunt business. According to Jack Judd, an amateur whipper-in at the time, *"Ashley's chief draw back was his quick temper and bad language to his whips"*. In a letter written many years later, Mr Judd recalls an incident in August 1931, when *"we were at Upper Gages Gill; I was on the railway bridge, with one or two labourers, [when] downwind, on the lovely summer's morning air, came Ashley's voice from a mile away, near Lyne, addressing Len (as Les was called). 'I due reckon as someone's gone and been and done something as wot he didn't ought to have gone and been and done', sagely remarked one of my companions!"*

Also around this time, reciprocal arrangements were made for subscribers to go out with adjoining Hunts. At the suggestion of the Crawley & Horsham, the minimum subscription was to be £10, plus £5 for the poultry fund and an additional £2 to the wire fund, for one day in the week [not Saturdays].

Words of Comfort to the Modern Mounted Field

"Miss Coles said, 'What amazes me is that you are still there when he has finished & and that you appear to retain complete control at all times'. 'Well, it's something if I appear to retain control', says I & off we went across the rabbithole field showing what a horse can do when a horse feels like bucking".

Saturday, January 20th, 1934

Beware of Flooded Streams in the Weald Country

"He had arrived at the ford full of enthusiasm &, undaunted by the very high floods, had charged in. He had almost attained the further bank when his horse, in attempting to scramble out, had fallen back into the water, shed his rider and firmly trodden on him. When Roger arrived he saw Prideaux sitting in the stream with his nose just above water blowing bubbles & emitting the most fearful noises: 'Guggle, bubble. Get my, bubble guggle, horse oo – oo, guggle, - off me, bubble!'. 'Here, hold my horse, I can swim!', cried Bill Hall plunging in, silk hat, scarlet coat, top boots & all. He swam across, removed the horse, which perversely returned to the near bank leaving John to scramble out on the other side where he was seen later lying in the middle of a field doing leg raising exercises!"

Saturday, November 9th, 1935
The Hunting Diary of Ruth Sewill

Notes

36 *In contrast, his younger brother seems to have played for Cambridge University and Sussex!*

37 *Apparently his surname was pronounced Aims.*

Peter Evelyn all set to hunt hounds, with one of the bicycle
brigade in the background.

For season 1935-36 it was agreed "*that the Chiddingfold be allowed to hunt in conjunction with the Surrey Union & by their permission the following part of the S U country. A line running west of Gallywood from Cranleigh – Horsham road along Wanborough Lane to Park House Green, then north along the road Winterfold, Hound House to Shere. Poultry claims to be divided equally. Each Hunt to pay its own damage, if any. This agreement to be for one year the season 1935/36, & to be reviewed annually, if both packs agreeable*".

At the commencement of the 1936-37 season, Mr Peter G Evelyn was co-opted to act as a joint-Master with Mr Heath and Major Roberts. In an effort to improve the Hunt's finances, it was decided that "*All those hunting, with the exception of farmers and children, be capped 2/6 per day for the Improvement Fund* [the successor to the wire fund] *and that occupants of cars following hounds be asked to give something. The 2/6 cap may be commuted to a payment of £2-0-0 for the season*". At the suggestion of Mr Evelyn, a Mr Leech was asked to act as "*Motor car Field Master & to be empowered to ask for cap money from cars*". A mandate was also given to Mr Evelyn to attend a meeting in London about the electrification of the Southern Railway and to put the views of the Hunt before it [see also Chapter: 28 – Hunting and the Railway]. At the end of the season, Major Roberts' term as joint-Master came to an end. To mark this retirement, Sir Benjamin Brodie presented a portrait to him at the Opening Meet at the Holly & Laurel Hotel, Holmwood, on Saturday, 6th November 1937. To much amusement, whilst expressing his gratitude for the gift, Major Roberts admitted that, "*the man he saw in the painting ... was much easier on the eye than the one he saw when he was shaving. He could only hope that his mirror was wrong and, the artist right.*"

At the start of the 1937-38 season, "*Mr Evelyn expressed a wish to hunt hounds himself on bye days. Agreed an excellent arrangement.*" It is possible that this did not go down too well with the huntsman, as there is an ominous minute from 4th October 1937 saying, "*The Master having made a statement re Ashley, Col. Barclay proposed & Maj Roberts seconded the resolution supporting the Master's action*". This was an awkward and most unusual time of year to seek a replacement huntsman to relieve Ashley and Mr Evelyn was fortunate indeed that Jim Goddard was available from the Southdown country, where he had been hunting Mr Dalgety's coloured pack. Goddard first started his career with the Old Berkshire before moving successively to Lady Craven's Harriers, the Duke of Beaufort's and the Southdown. In 1927 he was back at the Old Berks as 1st whipper-in, going on from there to the Belvoir and, in 1930, he was kennel huntsman to the North Hereford. Also during this immediate pre-War period, Frank Hazeltine was offered the job of second horseman and was soon promoted to 2nd whipper-in, before moving to the Crawley & Horsham in 1939, with the commendation in the Hunt Finds Book "*the boy should do well*". More will be heard of Frank Hazeltine in a later chapter.

CHAPTER 17

World War II and a Time of Austerity

"War declared Sept 3rd. Goddard carrying on for the present."

Entry in the Hunt "Finds" Book, *Season 1939-40*

This wonderfully phlegmatic entry really epitomises the initial Surrey Union approach to the outbreak of hostilities and the fact that hunting continued into March of 1940 demonstrates the extent of the 'phoney war'.

But to hark back to the beginning of the 1938-39 season, Mr Heath and Mr Evelyn were reappointed as joint-Masters. It also looks as though the request made to the Crawley & Horsham in 1930 finally came good, as a new loan agreement was entered into [although the minutes are silent on detail].

On 8th March 1939, Mr Heath died and, as a mark of respect, hounds did not go out again until the 16th. With his passing the Surrey Union Hunt lost a friend of irreplaceable stature and generosity, so it is perhaps fitting that the quality and breeding contained in the pack at that time should be a memorial to him.

He had put great faith in the blood of Morpeth *Dolphin*, to whom he constantly bred back. From *Dolphin* he bred *Prompter* [1929], a light-coloured, stocky hound with great bone: who became a great favourite of Mr Heath's. He may not have been fast, but his nose was exceptional and he was outstanding in his work. Mr Heath used *Prompter* extensively and, in the season 1939-40, *Prompter* offspring were the backbone of the pack. There was a spectacular run with these hounds on Saturday, 16th December 1939 that both showed their prowess and gave the few who took part in it something to enjoy in retrospect during the dark days of the Second World War.

"Hounds met at 'The Fox Revived' public house at Norwood Hill and found in Mr Berry's Rainbow Wood. They hunted up to Rowgardens before turning back to the farm buildings of Charlwood Place and, swinging right-handed, ran up the Stanhill sunken lane into and round Glovers, where more than one fox was afoot. Pushing their fox out of this big covert, hounds then ran by Beggars Gill to the Hammonds, Six Acre, the Snellings, Jessies Rough[38] to High Ridges and across the old point-to-point course at Brockham [on Mrs Trick's farm] to Betchworth Park [now the golf course]. Here he swam the river and was very nearly caught on the far side in the little covert known as Puddinghole [opposite Puddenhole Cottages, on the A25 Dorking-Reigate road]. He saved his brush, however, by slipping across both the main road and the railway to head for Box Hill. By that stage, with darkness coming on, neither man nor mount was prepared to face the steep ascent of the North Downs escarpment and so hounds were stopped. This was a 7½ mile point and a hunt of over 4 hours."

On the outbreak of the Second World War, Mr Evelyn rejoined his regiment, the Grenadier Guards. Unanimously, the committee decided to ask Mrs P G Evelyn *"to act as Deputy Master during the time Mr P G Evelyn is in France. Major Roberts to assist her in every way"* and it seems that Lt.Col. Bridges may also have assisted in a similar role, too. Hunting continued on a somewhat reduced scale for the 1939-40 season. Although hounds generally went out twice a week, on Tuesdays and Saturdays, they were stopped by frost and snow after Boxing Day until 21st February, bar one day. The last meet of the season was at the Holly & Laurel public house, Holmwood, on 30th March. After that, the Hunt had no option but to close down for the duration. Both whippers-in went away to war and because

This is believed to be a photograph of the meet at Holmwood on 30th March 1940, the last day of the season and the final time that hounds hunted officially until after World War II ended. Jim Goddard is on the grey and Percy Wright, the long-serving Hunt groom, is thought to be standing on the right, on foot. The few spectators are children from the nearby school and service personnel, all in uniform.

Notes

38 *It seems highly probable that a member of the field first wrote this long-standing account from memory. Although it is substantially correct, from evidence now available from the Hunt 'Finds' Book for the 1939-40 season and a report in Horse & Hound of January 19th, 1940, hounds were in fact stopped just beyond Jessies Rough because of their proximity to the electrified railway [a hound had been lost to this cause on 21st November 1939], but they immediately found again in that covert - thereby giving the impression of a continuous hunt to one following at a distance. It is also possible that they fresh-found in Glovers, where more than one fox was afoot.*

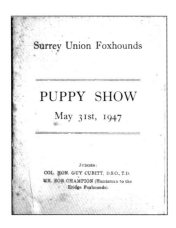

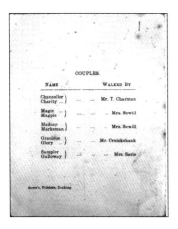

of food shortages only ten or so couple of hounds could be retained, in the hope that the pack might be built up again from this nucleus after the war. The rest of the pack had to be shot.

The RSPCA had stepped in to undertake this unwelcome task, but Goddard was so appalled by the first pathetic attempt by the 'official' detailed to do the job [the first hound was not killed outright] that he took the gun, ordered the wretch off the premises and did the devastating duty himself. Understandably, Goddard regarded this as the worst day of his life and it was something he never really got over.

As the War progressed, Major and Mrs Roberts took over management of the establishment at Oakwood Hill. Both the whippers-in were away serving in the forces and Goddard, although not 'called-up' [being over the age of 40], was required to do 'war work' [39], fortunately at the conveniently sited NAAFI located in the outbuildings at Farm Place. He was able to walk hounds out in the morning; they were let out into the grass-yard by Mrs Goddard [and their young daughter, Diana] in the afternoon and he would go straight back into Kennels on his return from work, often working by the light of a lantern as there was no mains electricity laid on at this time. As fallen stock was not readily available, finding food for the hounds was a great problem. Diana Goddard was often asked to pick nettles which, when boiled up, would be used as an additive to bread or anything else that could be scrounged from the nearby army camp. It was a hand to mouth existence. Now and then, when some Hunt members contrived to be on leave together and a horse could be borrowed for Goddard, a bye day would be arranged locally. On one occasion, whilst hacking home with hounds, Goddard was spotted by a lorry load of troops, causing them to exclaim, "*That's our bloody old bacon man!*"

During 1943, the sad news was received that Maj. Peter Evelyn was missing, believed killed, on active service in Tunisia and Major Malcolm Bovill, who had been Hunt secretary for 23 seasons, had also been killed in action.

In 1944, eight couple of Surrey Union hounds were loaned to Captain Vivian RN to hunt the Hambledon country, "*on condition they should be returned immediately they were wanted*". A further 2½ couple had been lent to the Chiddingfold Farmers' on the same conditions. It seems that a chap called Elborough had been assiduously looking after the tack all through the war and he was voted an ex gratia payment of £5 by the committee in October 1944, with the cryptic addendum "*with a further £5 to follow subject to work continuing*".

In the spring of 1945, a decision was taken to start hunting again the following season. Two new joint-Masters were appointed: Mr Nigel Tritton from Betchworth, who had connections with Barclays Bank and was the son of former Master Arthur Tritton, and Mr Roger Sewill of "Staggers Avon", Charlwood, a pre-war member of the Hunt. Both had served on the committee that had ably managed the Hunt's affairs during the conflict. Mr Sewill also took on the duties of Hunt secretary. With great energy and enthusiasm, the two new joint-Masters, assisted by an able committee, soon had the Hunt on its feet once more and started to show sport, which improved successively each season as one after another of the post-war problems was surmounted.

After demobilisation, Jim Goddard continued as huntsman, with Les Amess still as 1st whipper-in and assisted on Wednesdays by Tom Charman, a hunting farmer and haulage contractor from Forest Green, as an amateur whipper-in. Because Goddard never drove, Harry Moore, a wood merchant from Forest Green, transported hounds to meets in his old Dennis lorry and Tom Charman took the horses.

Notes

39 *Apparently his main task was cutting up sides of bacon.*

For the season 1945-46, the accounts show some 153 members and subscribers. An improvement fund was set up by placing a £5 tax on subscriptions [40], with the intention of opening up the country again, clearing rides in coverts, putting in new Hunt jumps, building replacement bridges and generally tackling the many problems that had arisen whilst hunting had stopped. The accounts also show that the Hunt had a deficit and, as ever, depended on external fundraising to make up the shortfall, especially from the annual point-to-point races and the Hunt Ball. Held in the old Dorking Halls during the 1940s and early 1950s, this latter event has been described in retrospect, by one of the organisers, as "*almost a Victorian affair: with chairs all around the dance floor, dance cards and some 600-700 people dancing to a London band*".

But all was not plain sailing and not everyone was quite so keen to see hunting resumed. The report for the 1947-48 season carried the admonition shown on the right.

The weather during the season 1946-47 was particularly harsh. There was continuous rain for most of the autumn and nine consecutive weeks of hunting were lost to frost and snow. The economic condition of the nation in 1947 was dire, there were fuel shortages and rationing continued. Accordingly, at the behest of the MFHA [the Masters of Foxhounds Association – the controlling body for foxhunting], there was a self-imposed return to austerity conditions at the start of the next season. But despite these privations and an outbreak of distemper, it proved to be a good season. There was "*one hunt with a six-mile point, six of four miles and many of three*".

Starting with 17 couple of hounds [made up of the residue of the post-war pack and £78-11s-10d worth of purchased drafts from the Duke of Beaufort's, Earl Bathurst's, the Essex Union and the Crawley & Horsham], a really good working pack was built up during these post-war years. In this regard, looking at the Hound List for 1949-50, it is clear that some limited breeding took place in the Surrey Union kennels during the War years, but drafts, particularly bitches, continued to be received from the Essex Union and the V.W.H. (Cirencester) to bolster the expansion of the pack.

One of the bitches kept during the Second World War was *Dewdrop* '40, a grand-daughter of *Prompter* '29. From her was bred *Dancer* '46 [by H.H. *Challenger*], who proved to be an outstanding hound. He was almost white and as good in his looks as in his work. Many were the tales told about him, usually along the lines of: "*and they came past me, a bloomin' great white hound leading them, and nobody with them at all*"! One great attribute *Dancer* did have was the ability to cast himself and to hunt on without human assistance, a priceless attribute when it was not always possible for the huntsman to be continually with his hounds during this period. In fact, so long as there was a whiff of fox in his nostrils, it seems to have been impossible to stop *Dancer* hunting. There was one occasion when late at night after a day's hunting, horses and hounds fed and sleeping, the huntsman came out for a last look round. There at the kennels at Oakwood Hill, clear as a bell, could be heard *Dancer*, still hunting his fox on top of Leith Hill. Truly, he was a quite outstanding hound for nose, tenacity and independence.

In 1949, the joint-Masters, through the good offices of the Hon. Guy Cubitt, former Master of the Crawley and Horsham Hunt, obtained an unentered draft from Major Trotter of the Berwickshire Hounds. These hounds were found to be the perfect counterpart to the *Dancer* blood, giving just that extra dash and speed necessary to kill foxes in the difficult country of that time.

Hounds hunted well throughout the 1948-49 season, with a tally of 15 brace, with 10½ brace to ground, which "*was approaching the pre-war average*". Perhaps the most memorable hunt was from a bye-day meet at Kennels,

---

WARNING

Westfield Farm, Charlwood (Mr Zambuni) is out of bounds to the Hunt, and any Member of the Field crossing it must be personally responsible for any claim which may arise. The farm lies between the Charlwood - Povey Cross and Lowfield Heath Roads immediately West of Brockley Wood.

Notes

40 *For the season 1946-47 these were: 20 guineas for one horse, 30 guineas for two, 40 guineas for three or more in a family and caps £2.*

Brendon Sewill [mounted] discusses the day in prospect with Les Amess, the 1st whipper-in, at a meet in the early 1950s.

where hounds met at 8am on 9th April. Scent was keen at that early hour and hounds picked up what was probably a travelling dog fox that took them 14 miles before getting to ground at Chenies.

At the annual meeting held at the Holly & Laurel public house, Holmwood, on 19th March 1949, the Masters quite properly chided "*some members who forgot to wait for people who had opened gates & sometimes also forgot to thank them for so doing*". Speaking on behalf "*of the car, bicycle and foot people*", Col. Lane hoped that "*they were not a nuisance...*" and went on to say, "*... but that they did enjoy themselves*". In reply, it was suggested that "*when the 'bicycle brigade' ceased to come out, it would it would be time seriously to consider giving up hunting*". These two messages had already stood the test of time when they were delivered, yet they are just as valid today: manners really do still matter in the field and hunting remains as egalitarian as it always was. It makes no difference if you are a Duke or a dustman: as a certain cockney grocer said, "*Tell me a man's a foxhunter and I loves him at once*", but also please never forget that "*manners maketh man*".

After Mr Tritton resigned in 1950, Mr H Michael Gordon Clark JP, from Mickleham, joined Roger Sewill in the Mastership and also took over the role of Hunt secretary. The senior joint-Master's son, Brendon Sewill, also began acting as a further amateur whipper-in on Saturdays and revelled in the tutelage offered by his hero, Amess. Whilst Brendon was an undergraduate at Cambridge University, every weekend during the season he had a frantic early morning train journey up to London, then taking the next available train to Horley, where Jack Richardson, the family groom, would pick him up and get him to the meet by 11 o'clock. During this period, the Saturday country was to the east of the Dorking-Horsham railway [and was considered distinctly 'superior'], whereas the Wednesday country lay west of this line.

Further drafts of hounds were purchased from the Berwickshire Hunt [a Mr G E W Lane making a contribution of 5 guineas towards their cost] and they travelled from Scotland by train, entirely unaccompanied.[41] The policy adopted by Mr Sewill was to cross-breed between the two packs, in the hope of securing the best qualities from both. He continued to breed back to *Dancer* and, by the season 1955-56, 10½ couple of his offspring were hunting, with a further 7½ couple of puppies coming on.

A notable run took place on 17th January 1953. Hounds met at Rusper and were put into Horsegills, where they found at 11-15am. Initially, the fox ran south to Northlands, but then turned back and ran by the Nunnery and Cophatch to the Prestwoods. Once hounds were through this big covert, having outstripped all the horses, they ran on down the hill almost into Charlwood village before turning left-handed into Glovers. They ran round this large covert, enabling the Hunt staff and some of the field to catch up with them, before crossing Greenings Park and going into Coopers. Running down the hill and pointing for the lowlands beyond Charlwood Place, the fox was dismayed to hear hounds ahead of him. He turned back, little knowing that what he heard was the Worcester Park and Buckland Beagles pursuing their hare across Charlwood Place. The fox ran across Edolphs, through the top of Coopers and once more regained the fastnesses of the Glovers. Hounds were close at him, however, and drove him right round the covert before he once more tried to make his point by way of Coopers. Yet again, he was headed by the Beagles and once more he returned to Glovers. Finally, when the Beagles had at last gone home, he made one more attempt and, running through Pit Covert, he was viewed crossing the road near Charlwood Place by members of the field who had abandoned their horses and taken to wheels. In the gathering dusk hounds ran on over Charlwood Place and Farmfields before finally being stopped in total darkness at 5.15pm, as they were

Notes

41 *See Chapter 28 - Hunting and the Railway*

crossing the road at Norwood Hill. They had been running continuously for six hours, made a seven-mile point and covered 33 miles as hounds ran.

With hounds out two days a week, it was possible to get in about 65 day's hunting each season. In 1954-55 they accounted for 37 brace: 25 brace being killed on top and 12 brace marked to ground. In 1955-56 they accounted for 41 brace: 22 brace being killed on top and 19 brace marked to ground.

What may well have been the fastest hunt with the Surrey Union was on 9th February 1955. Hounds found in Nuns Wood, near Rusper, and the fox ran due north to Temple, where he swung left-handed in a half circle to Lower Gages and from here due south to Langhurst. Turning again left-handed, hounds raced over Curtis's and Manns Farms to Court House, before turning north again almost into Rusper village. Here the fox turned back, but still running at the same tremendous pace, hounds hunted him through Cow Wood to kill at Baldhorns Park. This was a hunt of 75 minutes and 12 miles as hounds ran. From the moment that they found until they killed, they received no human aid and nor did they need it, for they never checked.

Following the retirement of Mr Gordon Clarke, Mr R C Dutton-Forshaw, from Pallingham Lock Farm, Pulborough, joined Mr Sewill as joint-Master at the start of the 1955-56 season. Unfortunately, Mr Sewill had a heart attack in 1956 and resigned as joint-Master at the end of the 1957-58 season. Shortly after being made CBE, he sadly died in January 1958. However Mr Sewill's magnificent contribution during his twelve successful seasons in the Mastership was made at a time when the fortunes of our Hunt were at a very low ebb and he may rightly be considered as a key instigator of the post-War recovery.

Two photographs of the meet on 31st December 1950 at Hurtwood House, home of Mr & Mrs R J Huggett.
[Upper] The original caption was, "*Squadron Leader G H Goodman in conversation with Miss I Touche as they wait for their horses*". It is not essential to own a horse in order to go hunting and then, as now, it was quite usual to ride hirelings. This is yet another example of how hunting puts money into the rural economy, in addition to the tailors, feed merchants, vets, farriers, boot makers and the myriad other trades that it helps to support financially.
[Lower] From left, Jim Goddard, Tom Charman, Mr R W Sewill MFH and Les Amess.

The Surrey Union Branch of The Pony Club

The Pony Club girls at Hurtwood House on New Year's Eve 1950. From left, Erica Burley, Thelma Burley, Susan Holloway and Jane Smith.

The Surrey Union Branch of the Pony Club was formed in 1936, the first District Commissioner being Ruth Sewill. The main tenets of the Pony Club are to:

- *Encourage young people to ride and to learn to enjoy all kinds of sports connected with horses and riding.*
- *Provide instruction in riding and horsemanship, and to instil in members the proper care of their animals.*
- *Promote the highest ideals of sportsmanship, citizenship and loyalty, thereby cultivating strength of character and self-discipline.*

The first President of the SUH Branch was Col. the Hon. Guy Cubitt of High Barn, Effingham. He was succeeded by Mabel Stuart-Hunt and subsequently by Rachel Fardon. Rachel is a legend in her own lifetime, having been involved with the Pony Club for well over 60 years and the erstwhile owner of a riding school in Dorking for more than half a century.

The Cubitt Award was introduced in the 1980s as a mark of appreciation for those who have served the Branch continuously for many years. Its recipients have included Naomi Lovering, Jill Burt, Elizabeth Ferrand, Michael Taylor, Peter Bolitho, Chris Cooper, Valerie Greenwell, Charmian Stow and Rachel Fardon. The current DC is Helen Dart, ably assisted by Jenny Kear. The secretary for the last 20 years has been Valerie Greenwell and her overall contribution, loyalty and devotion during this time has been exceptional.

CHAPTER 18

The Post-War World – A New Era

For the 1958-59 season Mrs Mabel Stuart-Hunt, the first lady Master in the history of the Surrey Union Hunt, joined Mr Dutton-Forshaw in the Mastership. Her accession as joint-Master was reported in the *Evening Standard* on 10th March 1958 as follows:

> *"For the first time the Surrey Union is to have a woman as joint master. She is Mrs Mabel Stuart-Hunt, wife of the chairman of the Billingsgate and Leadenhall Markets Committee. She is 41, has been riding with the Surrey Union since the war from her house at Newdigate ... ... Mrs Stuart-Hunt takes office on May 1st, opening of the new season. She is not sure what it will cost her: the hunt, which has a committee guaranteeing a proportion of costs, just pays its way."*

During this period it is recorded that the proceeds from the Christmas Bazaar funded the construction of four new bridges, 19 hunting gates, 22 heave gates and many new fence rails. These were put up at strategic points within the Hunt country, thereby making it much easier to cross. Additionally, Miss Molly Calvert undertook to run the Grand National Sweepstake and Miss Celia Cubitt organised the Hunt Ball.

The end of the 1959-60 season saw the retirement of Mr Dutton-Forshaw from the joint-Mastership after a five-year tenure. After 23 years as the Surrey Union huntsman, Jim Goddard also retired and a testimonial presentation of over £1300 was made to him in February 1961. In real terms, this was a great deal of money and was a clear demonstration of the high regard in which he was held within the hunting community.

The new huntsman, Frank Hazeltine, had had an eventful time during the War before returning to Hunt service with the Crawley & Horsham, the Essex and the North Warwickshire, where he had been 1st whipper-in for seven seasons. So, after an 18-year apprenticeship away, a local man had come back home to hunt hounds. Assisting him were Leslie Amess and the amateurs, Messrs Brendon Sewill, Tom Charman and David Rigby.

So, from the 1960-61 season Mabel Stuart-Hunt was the sole Master of the Surrey Union, but she seems to have been fortunate indeed to have had a strong team behind her on the committee and in kennel. The 1st whipper-in, Les Amess, retired from Hunt service in 1961, after 30 seasons of loyal and unstinting devotion to the Surrey Union [let alone his earlier work elsewhere]. His dedication was recognised by a testimonial from the Hunt. He was replaced first by Rodney Ellis and then, from the season 1964-65, by David Strivens.

Mrs Mabel Stuart-Hunt MFH, the first lady Master of the Surrey Union

The season 1962-63 was notable for the 'big freeze', which started on 20th December 1962 and lasted for ten weeks. In common with packs elsewhere, hounds were taken out on foot to hunt in the snow during this period, but with mixed success. Just to show the general cussedness of life, after the thaw Mrs Stuart-Hunt had a fall out hunting and cracked a rib, but it was on one of the best days of that season. From at meet at Ellen's Green, *"hounds had found well in Honeywood and went away on good scent to Wet Wood, Chapel Copse back over Kennels Farm, Ruckmans and on to Roman Wood and then back to lose at Ruckmans for just under 2 hours with only 2 checks"*.

Rails seem to have been smashed at a prodigious rate by the mounted field in the early 1960s, with 45 new or replacement ones being installed in 1963-64 alone. The Surrey Union was clearly ready for the advent of the tiger-

Frank Hazeltine, the very image of a professional Hunt servant. This photograph was taken whilst he was 1st whipper-in at the North Warwickshire.

Notes

42 *Anti-hunt protesters, later called hunt saboteurs - the "sabs". This change in nomenclature neatly describes the shift from peaceful protest to direct interference with legitimate hunting, often accompanied by yobbish behaviour or violence. The correct use of the apostrophe should be noted.*

43 *Presumably she meant a record for George Holder. In contrast, see tally for season 1955-56 in Chapter 17.*

44 *Including 26 boys, this membership rose to 177 the next season.*

trap! This new form of Hunt jump, a classic combination of both form and function, started to be erected from 1964 onwards and is now a familiar feature during a day's hunting in our country.

At the end of the 1964-65 season Frank Hazeltine moved on to the "HH". The new huntsman for the 1965-66 season was George Holder from the Monmouthshire, where he had been for the past eight seasons under the Mastership of Col. Harry Llewellyn, the famous show-jumper and Olympic gold medal winner. The whipper-in, Strivens, remained in post. From his former Hunt, Holder had brought six couple of hounds with him, and the introduction of this Welsh blood left a legacy of white or lemon coloured hounds [tracing their ancestry back to the Curre *Viscount* '60] for many seasons to come. Further Welsh blood was infused by the use of the Monmouthshire *Maxim* '63, *Master* '63 and *Lodger* '64 with Surrey Union bitches.

It is a well-known fact that the 1960s saw a time of change in society generally, not always for the better. Yet some shifts in attitude were long overdue, as this extract from the minutes of a committee meeting held on 19th January 1966 indicates: "*Boxing Day Meet: A discussion on the traffic congestion and damage to Ockley Green by horseboxes took place. It was agreed that the only solution was a greater number of police to control parking*". Including the honorary officers, there were 14 gentlemen and one lady present at this meeting, and that was the only solution that they could come up with? Ye Gods! The notion of self-regulation and insistence that, if requested by the Master, horse-boxes be parked at least quarter of a mile from the meet [as had been instigated Mrs Stuart-Hunt in 1963] seems never to have crossed anyone's mind. The blithe assumption that the constabulary had nothing better to do is astonishing. As it happened, both the committee and the police were soon find that they had more pressing issues to worry about on a hunting day, following the first mention of the word "*anti's*"[42] in 1965.

At the Annual General Meeting on 25th March 1966, Mrs Stuart-Hunt reported that, despite a very wet February, which necessitated moving some meets to the hills at short notice, it had been good season and that a record number[43] of foxes [28 brace] had been killed by George Holder to date. The chairman had previously indicated that the acting Master was considering resignation. Fortunately, Miss Jennifer Biggs [who was in her twenties] agreeing to share the workload and become a joint-Master with Mrs Stuart-Hunt averted this. The meeting was also told that the Surrey Union branch of the Pony Club was flourishing, with some 150 members[44], with Miss Jill Burt as the new secretary, in place of Mrs New who had retired after six years in the role. By the kindness of Lord Ashcombe, "*50 children had camped at Denbies the previous summer and had a very enjoyable time. The top ride was very lucky to be instructed by Col. Cubitt and a team was entered for the Inter-Branch Horse Trials. Miss Christine Sheppard also gave some tuition, which was much appreciated*". At the Ranmore meet during the 1966 Christmas holidays, some 250 children turned out, but not all were from the Surrey Union branch! Sensibly, it was decided that, in future, "*cards would not be issued to neighbouring branches in order to keep the numbers attending within bounds*".

Concerning the Hunt Ball, Commander Leslie Oldroyd expressed some candid views: "*... it was a waste of the Committee's efforts to have the Hunt Ball at the Burford Bridge Hotel where many people were unable to obtain tickets and the catering was not up to standard*". The Chairman responded by saying, "*... that many people wanted a change from the Dorking Halls and so it was decided to try the Burford Bridge. The financial result was not very different, only £46 less than in 1965 and that next year more room would be available and the catering better organised*". Another subscriber, Mrs Pearson, offered this revealing insight, "*... the food was good and plentiful, but did not circulate properly*".

In the summer of 1966 the Hunt finances were augmented by a new, and very welcome, source – the movie industry! Hounds and the Hunt horses visited Denham Studios and played a supporting role in *Gaiety George* with Richard Green. Not satisfied with one film part, they subsequently went on to appear in *Drop Dead Darling* with Fenella Fielding. Yet another film appearance was made in 1971, outside the White Horse, Shere, during the making of *The Ruling Classes*, starring Peter O'Toole.

There were hints of changes to come in December 1967. At a committee meeting, the chairman pointed out that, "*there was not room for both the SU & CF* [Chiddingfold Farmers' Hunt] *as at present constituted, and that the CF hunted mainly in our country loaned to them*". This theme was picked up by Mrs Stuart-Hunt, who pointed out that, "*the position worsened every year and that the CF had been warned over the past 5 years*[45] *that it was inevitable that the SU must have more of their country back*". Warming to this broad theme, Colonel Cubitt opined that, "*with the growth of towns & traffic and with the increase in shooting syndicates & intensive farming, hunting in the Weald was not really a feasible proposition. Hunts must have more heath and woodland*". It was agreed that the Chairman should write to the Master of the Chiddingfold Farmers', Mr Raymond Stovold MFH, saying that, "*while regretting the necessity, it was essential for the SU to reduce the country loaned to them …*" and that "*… there might be some form of amalgamation possible, but any such suggestion must be initiated by the Chiddingfold Farmers'. They had been hunting loaned country for 25 years, whereas the Surrey Union went back 180 years*". As it turned out, there was a short reprieve for the Chiddingfold Farmers' when the Chiddingfold & Leconfield Hunt loaned them extra country in 1968, but they finally disbanded at the end of the season 1968-69.

There was an outbreak of foot and mouth disease during the 1967-68 season and restrictions were not lifted until 1st February 1968. Even so, hunting was confined to the hills for some time thereafter. However at the close of the season some 25½ brace had been killed, which was more than for some full seasons during this period.

In September 1968 Mrs Stuart-Hunt wrote to explain that she, suddenly, had to move from the area and realised that this would "*present certain problems*". However, the upshot was that Mrs Stuart-Hunt did remain until the end of the 1968-69 season. This had proved to be another outstanding year for the Pony Club. Membership had risen to 200 and Jane Pelly [fresh from passing her 'A' test] and Daphne Field both got through to the Inter-Branch Finals at Stoneleigh, whilst the Surrey Union team were third in the Area Trials. Colonel Cubitt said, "*the SU Branch was one of the best in England, the quality of horsemanship being excellent both at the top and the bottom, due to help given by all instructors. It had produced 4 'A' candidates in the last few years. Anyone holding this certificate can get a job anywhere in Australia and USA and the standard required to pass was very high*".

Following the departure of Mrs Stuart-Hunt, the remaining joint-Master, Mrs Bolton [née Jennifer Biggs] of Ridgewood Stud, Sidlow, near Reigate, was joined by Mrs Elizabeth Armstrong for the next season. At their first committee meeting, at the Holly & Laurel, South Holmwood, on Friday 30th May 1969, these two lady joint-Masters indicated "*that Members should be invited to wear a yellow collar as formerly, but which had fallen into abeyance since the war*".

Unfortunately, Mrs Bolton died unexpectedly in the summer of 1969.

Notes

45 *Mr Roger Sewill had written to the Chiddingfold Farmers' Mastership expressing similar sentiments as early as 1956/7.*

George Holder takes hounds to the first draw. The Welsh blood in the pack is evident in their white and lemon colouring.

CHAPTER 19

The 1970s – The Start of a New Reality

Accordingly, Elizabeth Peace [46] Armstrong was left a sole Master. She had hunted, as a child, with the Enfield Chace and the Puckeridge. In 1939 she married an officer in the Royal Navy, who lost his life in the Battle of the Atlantic. Following her marriage to Colonel Geoffrey Armstrong after the War, living in Cranleigh, she had been a subscriber to both the Surrey Union and Chiddingfold Farmers'. With this background, Mrs Armstrong was ideally placed to take back the country previously loaned to the Chiddingfold Farmers' and to welcome the twenty or so newcomers to the Surrey Union from that now defunct Hunt.

When Mrs Armstrong assumed sole office, there were in kennels 36 couple of entered hounds, 2½ couple of unentered bitches and 12 couple of unentered dog hounds, and four horses in the Hunt stables. That summer, hounds had been shown at Ardingly and the Chiddingfold & Leconfield Open Day, as well as being paraded at the Greater London Council Horse Show on Clapham Common [47] and at the Epsom Horse Show. In the season 1969-70, there were 216 subscribers, with Mr D V Balls MRCVS [the Hunt treasurer] as field master for the east side of the country, whilst Mr P W W Parker [formerly a Chiddingfold Farmers' subscriber] led the field in the west.

In her first report as Master to the Annual General Meeting of the Hunt on Friday 20th March 1970, Mrs Armstrong asked [somewhat portentously, considering recent history], "*all members and subscribers to write both to the Home Secretary & their local MP protesting against the Govt giving time to an anti-hunting bill*".

It was never Mrs Armstrong's intention to be the sole Master and it is a mark of her fortitude that she carried the burden single-handed for two seasons. By common consent it was acknowledged that she had done a wonderful job, but clearly a second Master would be beneficial all round. Accordingly, Mr Peter Parker was approached and he agreed to be joint-Master with Mrs Armstrong from 1st May 1971. Peter Parker was born and educated in Suffolk, where his parents farmed. As a child he hunted from home and on Exmoor when visiting relatives. After the War, he ran a riding school in Devon and married Hilary. In 1949 the couple moved to Lockner Farm, Chilworth, where the family have remained ever since and hounds still meet.

The 1st whipper-in, Strivens, moved on to the South Devon as kennel huntsman and was replaced by Paul Shaw. Two amateurs, Tom Charman and Bob Robinson [another farmer, from Ranmore], assisted him. The next season, Shaw left to go abroad and was replaced by Edward Bailey [whose father was, for many seasons, the huntsman to the Hursley], again assisted by the two doughty farmers.

Incredibly, there were 260 subscribers to the Hunt for the season 1971-72, but not all of them necessarily rode to hounds. It was a sign of the times, perhaps, that the joint-Masters thanked "*the young members of the Hunt for the £37 raised by a discoteque [sic] held at Oakwood Hill Village Hall. This money would be used to put a roof over the skinning yard*".

At the end of the 1972-73 season, the Pony Club membership exceeded 250, thereby enabling the branch to enter two teams for inter-branch competitions. The District Commissioner, John Bullock, reported, "*the Horse Trials team won the Area trials at Coolham and came 13th out of 32 teams at the finals at Stoneleigh. The boys' tetrathlon team*

Colonel Geoffrey Armstrong and Elizabeth Armstrong, on the occasion of their marriage. This might appear to be an odd choice in a hunting history but, as befits the event, this is the best portrait of Mrs Armstrong currently to hand.

Notes

46 *She was born in 1918.*
47 *It was [and still is] part of our Hunt country, but how times have changed for Londoners.*

won the Area Competition at Ardingly and came 6th out of 14 teams in the final at Stoneleigh; Christian Brodie being first overall at Ardingly and third in the Championships".

In a further portent of things to come, Mr Parker told the Annual General meeting that, "*the MFHA were very keen that all hunting people should join the RSPCA and thus by their votes prevent the anti-hunting element from dominating the Society. The subscription was only £1 per annum*".

On 30th April 1973, the stud groom, Percy Overington, retired after virtually forty year's service to the Hunt. As he had to give up his tied accommodation, a council house was found and Mr Michael Taylor [of whom more will be heard later] organised and collected a testimonial for him.

There was also a need for some administrative housekeeping changes. The MFHA had advised that Masters should appoint committees to organise and run various outside activities and that the chairmen of these committees should be ex-officio members of the Hunt committee. This arrangement still pertains today. It was also decided that the Hunt required a set of rules and Mr C H H White agreed to be the chairman of a committee to be co-opted by him for this purpose. Although amended subsequently, this work still underpins the current Hunt constitution.

The single adult subscription was raised to £50 for the season 1973-74, with the others increased pro rata, and there was a possibility that intending subscribers "*might have to be put on a waiting list if the numbers hunting rose above the present level*", not that there is any evidence that this actually happened. However, with their ever-increasing numbers, some held the view that the manners of the Field had deteriorated. Whilst this season was a good one financially for the Hunt, the next season was less so. In a report dated 1st February 1975, the new Hunt treasurer, Mr I R Gilchrist [another of whom more will be heard later], said: "*As far as the 1974-75 season is concerned I estimate that the Hunt will have a deficit of about £1000. The main reasons … being large increases in the cost of wages, rates, horse and hound keep, petrol, coal and electricity. The income to date including that of outside activities is up on 1973-74 but unfortunately the increase in expenditure has overtaken the increase in income. In the near future the Hunt will need to spend money on improvements at the kennels; a new hound van will shortly be required and at least one new horse will be needed for next season*". As a review of how the mid-1970s inflationary period[48] affected hunting, the first part of this summary is hard to beat.

At a committee meeting held at the Red Lion, Ockley, on Friday 12th March 1976, Mrs Armstrong said that, "*it had been a good open season and all the Hunt staff had worked extremely well … … Few people realised the amount of work involved in the collection and skinning of carcasses, which was a continuous and tiring chore*". She paid tribute to the huntsman for being economical with purchases and also to the hon. treasurer, "*as the best she had ever known and the efficient way in which he controlled the expenditure*".

The crucial matter of proper headgear was also considered: "*After discussion it was agreed that owing to the impossibility of obtaining silk hats and the high cost of the nylon variety that gentlemen wearing a black velvet cap, with the ribbons removed or concealed, together with a black or tweed coat should not be considered to be improperly dressed*". From this peculiar wording, it may be deduced that gentlemen wearing red coats were, therefore, still expected to wear silk hats.

At the end of the season 1976-77, Mrs Armstrong retired from the Mastership, much to the regret of the Hunt committee, who sent her "*a warm message of thanks for all she had done*". To quote from the letter sent to subscribers

Notes

48 *In 1975, inflation was over 20% per annum.*

by Sir Ronald Wates on the setting up of a testimonial fund[49] for her, "*The fact that hunting in our part of Surrey has continued so successfully is due very largely to her enthusiasm, her wide knowledge, her energy and her remarkable ability to engender loyal support from so many people*". In accordance with tradition, Mr Parker tendered his resignation, too.

The acting joint-Masters appointed for the season 1977-78 were Messrs P W W Parker, M G M Taylor and R Davidson. The son of George Mercer Taylor, the Hunt treasurer during the post-War years, Michael Taylor lived at Great Brockhamhurst, Betchworth, and Raymond Davidson, a retired banker from the City, came from Woodcote Farm, West Horsley. Whilst Holder remained as huntsman, Bailey had departed to the Morpeth and Richard Bennett was set on as 1st whipper-in, assisted by the amateurs, Messrs Charman and Robinson [as before] and Mr Tim Barker from Barwell Farm, Chessington. At the start of the season, Mr Davidson spent a great deal of time, money and effort on the erection of hunt jumps and some pertinent points regarding the Hunt country were made at a committee meeting on 6th April 1978: "*It was agreed that opening up the country was expensive but well worth doing and subscribers were unlikely to cavil at money thus spent. That jumps should only be erected in consultation with the Masters and Area Managers[50], and that although some had been built and not used as yet, that was the difference between foxhunting and drag hunting*".

In view of what was to happen some twenty years later, the Surrey Union response to a request from the Secretaries of Foxhounds Association in August 1978 is telling. Working in collaboration with the BFSS [the British Field Sports Society] and MFHA, that Association was initiating a campaign "*to counter the present Threat to Hunting*". Hunt secretaries were encouraged to "*endeavour to obtain pledges from all Conservative, Labour and Liberal candidates before they were adopted for the General Election*". The joint-Masters had also received a similar request. The Hunt chairman, Sir John Prideaux, was of the view that "*there was a danger of making too much fuss and that although an election might be imminent he considered any precipitate action was to be avoided*". In the end it was resolved that "*a list of constituencies within the Hunt should be obtained with a list of the sitting MPs and potential candidates and that guidance should be given to members and subscribers for the headings of a letter to be written to them. These letters should be written individually and that the thread of field sports should be plugged rather than hunting*". To be fair, the initial brief was woolly, but readers can make up their own minds about the likely effectiveness of the Hunt committee's plan regarding this threat to foxhunting.

There are hints, too, that all was not as well as it might be in the mounted field, where a degree of laxity seems to have existed. In "*the cause of good relations with farmers*", the Hunt committee was asked to see that any instructions from the joint-Masters during a day's hunting were received and understood by the field. Furthermore, for the season 1978-79, gate shutters were to be appointed, although they were not to wear armbands, "*as this was inclined to cause some followers not to bother to shut gates*". This latter point caused some further debate as the season progressed, resulting in the decision "*that a member of the Committee or senior member should be asked to bring up the rear and check that gates were shut, push on stragglers and prevent any misbehaviour and generally control the rear of the Field*".

At the general meeting on 26th April 1979, Commander Douglas made two shrewd points that seem to sum up the general feeling at this time, "*... he thought that finance matters rather than legislation were more likely to end hunting and to survive it must be enjoyable for those taking part. He asked that the Field should be told what is going on and told at the Meet the plan of the day & which Master is acting as Field Master*".

Mrs Goodchild was a long time Member before becoming Hunt Secretary and eventually joint-Master. She is riding her hunter, *Biscuit*, at a meet at Woodcote in November 1977.

Notes

49 *A painting in watercolours of Mrs Armstrong with hounds on Holmbury Hill was commissioned from the artist, John King. The sale of prints from this work had raised £950 by the spring of 1978.*
50 *The area managers operated as agents for the joint-Masters, liaising with farmers and other occupiers.*

Michael Taylor, in characteristic pose [left], and Peter Parker.

These concerns carried forward into the following season, 1979-80, as the minutes of a meeting held at the Punchbowl Inn [51], Oakwood Hill, on Thursday 29th November 1979 show. They record that *"the subject of Field mastership was discussed and left in the hands of the Masters to be solved for next season"*. It was also intimated that subscribers were being lost because, *"we were not getting as much fun as previously and not getting sufficient jumping"*. The Masters' response to these criticisms is illuminating, as is the Chairman's summing up: *"Mr Parker replied that, although boring to some of the mounted Field, digging was essential in our country and that to kill a fox in the open was a rarity. The Chairman agreed that followers must be kept interested but that the Surrey Union was a very difficult country to hunt and was becoming increasingly more so. Ever increasing costs could price it out of existence and that in these days of intensive farming, farmers could well prefer drag hunting"*.

As far as one can see, even after the next annual general meeting in March 1980, there was no tangible solution that resolved the subscribers' clearly expressed worries. However this probably unrelated outcome might cause some raised eyebrows amongst readers today: *"It was decided after discussion not to allow visitors on Saturdays except in exceptional circumstances"*. This seemingly draconian view was slightly modified early the next season, when it was decided *"that whether or not visitors were acceptable on any particular day to be left to the discretion of the Masters or hon. secretary"*. Perhaps readers might like to consider the implications of this policy, too!

On reading this, is it fair to say that the plot was in grave danger of being lost? Admittedly, it is a difficult balancing act, but the tensions that inevitably exist between the essential raison d'être of a Hunt [the control of the fox population]; the wishes of the farmers; the demands of the Field and the imperatives of cash-flow all need to be kept in harmony if overall success is to be achieved. Ignore any one of these elements and the whole entity will soon get out of kilter.

At the end of this season, Mr Davidson decided to retire from the joint-Mastership. He was described by Mr Parker as being *"both game and brave"*, having *"continued to hunt despite one or two nasty falls"*. And so it was that Messrs Parker and Taylor were re-appointed as acting joint-Masters for the season 1980-81.

Notes

51 *Probably the first time that the Punchbowl was used as a venue for a formal Hunt meeting.*

CHAPTER 20

The 1980s – The New Reality Takes Hold

"There must be unanimity and concord or we shan't kill no foxes."

Mr Jorrocks in **Handley Cross**, *R S Surtees 1854*

Despite the promises made early in the previous season, it is significant that one of the items discussed at a committee meeting held on 6th November 1980 was *"a plea put in either to appoint a permanent Field master or inform the Field before moving off who was in that capacity for the day"*. This ostensibly avoidable problem simmered on through the rest of the 1980-81 season and reached a climax at the committee meeting on 12th March 1981: *"It was agreed that some members & subscribers were not entirely happy that the hunting was being managed in the best possible way. The lack of a permanent Field master was deplored and the need for firm and cheerful leadership was stressed. Also that the huntsman should be given positive orders, particularly as regards the time spent digging. It was agreed that a sub-committee of Sir John Prideaux [the Hunt chairman]; Sir Ronald Wates; Lord Onslow; Col. Drew; Mr White and the hon. secretary [Col. Girling] be appointed to consider the future arrangements and report its findings to the Hunt committee ..."*.

The hunt committee duly reconvened in Ockley Village Hall on Friday, 10th April 1981. It is recorded that *"The under-mentioned points were put forward by Lord Onslow and agreed:*

1) The Huntsman must have clear instructions and remain mounted.

2) The terrier-men should be left to do the digging.

3) An additional man should be employed in Kennels.

4) There should be a rota of gate shutters to bring up the rear of the Field.

5) A fence repair party should follow the Hunt.

6) That the hills were hunted too frequently.

7) The Hunt staff should build fences during the summer.

8) That more Committee meetings should be held."

Astute readers will note that there is no mention whatsoever of the Field master issue. However, under the heading *"Discipline"*, it was agreed, *"that the Field should be requested to keep up and not to straggle and so make the gate shutter's role less difficult. And as laid down in Rule 20, only the Masters may give instructions or requests to the Hunt Servants"*. On reading this last sentence, one is immediately reminded of the essential principles enunciated at the Hatchlands Park meeting in 1802 [see Chapter 3]. Plus ça change, indeed!

To round off this review of a momentous meeting, the hon. treasurer forecast a deficit of £2000 for the season 1981-82, even if subscriptions were raised. To this, Mr White responded pragmatically *"that those who wanted to hunt should be prepared to pay for it and that outside activities should be limited"*. The view of Mr Taylor was that *"he would like to bar visitors altogether"*. It was agreed that this was not feasible, but *"as far as possible, they should seek permission from and be vetted by, the hon. secy"*. This latter point is perfectly reasonable and all visitors or newcomers should, as a matter of course, always contact the secretary of any Hunt with which they wish to venture out.

At the start of the season 1981-82, Mrs Rosemary Peters joined Messrs Parker and Taylor as an acting joint-Master. Keeping the country open was a huge problem for this Mastership [as, unfortunately, it still is]. The proximity to

London, fragmentation by roads and railways, paucity of large 'hunting' estates and the expansion of towns and villages was compounded from this time by the 'asset stripping' of farms. Frequently when a farm came on the market for sale during this period it was bought not by a farmer for its intrinsic agricultural potential, but by a developer who would split the holding up into more manageable lots. Thus the house and a paddock or two might be sold on as a single entity, the barn and the other buildings would become 'conversions' and the residual land sold off piecemeal to adjoining owners. So, instead of having one occupier to deal with, a joint-Master might now have half a dozen or more. To help cope with this seemingly overwhelming workload, the joint-Masters used a complex system of Area Managers to act as their 'eyes and ears' and ambassadors for several seasons. By the summer of 1985, there were 26 such Area Managers, each looking after two or three parishes close to their homes and opening up country as an opportunity presented itself.

Early in her time as joint-Master, Mrs Peters had to visit Oliver Reed, the [in]famous film actor, at Broome Hall to discuss crossing his land. She has subsequently recollected, "*I was shown into the grand hall, with an even grander fireplace. Oliver Reed welcomed me with a whisky bottle in one hand and two glasses in the other. He handed a glass to me, which he filled; generously topped up his own and proceeded to throw the not so empty bottle into the fireplace where it joined all the other smashed bottles. I did not stay longer than I had to*".

At the end of April 1984, Mr Parker retired from the joint-Mastership and Sir John Prideaux stepped down as chairman of the Hunt. Sir John had hunted for many seasons and, when he finally retired in 1987, had served on the Hunt committee for 54 years. For the season 1984-85, Mr Taylor and Mrs Peters were reappointed as acting joint-Masters. The establishment in Kennels remained largely unchanged: George Holder stayed on as huntsman, with Austin James as 1st whipper-in, assisted by the amateurs Tom Charman, Bob Robinson [until a hip operation intervened], Tim Barker and Fred Trinder. The kennelman was Adrian 'Sage' Thompson and Elizabeth Joinson looked after the horses.

A spectacular Hunt Ball was held at the Mansion House in London on 25th January 1985. By the kind invitation of the Lord Mayor of London and the Lady Mayoress, Sir Alan and Lady Traill, some 350 guests were received in the Old Ballroom. Dinner was served in the Egyptian Hall and adjoining rooms and the band, *The Dark Blues*, played throughout the evening until carriages were called at 2.00am. It is understood that no member of the Mansion House staff could recall a Hunt Ball ever being held there previously.

Rather more prosaically, but just as importantly, some 300 farmers and landowners attended the Farmers' Dinner on 19th February 1985. The Pony Club successes also continued, with Rebecca Cooper being placed second in the Dressage Championships for the 14 years and under competition and an impressive eighth overall. Now 'Becca Gibbs, she has gone on to become an established, top-level, three-day event rider.

But in the season 1985-86, things really started to unravel. It is essential that a huntsman has the respect of his hounds and has absolute control of them at all times. For a variety of reasons, the 'unseen thread' linking George Holder to the Surrey Union pack was showing signs of strain and consequently moves had to be made by the joint-Masters to resolve this issue. At the best of times it is also equally imperative that Hunt servants have the trust of the Mastership [and vice versa], and particularly so in times of difficulty. Unfortunately, what was already a delicate situation continued to deteriorate as the joint-Masters, the new Hunt chairman [Colonel Drew] and members of the committee endeavoured, unsuccessfully, to find a solution mutually acceptable to all parties. Inevitably, as some members and subscribers considered that the Hunt committee had failed to reflect their feelings [in their view, Holder had been a loyal servant for some twenty years and, on account of his age, he was unlikely to get another job as a huntsman], the problem began to create factions within the Hunt and it rumbled on deleteriously into the next season.

In the meantime, at the end of April 1986, Austin James left to go to the Albrighton Woodland as kennel huntsman and Peter Ellrich, who at one time earlier in his career was with the Beaufort, came from the Colchester Garrison Beagles to replace him. The kennelman, 'Sage' Thompson, also moved on [he is now huntsman at the Chiddingfold, Leconfield & Cowdray].

In August 1986, matters came to a head when Holder was suddenly dismissed summarily from Hunt service by the joint-Masters. Whilst their action was perhaps explicable to some degree, this proved to be a very controversial move indeed. As a consequence, some hard decisions had to be taken during the formulation and execution of a recovery plan that would allow the Hunt to be held together.

Rosemary Peters smiles for the camera as she canters by.

The remedy was radical and immediate. It was decided to disband the existing pack of some 35 couple and to promote Ellrich to the role of huntsman. He then had the task of blending the remaining hounds and the replacement drafts into a more wieldy pack of about 20-25 couple. In view of the timing, it was difficult to find a replacement whipper-in and the amateurs filled in, with other valuable help coming from neighbouring Hunts. By October, Tony Grinstead had taken on the role of 1st whipper-in on a part-time basis [he was, however, available every hunting day] and Tom Robinson was employed as kennelman.

But the debate raged on and the divisions within the Hunt continued to deepen. The pervading gloom was further intensified when it became apparent that the income from subscriptions had fallen very far short of expenditure and that the negotiated settlement with Holder would severely deplete the Hunt's financial reserves. As is now apparent, it was a situation the Hunt had faced several times before, although it is doubtful that the joint-Masters or any of the then Hunt committee realised that. Their solution was sound, broadly following the historical precedents – an appeal was made for more money.

To maintain overall solvency and cash flow, a target of £12,000 was set. To raise this sum the committee called upon all friends, past and present, to make a one-off gift of as much as could be individually afforded. Perceptively, the hon. treasurer pointed out that the payment to the ex-huntsman had only brought forward these financial problems and had not been the cause of them. But no matter how one looked at it, the Hunt was in trouble.

On a more cheerful note, at a committee meeting held at the Punchbowl on 19th March 1987, it was decided to provide Mrs Olivia Jordan with a memento in recognition of her secretarial work for the past sixteen years in connection with the hunter trials. She was duly presented with a rose bowl at the annual general meeting in April.

Yet, despite the furore, hounds carried on hunting, subscribers continued to renew their subscriptions and outside activities were particularly successful. Following some astute financial management, the accounts for the season 1986-87 actually showed an overall surplus of £4,612 [compared with a deficit of £10,030 the previous season] and the appeal fund exceeded its target. The Hunt committee also had a new chairman, the energetic John Plummer from Waterlands Farm, Forest Green.

John Plummer, about to give a commentary as hounds are paraded at Cranleigh Show. When a rousing view-halloa from the far corner of the ring echoed around the showground, his laconic, *"I think the whipper-in may have seen a fox"*, brought the house down.

Notes

52 *That the Countryside Alliance strategy some ten years later followed a similar path speaks volumes for the insight confidently displayed in this paper.*

At the committee meeting held on 23rd April 1987, Mr Plummer stressed *"that the Hunt must become a unified force and that everyone must pull together. There was no room for complacency and having reached the £12,000 appeal target, we must forge ahead, make improvements and attract new subscribers ..."*. He also announced that there was to be a general review of the Hunt, *"with the object of making it more efficient"*, although an exception to this scrutiny would be the actual hunting arrangements themselves. They were, and remained, the responsibility of the acting joint-Masters.

As part of this review, Major J F V Vandeleur-Boorer produced a paper setting out his views, which he described as *"radical, unflattering and provocative"*. But be that as it may, being skilled *"as an administrator in modern management practices"*, he produced an incisive analysis and proffered practical ideas to ameliorate the bleak position in which the Hunt found itself. These extracts from his forthright study demonstrate an understanding of the direction that needed to be taken and, additionally, they provide a series of tenets that still hold good today:

> *"... It is obvious little or nothing was done and the unsatisfactory position was allowed to continue which indicates to me a fundamental problem of management. If a huntsman proves to be unsatisfactory then the Hunt committee and Masters must act decisively before the situation deteriorates and affects hunting within the country. To do nothing, or little, reflects a weakness on behalf of the committee and Masters, which in my opinion is the reason for the crisis today. Combine this weakness with the lack of hunting lore and expertise on behalf of those responsible then naturally the professional huntsmen will lose all respect for his Masters and those in authority.*
>
> *... This means that we must form a marketing strategy which will promote the Hunt in the best possible way, initially by personal visits to every landowner, farmer, gamekeeper or forester on whose land we hope to cross and also those subscribers and supporters who left us last season. We must explain and discuss our aims for the future and seek their help and cooperation. Goodwill visits and close-working relations must be maintained with the Police and Editors of the local press. A series of articles about hunting should be offered for publication. Any item of good publicity must be exploited to the full ...*[52]
>
> *... My perception of the present division of the responsibilities between our Joint-Masters is one of disproportionate workload, which now requires close examination. This I consider to be the key to our future success. In our present position we must have Masters who are prepared to overcome enormous difficulties and give every free moment they have to the benefit of the Hunt. Not only must they be highly motivated, but possess the character and charisma of a positive leader with a committed sense of duty, a detailed and proven knowledge of hunting and the respect of all those who support and follow hounds throughout the hunting country. In all honesty I do not believe, under the existing circumstances, our Masters can claim that situation exists ...*
>
> *... If these duties could be shared between four Masters then I feel the workload would be more acceptable and can only benefit the Hunt."*

Probably for the first time in the history of our Hunt, an opportunity was being presented that might lead away from the blind reaction to events and towards a future where we might exercise some control over our destiny by proper planning. The markers had been set out, but would they be followed?

Broadly, the answer is probably yes. It is never easy converting principles into practice, but John Plummer and the Hunt committee had a jolly good go at trying to do so, as did Mr Taylor and Mrs Peters. A problem quickly recognised was the paucity of talent available to expand the joint-Mastership and so, for the season 1987-88, there was only one addition to their number, Mr N L Fawcett. Living at Midhurst, Nick Fawcett was an insurance broker with a business in Surbiton and had previously hunted with the Chiddingfold, Leconfield & Cowdray and Mr Goschen's.

As far as the establishment was concerned, Grinstead was taken on full time as 1st whipper-in [he also looked after the Hunt horses] and Robinson was promoted to 2nd whipper-in. The quality of the pack was still being improved and drafts were received from the Duke of Beaufort's, the Isle of Wight and the Chiddingfold, Leconfield & Cowdray to further this aim.

During the night of 15-16th October 1987, the South-East of England was hit by an unexpected hurricane. There was considerable damage to property and not only were kennels badly damaged [especially the Horsham 'slate' stone roofing of the hound lodges], but a great many woodlands were flattened or laid waste by this storm. Working parties from the Hunt were arranged to help clear up the mess and areas at Abinger Flats, Blackheath, Farley Heath and Holmbury Hill were declared "*passable*" at the start of November, although all sporting activities on Forestry Commission and National Trust land were suspended until the end of that month. The Opening Meet that season was on Wednesday 4th November 1987, at Newhouse Farm, Newdigate, by kind invitation of Mr Tony Crutcher and his wife, Carrie.

As for the season generally, there is a degree of buoyant optimism in the joint-Masters' report given at the general meeting on 14th June 1988:

"*… we finished the season … with a quite noticeable improvement in the hunting of our hounds, which had in fact been taking place from the very beginning of the season. Our hounds have now blended together in a most remarkable way under the care and attention of our kennel staff. Compliments have appeared from all quarters, particularly from the well-informed in the visiting Masters and huntsmen that have come out with us. We are, of course, appreciative of those who have drafted us hounds, and who continue to do so. We hope that all of you will be with us at our Puppy Show on 3rd July [53] when you will be able to see just how well they look thanks to Peter and Tony, and indeed how well mannered and attentive they are to our huntsman. At the same time I hope that you will appreciate the improvements that have taken place around the kennels. Not all the gale damage has been dealt with, but this is in hand and should soon be finished*".

At the end of April, Robinson moved on to the New Forest and in May there was more lucrative media work when hounds appeared in a television advert for *Tiger* beer, shot on the 18-20th May.

The same three acting joint-Masters were appointed for the season 1988-89 and, in kennels, the establishment remained the same. The Opening Meet was at Elderslie, Ockley, by the kind invitation of Sir John Prideaux. A visit was made to the Hursley Hambledon, where Mrs Peters' daughter was a joint-Master, and a good day was enjoyed from their meet at Upham. The same acting joint-Mastership carried on into the next season and the whipper-in, Grinstead, was replaced by Stephen James from the East Essex. The hunting continued. Perhaps things were beginning to settle down onto an even keel once more?

Notes

53 *The judges were Mr & Mrs Nigel Peel, joint-Masters of the North Cotswold.*

Three Generations of Terriermen

Lenny Moore in the 1940s.

Keith Nickolson in 2003.

[left to right] Tom Dale [the farrier]*, Rodney West and Bill Johns in the 1970s.

* Not to be confused with Tom Dale [the farmer] on the Hunt committee.

78

CHAPTER 21

The 1990s – The Old Order Changeth

"Great 'eaven! Wot a many things are wantin', to 'unt a country plisantly."

Mr Jorrocks [again]

The season 1989-90 started well. Harvesting finished early and hounds were able to go out on 16th August, which was considered to be a record, and three days a week thereafter. There had been a particularly successful point-to-point, a 'Midnight Steeplechase' at Beare Green had raised a lot of money for charity and the Hunt team were runners-up in the Beefeater Team Competition at the South of England Show at Ardingly. Yet, at a committee meeting held on 11th January 1990 attended by fifteen people, the resolution, *"The Hunt Committee recommends the dissolution of the Surrey Union Hunt"*, was passed with twelve votes in favour and three abstentions. How could such a state of affairs have come to pass?

At an earlier meeting, on 30th November 1989, the Hunt committee was told that the huntsman, Ellrich, had decided to leave at the end of the season. [He went to hunt hounds in the USA.] It was also explained that the pressures on the Hunt country were such that it might not be possible to fill the meet card for the next season and that the acting joint-Mastership intended to retire on 30th April 1990. On this last point, the joint-Masters suggested that a solution for the next season would be for them to be re-elected, together with two additions to their number. That way, their burdens [which were particularly heavy on Mrs Peters] could be shared more evenly. Alternatively, the committee might wish to accept their resignation and appoint others, with or without any of the present joint-Mastership, or even try to find an amateur huntsman. The committee decided, *"that the predicament was too profound a subject to resolve without time to discuss all implications in detail"* and a further meeting was arranged for 5th December.

At that next meeting, the subscription lists for the two previous seasons were reviewed and *"these gave rise to great optimism for the future"* and, when allied with the excellent order of the kennel premises and Hunt motor vehicles, the chairman thought that *"this was a good and sound foundation to build on for next season"*. So, *"after a lengthy and full discussion"*, it was decided to accept the retirement of the joint-Masters, as they had requested in their report to the November meeting. The chairman went on to say, *"how indebted the Hunt was for all they had done and recognition of their help and hard work would be made at a later date ... it was hoped that they would remain associated with the Surrey Union. Their expertise was valued. The committee hoped that the season would continue on the high note that exists at the moment. We are looking forward to the future with confidence"*.

A further committee meeting was convened on 18th December to explore the possibilities, but apart from setting up a sub-committee to *"find a new Mastership for the 1990-91 season"*, nothing of substance was resolved. Discussions with several interested parties seem to have taken place over the Christmas period and, early in the new year, Mr R C A Hammond outlined to this sub-committee his initial proposals for taking on the Mastership, in conjunction with others. As the minutes of the committee meeting held on 11th January 1990 make plain, this proposition was not accepted and no other viable option seemed available, other than dissolution.

". . . anyway the Hunt problems were not due to lack of finance, only to lack of country."

Fred Trinder, Hunt Committee meeting 11th January 1990

". . . it wouldn't be the antis that finished the hunt, it would be the lack of money."

John Funnell MFH, Hunt Committee meeting. 8th January 1991

Christopher Hammond in typically benign mood
September 1994.

However, by the next committee meeting on 30th January, Mr Hammond had produced a detailed document '*Surrey Union Plan 1990-93*' and started a collaboration with Mr A Drysdale. Soon after, on 4th February, the Hunt committee was able to resolve that:

"a) The Hunt Committee accept in principle Mr Hammond's proposal,

b) Appoint as provisional Joint Acting Masters:-
*   Mr A Drysdale   Mr C Hammond   Mrs D Goodchild*
*   - subject to later formal endorsement.*

c) The provisional Masters are authorised to explore its feasibility.

d) The provisional Masters are asked to report back to the Committee by 30th March 1990

e) With a view to the Hunt Committee making an appropriate recommendation to the adjourned Annual General Meeting by 15th April 1990."

Hence the makings of a rescue package were in place, but who would hunt hounds? After considering several alternatives, the provisional acting joint-Masters recommended Mr J Funnell, who would join their number. All of these suggestions were ratified by the general meeting of the Hunt on 18th April, together with some constitutional changes and the appointment of Lord Hamilton of Dalzell and Mr Patrick Evelyn as President and Chairman of the Hunt respectively, with Mr Gordon Lee-Steere as Chairman of the Landowners' Council and Mr John Plummer as Chairman of the Executive Committee of the Hunt.

So, from 1st May 1990 there was a complete change of Mastership and establishment. The outgoing joint-Masters were duly fêted – Mr Taylor was presented with a silver hunting horn, Mrs Peters an antique silver sugar castor and Mr Fawcett a packed hamper[54]. As a reminder that the Surrey Union hounds were paraded at the Grand Military race meeting at Sandown Park and as a postscript on these times, Mrs Peters recently recalled that, *"After parading hounds at Sandown in 1990 I was asked to present flowers to the late Queen Elizabeth, the Queen Mother. On arriving at the lift I found the royal party led by the Queen Mother waiting there. She smiled at me explaining the lift had broken down and I had better wait until we were all upstairs before presenting my bouquet. In conversation the Queen Mother, who was always well informed, said how sorry she was to hear about the problems of the Surrey Union Hunt"*.

But just who were all these new acting joint-Masters? A businessman and former Royal Navy officer living at Holmbury St Mary, Christopher Hammond had been a subscriber to the Surrey Union during the late 1970s and his wife, Bar Hammond, had competed on Great Britain's three-day event and dressage teams. From his home in Hookwood, Andrew Drysdale had hunted with the Old Surrey & Burstow and was a joint-Master of the Coakham Bloodhounds. As the Hunt secretary, Prudence Goodchild had been with involved with the inner-workings of the Hunt for many years and had been a member and subscriber for many years before that. Aged 53, John Funnell had been Master and huntsman of the Tickham until their merger with the West Street. He was also involved with the manufacture and marketing of the *Claydon* horse exerciser.

By the time the 1990-91 season got fully underway, the Hunt was being run like a commercial company on business-based principles, with a very clearly constructed organisational structure. There was even a computer installed in kennels, operated by a paid secretary. The relationship between the acting joint-Mastership and the Hunt committee was clearly defined and the overall intent may be gauged from the opening paragraphs of the agreement: *"An atmosphere of open debate is imperative to maximise potential. Survival is not success. Only when we have tapped the potential of the country and those people interested in hunting can we start to think of success. A large measure of* [that] *success will depend on the degree of frankness maintained by the Masters with the committee*". All sound concepts and essential to the build up of trust; clearly the lessons of recent history had been taken to heart.

To whip-in for him, John Funnell initially had John O'Donnell from Ireland and later Richard Scrivens from the Beaufort. The experienced amateur whipper-in and committee member, Fred Trinder, assisted them. The Field master was often Tim Barker and the terrier men were Rodney West, Tom Dale, Rob West and Phil 'Wagbi' Overton. Always a bit of a character, Phil was a local gamekeeper who often rode out with hounds, carrying his terrier in a side bag. In January 1991 another new Surrey Union trait was introduced, as Mrs Mandy Agnew and Mrs Jenny Barker became the joint-honorary secretaries.

A partial solution to the shrinking country problem presented itself when the northern part of the country formerly hunted by Mr Goschen's Hounds became available for the season 1991-92. The disbandment of Mr Goschen's Hunt brought several of their former subscribers over to the Surrey Union, including Mr M G Sprake, who joined the acting joint-Mastership. A proprietor of a riding school at Eashing, near Godalming, Mark Sprake had formerly been an amateur whipper-in to the late Richard Barlow MFH of the Chiddingfold, Leconfield and Cowdray. He had also whipped-in, looked after country and acted as Field master to Mr Goschen's pack.

John Funnell, ever cheerful, was particularly popular with the gamekeepers in our country.

At the annual general meeting on 18th February 1992, Mrs Goodchild was able to report that, "*Our thanks must go to John Funnell for providing such enjoyable days. The hounds were now second to none and the way they hunted was the envy of many. His back-up team of Mrs Jan Funnell, Peter Hoare and Richard Scrivens must not go unnoticed and thanks were due to all at the kennels . . . Nor should the landowners and farmers be forgotten since it was only with the co-operation of these that hunting was possible. It was noted that landowners and farmers were very pleased with the conduct of the Hunt*". At the end of the season, Mr Drysdale retired from the Mastership and eventually moved to the West Country.

On the hound-breeding front, John Funnell reported to the summer general meeting on 15th July 1992 that he had managed to find hounds at the Monmouthshire whose bloodlines went back to old Surrey Union hounds. He had been given a number of puppies and intended to use one of their stallion hounds next season, to keep the lines going. That season, there had been 14½ couple of new entry. At the end of April 1993, John Funnell resigned as joint-Master and huntsman, after three years of hard work and showing some exceptional sport. He had developed a particular rapport with gamekeepers and, as a consequence, managed to open up a lot of country that had formerly been closed to us. In a phased handover, Mark Sprake took his place as huntsman. In fact, Mr Sprake first carried the horn with the Surrey Union on Friday, 19th March 1993. As Mrs Goodchild said at the summer general meeting on 23rd June, "*. . . and as anyone who was out that day would agree, it gave great heart to go into the current season*".

A further change from 1st May 1993 was the addition to the acting joint-Mastership of Mr I R Gilchrist, the Hunt treasurer. Having taken up hunting whilst at Cranleigh School, "*to avoid games*", Ian Gilchrist had come to the Surrey Union when the Chiddingfold Farmers' disbanded in 1969. As a partner in an accountancy firm, he had proved to be a most effective treasurer, having managed the financial affairs of the Hunt with considerable acumen – his adroitness had helped it avoid many perils since 1975. He immediately embarked on a long-term drive to open up the Weald country; a campaign that slowly showed dividends in the ensuing seasons and his success in this regard is now apparent to all who currently hunt with us.

Later in the season, John Plummer finally retired as chairman [something he had being trying to do for a number of years!] and was succeeded by Tim Barker, a popular member of the Hunt and sometime amateur whipper-in and Field master. At the general meeting on 19th April 1994, Mrs Goodchild reported that since the Opening Meet there had been 45 day's hunting, with only three lost to the weather, and of the eleven scheduled for Saturdays, ten had been successfully held. This return to Saturday hunting was particularly welcome, as during the two previous seasons hunting had been restricted to weekdays only. Great fun was also had, she said, at the Hunt Breakfast[55] at the end of the season, when an incredible 270 "*proper hunting breakfasts*" had been cooked and served. To attract new subscribers and improve cash flow, a successful marketing exercise had been undertaken at the start of the season and the treasurer also described at this meeting how there were now more people subscribing, more caps and more field money.

For the season 1994-95, the 'marketing' of the Hunt continued, with promotional material and financial incentives. Jamie Bryant neatly summed up the underlying philosophy behind this policy at a committee meeting on 11th January 1995: "*If a product lived up to the consumer's expectations, then he would buy again. People were having fun hunting and expectations were being amply fulfilled*". Whilst locally the support for the Hunt was increasing [there were 40 lawn meets during the season[56]], it was becoming ever more clear that the political pressures against hunting were beginning to grow. To combat this threat, the now familiar Campaign for Hunting was launched.

Rather earlier in this season, Rob West, a foot-follower and staunch supporter of our Hunt, had died suddenly and a memorial collection of some £350 was collected as a tribute to him.

There were changes at kennels at the end of the season: Kevin Boyles did not stay long and moved on to the Garth & South Berks and Peter Hoare took over as non-riding kennel huntsman. David Marr was also employed as a professional whipper-in, although soon after taking up duty he went down with appendicitis.

Further evidence of the resurgence of hunting's popularity came from the numbers in the field – at the start of the 1995-96 season there were over 100 mounted followers at the Opening Meet at Elderslie, 76 at the Stileman's meet and over 50 at Albury Heath. That autumn, Jamie Bryant temporarily took over the role of Chairman. He was keen that the Hunt committee should be a proper executive committee and that every member of it should have a clearly defined role. He identified 17 separate committee functions, such as fundraising; social activities; managing structural repairs at kennels and construction of hunt jumps; Hunter Trials courses; police liaison; PR; marketing and the Pony Club. Unfortunately nothing more came of this enterprising view[57] following his retirement from the role of chairman and the election of Ian Agnew to this key post. But as Ian Agnew came in, Mandy Agnew went out. She retired as joint-honorary Hunt secretary and was presented with a silver fox, and a residue of the collection in cheque form, sufficient apparently for a pair of new boots! Her joint-secretarial role was ultimately taken over by Rita Boggiss.

At the end of the season, Peter Hoare moved on and Mrs Goodchild retired from the acting joint-Mastership. At a committee meeting on 24th January 1996 the chairman wished to "*minute the debt owed to Mrs Goodchild for all that she had done in the past but was prevented by Mrs Goodchild herself from expanding on just how great that debt had been*". And that remains the measure of the lady: very few realise quite how much good she did for our Hunt during her years as secretary and joint-Master and, indeed, has done subsequently, ranging from, amongst many other things,

Notes

55 *These are still a revered part of Surrey Union tradition and a direct link with our 18th-century roots.*

56 *Indeed, the next season there were more invitations than hounds could accommodate.*

57 *An idea essentially overtaken by events when the Hunt returned to a full joint-Mastership, with guarantee [see later].*

her determined stance when negotiating with the Surrey constabulary [which obliged them to adapt, change and on occasions entirely re-think their response to policing legitimate hunting] to quietly funding a social event.

From 1st May 1996, Mrs Katharine Meller joined the remaining acting joint-Masters and Daron Beeney was set on as kennel huntsman and 1st whipper-in. Previously, Daron had been kennel huntsman at the Vine & Craven and prior to that was 1st whipper-in with the H.H., where he had moved from the Curre with Bob Collins. His wife, Alison, was responsible for turning out the Hunt horses.

The season 1996-97 showed that the popularity of hunting in our part of Surrey was still being maintained, with 120 mounted followers at the Opening Meet. When the season finished, David Marr moved on to the Albrighton Woodland and was replaced by Matthew Cook, from the Chiddingfold, Leconfield & Cowdray, as 2nd whipper-in and kennelman.

Ian Agnew explains the finer points of hound showing to his granddaughter, Abigail, at the Kennels Open Day in June 2006.

Readers will have noted the assiduous use of the term 'acting joint-Master' in this history since the late 1970s. As an explanation, when asked what the benefit of Mastership over acting-Mastership was at a committee meeting on 10th October 1997, Mr Hammond replied that, "*Masters often felt frustrated by the committee and that the change of system would make them masters of their own destiny and give them a measure of control which they did not at present possess*". Essentially, he was seeking a reversion back to a full joint-Mastership, whereby the Mastership team would be given a guarantee to run the Hunt in their own right, rather than as agents of the Hunt committee. Under such an arrangement, the Hunt committee would remain responsible for raising this guarantee and for recommending a Mastership to the annual meeting of members and subscribers. The joint-Masters would not be *ex officio* members of the committee, although a representative would attend meetings. The crucial difference would be that the joint-Masters would make up any expenditure in excess of the guarantee themselves. A proposal that there should be a change to full joint-Mastership, with guarantee, for the 1998-99 season was carried unanimously.

From 1st May 1998, Mr J. Ford joined the joint-Mastership. With a natural ability to ride across country, Jonathan 'Freddie' Ford had already made his mark as a proficient Field master. With his family farming background and connections in the Weald country, he was considered a useful asset indeed. After five seasons hunting hounds, Mr Sprake passed the horn on to Beeney and, from the West Norfolk, Ian Shakespeare was taken on as 1st whipper-in. To complete all these changes, Jenny Barker retired after six years as joint-honorary Hunt secretary and was replaced by Miss Clare Rickard.

With a view to arranging fundraising activities that would appeal to the younger members and subscribers, a junior committee of the Hunt was formed. They assisted with fund raising efforts and liaison with the Pony Club, and were responsible for around 50 children coming out hunting over the Christmas holidays. One member of that committee, Dominic Jones, who had also been an amateur whipper-in, was appointed Master/huntsman of the Royal Agricultural College Beagles at Cirencester. Currently [season 2006-07], Dominic is joint-Master of the Cotswold, hunting hounds.

On 6th July 1998 the General Meeting was told that at the national Hunt Secretaries AGM it was reported that the Surrey Union were regarded as "*one of the best organised and best run Hunts and that our Masters should be congratulated*". It must have been gratifying to all concerned to receive such recognition, especially in view of the difficulties experienced over the previous dozen seasons or so and the ensuing hard work to overcome them.

As the putative 200th anniversary of our Hunt approached, at a committee meeting held on 7th September 1998, Mrs Goodchild outlined her plans for a party to be held at Okewood Village Hall. Having obtained donations to underwrite its costs, a large assortment of people with past associations or involvement with Hunt, together with an array of past Masters, members and other supporters duly gathered on 25th October to mark this historically significant occasion.

Unfortunately, hounds suffered an outbreak of the virus, *Pasturella*, and had to be rested for two weeks on veterinary advice. As a result, the Opening Meet had to be put back until 14th November. According to a report in *Horse & Hound*, "*Our kind hosts, Mr and Mrs Bryant, generously entertained a field of 104 mounted followers, augmented by a substantially larger number on foot. Huntsman, Daron Beeney, with whipper-in, Ian Shakespeare, hacked a mixed pack of 15½ couple the short distance* [to Elderslie, Ockley] *from kennels at Oakwood Hill. Three resounding cheers for the future of the Hunt followed a rousing speech by Hunt committee chairman, Ian Agnew, before the pack moved off*". As it turned out, the virus was difficult to eradicate and for the early part of the season hunting was undertaken with fewer hounds than normal.

In December, Jim Saunders retired as an amateur whipper-in, a role he had undertaken since coming to the Surrey Union in 1991 following the demise of Mr Goschen's Hunt. He had contributed a great deal of hard work, both in the field and in kennels.

At the general meeting held on 28th January 1999, it was announced that Ian Gilchrist was to retire as Hunt treasurer. "*As a mark of our respect for seeing us through thick and thin*", Ian Agnew presented him with a crystal port decanter, with an engraved silver collar. The chairman went on to thank him "*for all he had done in the past 25 years*" and said "*Ian's accountancy skills had kept the Hunt going*". This was a truly accurate summary and Nigel Morland had the unenviable task of taking on the responsibility as Hunt treasurer from 1st May 1999.

The Bicentennial Hunt Ball was held at Hurtwood Polo Club in February 1999 – a glittering and memorable occasion for all those attended. This celebration was a culmination of a great deal of time and energy expended by the organising committee, comprising Jamie Bryant, Clare Rickard and Freddie Ford.

As the Labour government [elected with a huge majority in 1997] started to find its feet, the insidious pressure against hunting started to mount. Although this aspect of our history will be expanded upon in Chapter 23, from the outset there was clear evidence to show that our Hunt was winning the battle for hearts and minds locally. In this regard, the unsolicited letter published in *Horse & Hound* on 25th February 1999 is hard to beat [see left].

But such a public perception could not be taken for granted. Speaking at the Annual General Meeting on 27th January 2000, Mr Sprake said, "*The country was divided among four Masters; the management of the Weald had gone particularly well under Mr Gilchrist; Mr Ford had done much to improve access in his country* [The Kennels Area]*; Mrs Meller had earned the admiration of all her fellow Masters in the way she ran her country* [The Hill Country]*; and he himself had succeeded in opening up long closed areas* [The 'Other Side']*. In the mean time public perception was crucial and good behaviour essential. Please do not be afraid to tell people that they <u>must</u> act with courtesy.*"

It seems that the members and subscribers took Mr Sprake's words to heart, as the letter published in the *Farmers Weekly* of 2nd June 2000 demonstrates [see opposite].

At the end of the 1999-2000 season Beeney left and went to hunt the Eglinton hounds in Scotland. It was also a time for the reorganisation of the duties of the joint-Hunt secretaries. Following a thorough review, it was clear that the requirements of the job were becoming ever more onerous, even for two people. So, with Clare Rickard having relinquished her role, a most effective team of four, Rita Boggiss, Rachel Brooker, Geraldine Firth and Judeth Chamberlain, became the new joint-honorary Hunt secretaries from 1st May 2000.

For the season 2000-2001, Simon Richmond was appointed as the new huntsman. However, his resignation after a few weeks led to the brave decision by the joint-Mastership in September 2000 to promote the young Ian Shakespeare to 1st whipper-in, hunting hounds. He was assisted by Keith Nickolson, who arrived during the autumn of 2000 to act as kennelman, together with Antonia Jones and Fred Trinder who also helped in kennels.

Andrew Hazeltine has been an amateur whipper-in for many seasons. His musical calling up of hounds is always a delight to hear.

Tom Zamoyski was the last person in our Hunt to wear a swallow-tailed coat and top hat regularly. He finally "hung up his boots" at the end of the 2005-06 season.

Nigel Morland, the honorary Hunt treasurer. Not only does he keep the books with aplomb, he can also be relied upon to make a fine speech.

Some Hunt Notables

Graham Rand is often appointed Field master, particularly in the Weald country. In this photograph, neither drink nor cigarette seem to be at hand! Hunt Committee member Danny Davies is in the background.

The first President of the Surrey Union Hunt, the late Lord Hamilton of Dalzell. Just before this book went to press, Corinna, Lady Hamilton, had kindly consented to become our next President.

John Lea is looking pretty pleased with himself, having just won a bottle of port in the draw at the meet. John is one of several intrepid foot-followers who tramp miles during a hunting day.

CHAPTER 22

Into the New Millennium

"There is not a subject under the sun that is better suited to us for raising our morale in the constituencies than a ban on foxhunting"

Dennis *"The Beast of Bolsover"* Skinner MP, House of Commons, 17th June 2004

Just as this new establishment was settling down to its demanding tasks, in February 2001 there was an outbreak of foot and mouth disease [FMD], which rapidly spread nationwide. In consequence, hunting was immediately suspended voluntarily.

For reasons best known to itself, the Department of the Environment, Food & Rural Affairs [DEFRA] refused the offers of help from Hunts and the outbreak continued to spiral out of control. Such 'political' niceties were soon subsumed by practicality when the Army took over the handling of the emergency and our Hunt servants were put on stand-by for culling duty in the event of an outbreak in the south-east of England. At the height of the crisis in March, Ian Shakespeare was posted to Cumbria for two weeks, but such was the 'sensitive' nature of this deployment that DEFRA managed not to pay his legitimate expenses until many months afterwards. The devastation caused by the outbreak continued throughout the spring and summer, effectively putting the countryside on hold until the spread of the disease was finally checked.

From 1st May 2001, Ian Shakespeare was formally appointed huntsman, with Keith Nickolson as 1st whipper-in. There was no point-to-point racing during 2001 and the formal start to the 2001-02 season was further delayed by a fresh outbreak of FMD in Northumberland.

By November, it was becoming clear that hunting could be resumed, but only under tightly controlled circumstances. Hunts were required to obtain a permit from the local DEFRA office for each and every day they wish to hunt. The granting of such permits was dependent on strict compliance with statutory regulations and Hunts had to be scrupulous in their adherence to the rules. One small moment of cheer was provided when the civil servants in our Hunt [who, regretfully, must remain anonymous] beat DEFRA at their own game and produced a comprehensive working guide to these complex regulations, complete with forms, long before the official version was ready. Yet again DEFRA inexplicably chose to decline our offer of help!

With such competent work by its staff, the Surrey Union was the first Hunt in the country to resume after the withdrawal of the FMD restrictions. Our licence was issued at ten minutes past nine on 17th December – by nine thirty, hounds were in covert. However, as the new entry from the previous year had not had the benefit of a complete season's hunting and the current new entry had had no autumn hunting experience at all, a succession of low-key days was to follow until Christmas.

At the Annual General Meeting held on 25th January 2002, the Masters were given due recognition for their efforts in getting hunting resumed so promptly and efficiently, whilst the secretaries were applauded for their effective handling of all the resultant paperwork! Grateful thanks were accorded to all those who had continued to pay subscriptions during the layoff and to the organisers of the various events that were so successful in raising funds. These included the joint-Masters' 'fun rides' on Saturdays; a Summer Dance organised by Charlotte Heath-Bullock

Levity and Seriousness. Ann Metson sees the funny side, whilst Catherine Heilbron contemplates the next move …

… which might just involve a fall! Happily both horse and rider were unscathed in this incident on Boxing Day 2005.

Keeping the Hunt country open requires a lot of hard work by the Mastership. This sign in the Weald instructs the Field to walk over a vulnerable private driveway that provides a crucial link between strategic parcels of farmland.

and her team; Mrs Meller's Sponsored Ride; Sarah Dunsdon's 'Host-a-Roast' and the Surrey Union Hunt Supporters' Club's lucrative auction of promises.

This meeting was also told that Mr Hammond was standing down as Master, after 12 seasons. It was wholly appropriate that the Chairman opined that "*a huge debt of thanks was due for his input to the Hunt since his appointment in 1990*". Without his drive, determination and businesslike approach at a time of crisis, there would be no Surrey Union Hunt today.

Also standing down from the joint-Mastership was Freddie Ford, whilst Geraldine Firth resigned as joint-honorary Hunt secretary. After relinquishing her role as chairman of the Surrey Union Hunt Supporters' Club, Jane Williams became Geraldine's replacement.

A visitor from the USA, Mr Brent Lane, had been sitting in on the meeting and asked to say a few words. He spoke warmly about the welcome he had enjoyed when he hunted with the Surrey Union in 2000. He continued with the shrewd observation, "*Knowing little about hunting he had come with an open mind and open heart and was pleased to be received in the same spirit. We had a wonderful tradition. But having heard some of the earlier remarks with regard to etiquette and dress, he advocated flexibility. Traditions that were kept purely for the sake of those who understood them would become dying traditions if their strict observance were to discourage newcomers*".

Having eventually got towards the end of a very difficult season, a further blow fell when kennel cough put a premature end to hunting for our hounds. Undaunted, our joint-Masters made a virtue out of necessity and, with the kind co-operation of the Masterships of adjoining Hunts and their respective staffs, organised the 2002 Surrey Union festival of hunting. The Crawley & Horsham brought their hounds to Coldharbour and were royally entertained at the meet by Mr & Mrs Yeomans; the Chiddingfold, Leconfield & Cowdray enjoyed the generous hospitality of the Ford family at Beldham's Farm and, on the last day of the season, the Old Surrey, Burstow & West Kent came to the William IV at Little London and our traditional Hunt breakfast. In this last regard, John Murray's sausages really did deserve a wider audience! All our visitors provided an interesting diversity of hunting days and thereby ensured that the 2001-2002 season concluded on a suitably upbeat note.

At the start of the 2002-03 season, Messrs O'Reilly-Hyland and Gumbley joined the new joint-Mastership. In the kennels, Nicholas Prior replaced Keith Nickolson as 1st whipper-in. After six years as joint-honorary Hunt secretary, Rita Boggiss retired from the post [subsequently moving to France] and Penny Wilson was appointed in her stead from 1st May 2003.

CHAPTER 23

Modern Times

"For most of the MPs who voted for a ban, it was all about pay-back time for the miners"

Llin [now **Baroness**] **Golding**

Bearing in mind that the political consequences of the desperate attempt to ban hunting are currently far from being played out, it will be for a future generation to analyse in detail the part that the Surrey Union Hunt played in the events surrounding the creation of the Hunting Act 2004. That said, there is no aspect of this peculiar piece of modern history where we failed to play our part in the campaigning that went on before this singularly unprincipled piece of legislation was passed, and that has been carried on with equal determination since. [Anyone still harbouring a naïve notion that this issue was in any way concerned with improvements to 'animal welfare' is encouraged to read *Rural Rites – Hunting and the Politics of Prejudice*, a book by Charlie Pye-Smith that sets out the inner workings of the whole ignoble affair in some depth.]

From long before the moment when the idea that a ban on hunting should become "*totemic*" to the government, the Surrey Union Hunt had been in the front rank of those pointing out the follies of such a policy. In the public arena, we initially rallied in Hyde Park and twice marched with hundreds of thousands of other like-minded folk through the streets of London. We picketed Cabinet meetings, held night vigils and the ladies of the Hunt even strung out their knickers before the House of Commons in their 'pants to prejudice' protest. We literally shone our light on the political prejudice in Parliament one evening, and were baton charged at the canter by mounted police for our trouble. We rallied in Parliament Square at significant times during the passage of the various bills through Parliament. On the last occasion, for the second reading of the final Hunting Bill on 15th September 2004, we were again met with the full force of the Metropolitan Police intent on "*protecting Parliament*" and, in so doing, they were clearly prepared to use their batons indiscriminately against the unprotected heads of our Hunt supporters.

More locally, our Hunt has held newcomers' days that have enabled dozens of beginners to sample hunting for the first time and to see for themselves what it is all about. We have invited politicians of all political persuasions to visit our Kennels, to learn at first hand what we do and how hunting has an effective and symbiotic role in the countryside, in both the management of the fox population and the disposal of dead farm animals, as well as the wider stewardship of the rural environment. In addition to writing letter after letter to MPs, members of the House of Lords and newspapers, we also developed more subtle forms of protest. A new sport, "hounding the Ministers", was soon discovered and this proved to be a surprisingly effective, albeit not so well publicised, tactic. One of our number became a veritable thorn in the flesh of a certain DEFRA minister and became very adept at inducing him to use singularly unparliamentary language in public, in addition to demonstrating quite how poor security arrangements for politicians actually were at that time.

Being close to London, we have also had to get used to the media spotlight and it became commonplace, certainly in the season 2004-05, for the Surrey Union Hunt to appear regularly on the television, in radio broadcasts and in the newspapers, both at home and abroad. In an age of instant celebrity, Jeremy Gumbley, our youngest most dashingly handsome joint-Master, even managed to get a leading role in a television documentary on BBC3. Another

Tally-over! The early morning sun illuminates a classic autumn hunting moment.

Two recent products of the SUH Branch of the Pony Club enjoy a stirrup cup at Rolls Farm, a meet hosted by Fraser and Lynne Norton on 19th February 2006. Jenny Womersley [left] is now one of the younger members of our Hunt, whilst Camilla Kear was, at the time, hunting the Kent & Surrey Bloodhounds following a serious riding accident suffered by her father, Bill Kear [who is yet another product of the Branch!].

particularly memorable moment came shortly after moving off from the Opening Meet in 2004, when Charlotte Heath-Bullock's recorded interview for Radio Suisse Romande, from horseback and in fluent French, was suddenly interrupted by a ruddy-faced foot-follower exclaiming, "*Écoutez! Ils ont trouvé un renard!*" as glorious hound music suddenly burst out of the adjacent covert. In similar vein, our Hunt Campaigner's casual, spur-of-the-moment comment, "*Look at us now – we're not toffs, we're desperados*", found itself syndicated throughout North America. The mellifluous tones of farrier and terrier-man, Rodney West, were heard on BBC Radio 4 and Jane Williams was described in *The Independent* on 20th November 2004 "*… as a suburban housewife. She's the sort of suburban housewife that can handle a four-wheel drive down a vertical muddy hillside while maintaining perfect composure*". But out of all the voluminous reportage, by far the most unlikely piece came from BBC Brasil, complete with Mark Sprake's unforgettable description of the ban as "*um pouco como um luto*" ["rather like a bereavement"].

But despite all this effort, the politicians finally got their wicked way and our last day of hunting under the old order was on 17th February 2005. A piece in *Horse & Hound* [see Appendix: 8] accurately described the mood at the time and hinted, quite rightly as it turned out, that all was not necessarily lost.

Owing to the curious way that the Hunting Act is drafted, its exemption provisions still allow certain types of hunting. Furthermore, there are aspects of its wording that tend to make successful prosecution difficult and, as this law is brought ever more into disrepute, it is becoming increasingly clear that this is now nothing more than just a temporary 'ban'. To slightly adapt the maxim of Fredrick Nietzsche, "*that which does not kill us makes us stronger*" – and the passing of the Hunting Act has certainly done just that.

No Hunts have disbanded as a result of this legislation and the whole of the hunting community has become politicised in a way that would have been unimaginable only two decades earlier [see Chapter 19]. At the 2005 election, for example, the 'political wing' of the Surrey Union Hunt actively helped to oust anti-hunting MPs from their seats. Having a clearly identifiable 'enemy' that one can effectively oppose does wonders for morale and the focus on survival within our Hunt is remarkable, wherever one looks.

To augment this resolve, we are currently very fortunate indeed to have strength in depth in every department of the Hunt. People come and people go, of course, but the modern essence of the Surrey Union has been formed and forged during this struggle. Combined with the lessons that we have learnt from our own history, this makes for a very potent force indeed.

The senior member of our team of joint-Masters is Mr Mark Sprake. One only has to be in his company for a few moments to realise that he is an excellent and enthusiastic communicator and is, therefore, the principal spokesman for the SUH. His energy and belief in the hunting cause have helped to carry everyone in our Hunt through the recent uncertain times. On a hunting day, Mark likes to keep people informed about what is happening and what to expect. His running commentary on events as they unfold is always worth listening to and his patient explanations of the intricacies of hunting lore have encouraged many, both young and old alike.

As has already been outlined, Mr Ian Gilchrist has hunted with the Surrey Union for 37 seasons and has been a joint-Master for the last thirteen. As a consequence Ian is exceedingly knowledgeable and is well versed in the hunting tradition. He continues to run the Weald country and works hard to make sure there is a good day to be had there. Whilst not always choosing to be out mounted these days, he is usually to be found around every corner, checking the day is going to plan.

Our sole lady joint-Master is Mrs Katharine Meller. She started hunting in about 1947, when, together with her sister, she would ride her pony, *Dingle*, to any meet that was within a two-hour hack of her parents' Burstow home. This often meant leaving in the dark and certainly returning home in the dark after a long day. So, as another joint-Master of the 'old school', she looks after the landowners in her country diligently and is particularly well informed on hounds and their breeding. She undertakes the organisation of the annual Puppy Show and is the guiding hand behind the Surrey Union Hound Show, which is held the Sunday prior to the South of England Hound Show at Ardingly and used by many Hunts as a rehearsal for that prestigious event. But it is as a fund-raiser that Katharine is second to none! She will collect for the raffle at each meet and always manages to appear, seemingly from nowhere, to collect the £5 "tumblers' club" fee should anyone have the misfortune to have a fall. Seemingly tireless, she will hunt three times a week if required – unfailingly first out and last to return.

Running the Kennels country is Mr Jeremy Gumbley, the youngest of the five joint-Masters. As befits a former Formula 3 racing-driver, he is young, dashing and possessed of a keen sense of humour. As is apparent from his media work, Mr Gumbley is also considered extremely photogenic. Unfortunately his looks have been somewhat spoilt recently, following a sponsored haircut [perhaps shearing might be a more accurate expression?] at the 2006 Opening Meet.

Always looking as smart as a new pin on a hunting day, huntsman Ian Shakespeare with a typically wry smile.

Last, but by no means least, is Mr Edmund O'Reilly-Hyland, an Irish property developer, who, like Mr Gumbley, has been a joint-Master master since the start of the 2002-03 season. He is not in the thrusting Field master category: more the sensible, benevolent and mature, "*sit back and wait for the jump*" character. Edmund has hunted extensively in Ireland with, amongst others, the Wicklow, the Scarteen and the Galway Blazers. A quiet, unassuming and dependable joint-Master, he makes a fine statement on a big horse.

The Hunt committee, under the able Chairmanship of Ian Agnew, is made up of a variety of individuals, each of whom brings their experience and an assortment of professional or practical skills to bear in the management of the Hunt. A full list of the Hunt committee and other officers for the season 2006-07 appears as Appendix: 12.

Our huntsman, Ian Shakespeare, shows a maturity beyond his years and his happy knack of being able to concentrate on the job in hand despite the unwelcome distractions that may sometimes occur on a hunting day is a calming influence on all around him. It is clear that hounds simply adore him and the biddability of our pack is regularly demonstrated in the field and also to great effect at agricultural shows, particularly when hounds from a variety of Hunts are mixed up together. When the time comes to sort them all out, the Surrey Union hounds readily return to Ian without demur. Indeed, amongst those that are old enough to remember, there are some who think that Ian's style of hunting and hound control is reminiscent of Jim Goddard. If this true, then it would be very high praise indeed. Until recently, he was ably assisted as 1st whipper-in by Nick Prior [who has now gone to the Chiddingfold, Leconfield & Cowdray], a role taken over by Kent Lock from the start of the season 2006-07. On a hunting day, Andrew Hazeltine and Danny Murphy assist the professionals by acting as amateur whippers-in. Alison West looks after the Hunt horses.

Master Jeremy Harvie represents the future and is often to be seen in the mounted Field.

As its title suggests, the Surrey Union Hunt Supporters' Club [SUHSC] exists to sustain our Hunt through the organisation of fund-raising events, the personal involvement of members in events run by the Hunt itself and general support in the field on a hunting day. The monetary donations from the SUHSC contribute very significantly to the Hunt's general funds. In addition, the SUHSC has generously purchased specific capital items for the use of the Hunt, including horses, a succession of most useful marquees and a steam cleaner for Kennels. Currently [November 2006], under the chairmanship of Danny Murphy, the SUHSC is a thriving organisation run by a strong committee, comprising: Zoe Edge [Secretary 2003], Nikki Selby [Treasurer 2003], Simon Autie, Trisha Bicknell, Becky Seviour, Keith Nickolson, Sharan Braham and Sue Porter, with joint-Master Jeremy Gumbley attending in an *ex officio* capacity. This team is always active and inventive in devising new ways of fundraising, at the same time as providing great entertainment. Throughout the year the SUHSC is responsible for events such as the Terrier Show, quiz nights, an auction of promises, pre- and end of Season parties and the ever-popular 'Lukyns Lunch', kindly hosted by Mrs Sarah Dunsdon.

The close and inter-dependent relationship between hunting and shooting still exists, as it has done for over 150 years. In recognition of this, a clay shoot is held in September each year as a "thank-you" to the landowners, farmers, gamekeepers and shoot captains with whom our Hunt comes in contact during the hunting season. For several years this shoot has been organised and run by Gary and Bonnie Yeomans, and so it was particularly fitting that in 2006, a year with a record entry of 56 teams, Jamie Yeomans won the junior cup.

In April, after the hunting season has finished, the Hunter Trials are run. For many years they were held at Brook Farm, Albury, owned by Buck Jones, the racehorse owner/trainer and former jockey. However, three years ago this annual event was transferred to Heath Farm, Munstead, near Godalming, the home of Rebecca Harvie [née Metson] and her course-builder husband, Rupert. As the course is used for an affiliated "intro" event the previous week, our Hunt has the benefit of those preparations. The day itself is organised by two Hunt members, Geraldine Firth and Ann Metson. With the help of Ann's husband, Nigel, they recruit other members and supporters to assist with jump judging, catering and the many other jobs that need to be done. Catering is usually in the capable hands of Liz Potts or Penny Wilson and their teams.

And so one could go on, listing all the hard work that many dedicated people carry out on behalf of our Hunt. One only has to think how many sandwiches are made, cakes baked, scones buttered and cups of tea are drunk at the Puppy Show to realise just how many people are involved in making our Hunt function. Unfortunately there really is not the space to list all these willing volunteers, but each and every one is cherished and all their efforts, no matter how small, are very much appreciated.

But why does our Hunt have such a passionate following? How better to provide the answer than to read what our members and subscribers have to say for themselves:

"Hunting is not just a sport, it is a way of life, and the SUH in particular is not just a hunt but our extended family. Hunting means to me – crossing country on a good horse watching hounds do the job they have been bred for generations to do, the look in the huntsman's eyes when they have done that job well – and, the greatest thrill of all, seeing the huntsman putting the hounds on a line and knowing for one short moment in time that I am an intrinsic part of this great tradition we call hunting." Rita Boggiss

"I have been attached to the SUH for over 30 years and I can say without exception that I have never met such a nice group of people and made so many friends. To follow hounds in full cry across open country with a few stiff hedges is to people who love horse and hound the greatest pleasure; and long may it be so." Graeme Boggiss

"It is a perfect way to forget all about everyday life and just enjoy the countryside watching the hounds work and seeing the wildlife." Rebecca Harvie

CHAPTER 24

The Hunt Steeplechases & Point-to-Point Races

"Hosmer, [58] *for instance, tells us that a hostrich can outstrip an 'oss but what matter does that make, seeing that no one would like to go cutting across country on a hostrich."*

John Jorrocks Esq MFH, from **Handley Cross**, R S Surtees 1843

Quite.

But such is human nature that, if one man has a horse, another owner will claim that his will be the faster of the two and competition will inevitably result.

Although there are many lurid tales of how steeplechasing first started, officers from the 1st Life Guards were, by 1830, organising regular steeplechase meetings near St Albans. Although Surtees was later to call such events *"crude ill-arranged things"*, being *"neither hunting nor racing"*, both the Surrey [now Old Surrey & Burstow, West Kent] and the Union [now, of course, Surrey Union] Hunts were soon to follow this new trend, holding annual two-day steeplechase joint-meetings on Reigate Heath in the years from 1834 to 1838. These were organised by a committee of Reigate businessmen *"to make some return and to give some encouragement to the farmers in the neighbourhood over whom [sic] the Gentry and the Sporting Men of the Country have been in the habit of hunting"*.

The principal race on the first day was for a gold cup valued at no less than 100 Guineas. On the second day, the main attraction was the race for the Farmers' Plate, *"for horses not thoroughbred the property of farmers residing within the limits of the Surrey and Union Hunts"*. Improvement work on the course, including turfing and the erection of a temporary building *"for the weighing in of the Gentlemen Riders and Jockies [sic]"* was undertaken in 1835. The course was further enlarged the following year. After 1838 it seems there were no more races on the Heath until 1863 and 1864, but these proved unpopular with the Reigate townsfolk, owing to the undesirable characters that they thought might be attracted to the neighbourhood. A similar view of such crowds was expressed by Surtees in *Mr Sponge's Sporting Tour* [1853]:

"The same sort of people commingled that one would expect to see if there was a balloon to go up, and a man to go down, or be hung at the same place ... ... sweep[ing] down upon the spot like flocks of wolves."

Oh dear!

Unfortunately, things would continue to get worse before they improved.

The Hunt Point-To-Point Races

Throughout the reign of Queen Victoria and into the first part of the 20th century, the sport of racing horses over a course of fences slowly transformed itself into the two distinct activities, as they are understood today, of steeplechasing [professional riders and trainers] and point-to-point racing [amateur]. Although there is no record of the first Surrey Union Hunt Point-to-Point, it seems likely that such races started some time between the closing down of the Reigate steeplechases and the year 1899, when the point-to-point held at Slyfield, near Cobham, was described as *"the annual meeting"*. In the end, this particular race meeting came to naught *"as sufficient time had not been allowed for the meeting to be registered, it had to be abandoned after all the ladies and gentlemen were assembled"*.

The race card for the point-to-point races held at Slyfield Farm on Saturday, 21st March 1914. There were four races: the Heavy Weight Race at 2pm [won by Mr Cuthbert Heath's *Kilrowan*], the Light Weight Race at 2.45 [won by Mr A G Cubitt's *Priscilla*], a Nomination Race at 3.30 [won by Mr H S Ellis's *Stepping-Stone*] and The Farmers' Race at 4 o'clock [won by Mr Poole's *Farmer Bill*].

Notes

58 *William Osmer, a veterinary surgeon, was reckoned to be a fair judge of thoroughbreds in his time and his principal work, "A Dissertation On Horses", published in 1756, outlined the basic principles of bloodstock breeding.*

The Surrey Union Hunt Races

ADMIT TO
Carriage Enclosure
SATURDAY, APRIL 20, 1929
ase bring this Ticket.

By 1929, the world of the motor car had arrived, but the wording for an earlier age pertains. In contrast, this is the earliest use of "our" fox logo that has been found – but is it an improvement on the fox appearing on the meet cards of the late 19th century or the race card on the previous page?

Notes

59 *However, from 1929 to 1967, they were only permitted to ride in races confined to lady riders.*

60 *Before the airport development it was once a famous racecourse. The Grand National was run there during the Great War, in the three years 1916-18.*

Not surprisingly, perhaps, *"a great deal of dissatisfaction was expressed"* and this caused the Master, Mr Labouchere, to resign. [The full story behind this resignation is in Chapter 10.]

In the early 1900s Shellwood seems to have been the venue for the race meeting. Sometime between 1906 and 1908 it moved to Charlwood Place, but in 1909 it was held at Shellwood again. A return to Slyfield was made in 1912 and the bar [ie barristers from the legal profession] was invited to join in with races. This was not an auspicious reversion, as the 1913 meeting only had four entries and had to be abandoned. By a twist of fate, the farmers still got their luncheon and tea, being conveyed to the bar point-to-point instead!

Initially, these Surrey Union Hunt Point-to-Point race meetings were run under their own local rules. However, in 1913, the Masters of Hounds Point-to-Point Association established a set of rules applicable nationwide. Crucially, these rules did not preclude lady riders, who were regular competitors and often rode side-saddle [59]. So, following a return to Mr Crow's farm at Shellwood in 1921, the scene was set for a Ladies' Race to appear at a Surrey Union point-to-point race meeting. Despite the disapproval and foreboding expressed by the more reactionary forces within the Hunt, there were at least four starters and the Ladies' Race was here to stay. A press report of this race meeting is contained in Appendix:10.

But the misery for the organisers continued. The Shellwood meeting of 1922 was abandoned owing to lack of entries and that of 1925 had to be cancelled owing to an outbreak of foot and mouth disease in the district. Eventually matters started to improve and point-to-point races were held there for some years thereafter. Until stopped by the Second World War in 1940, the races were held for a number of years at Mrs Trick's farm at Brockham, before being moved to Kemp's Farm, Buckland. This proved an excellent course at the foot of the North Downs and, with much of it being on the chalk, the going was good whatever the weather.

Another course was at Holmwood Farm; this was not so successful. Here, on one very wet day with a bitter northeaster blowing, only a few cars got on and into place and those that did had to be dragged out again by tractor or horse power. With the present configuration of the A24 dual carriageway and new housing developments, it is hard for the modern observer to imagine this ever being a site for a point-to-point course.

After the war, in 1946 and 1947, the meetings were held at Rowgardens on Norwood Hill, This was a very popular course as the horses could be seen all the way round from any point on the hill. In 1948, owing to petrol rationing, a joint meeting with the Old Surrey and Burstow was held at the still requisitioned Gatwick racecourse [60]. This meeting attracted an estimated crowd of 20,000 and, despite police intervention, it is thought that some 7000 managed to gain entry without paying after the barriers at the turnstiles burst. Free admission was given to 1200 farmers.

With the economic position improving, it was possible to return to Rowgardens in 1949, but the problems encountered by the organisers were still far from over. Promoters of the early Point-to-Point races had no traffic problems to contend with, for it was but a simple matter to get horse-drawn carriages, traps and brakes across country and onto the course. Even when the motor car began to make its appearance after the First World War, the early models were high off the ground and relatively able to cope with unmade ground. After the Second World War, things were very different. Cars were much more low-slung and the crowds were increasingly comprised of townsfolk, used to driving on tarmac. So tracks and firm going for the spectators' vehicles, as well as a good course for the races, became imperative. Unfortunately, Rowgardens delivered two successive postponements on account of the wet ground and a further meeting where cars had to be towed in as well as out. A new venue was needed.

For the three years, 1953-55, the Point-to-Point race meetings were held at Canons Farm, Banstead. This was a very pretty course, on sand, and exceptionally large crowds assembled there to enjoy some very good racing. But the grumbling persisted – some felt it was too far from the southern end of the Hunt country and others that it was too near London! So, in 1956 the venue was changed once more. By the kind invitation of Mr McAndrew, the owner and the Chiddingfold and Leconfield Hunt, the Surrey Union was able to share the beautiful setting of their course at Tisman's, Rudgwick.

In 1969 the event moved to Tweseldown. Held on 7th May, it was the fifth meeting there that season, but it was blessed with good weather and a large number of entries. The following year the point-to-point moved to the former Chiddingfold Farmers' course at Peper Harow, where our race meetings have been held ever since. It is a most unusual course, based loosely on a figure of eight, with the finishing straight up the middle and some very tight turns. It was just possible, at one time, to watch the racing all around the track [although few will remember that!]. Over the years, what was once a new conifer plantation has now grown into a veritable forest that obscures much of the action in the west, even for commentator in his "cherry-picker"! But despite its idiosyncrasies, the course is on sand, which gives good going and, in conjunction with ease of access to the nearby A3, allows reasonable vehicular access whatever the weather. It is a popular venue and the Peper Harow point-to-point is a well-established part of the Surrey social scene for the many thousands that attend annually. According to *Horse & Hound* it is "*the place to see and be seen*" and "*numerous TV and pop stars are regularly spotted enjoying the atmosphere and having a wager incognito*".

Thrills and spills at Kemp's Farm, Buckland. Mr E Salaman takes a tumble, whilst others gallop on strongly.

The Surrey Union Point-to-Point Today

As we have seen, point-to-point racing, "between the flags", has been a uniquely enjoyable sport for about 200 years. Restricted to amateur riders and to horses that have qualified with the local hunt during the months leading up to January (the start of the season for these races) point-to-points have become an increasingly popular spectacle. For the owner and rider they are tremendous fun at a reasonably modest investment. The average pointer, always a thoroughbred, probably costs about £3000 – £5000 to buy.

Many racehorses have started and ended their careers in point-to-points. In the meantime they may have gone on to considerable success in National Hunt racing or, perhaps, been something of a disappointment. In times past, a local farmer might have run a point-to-pointer as a hobby, but alas the farming element of ownership is declining and many owners now keep their horses at livery while they hold down demanding jobs.

The current Secretary of the Point-to-Point committee, Mr Andrew Ayres, is a retired solicitor and has been both an amateur jockey and racehorse owner. It is he who has the responsibility for the administrative organisation of the meeting. Essentially, this means making sure everyone turns up on the day! Increasingly, there is much "red tape" to comply with ensuring, amongst other things, that the Jockey Club regulations and Health and Safety regulations are adhered to.

The Clerk of the Course, with the help of the fence builder and others, is responsible for the preparation of the course and ensuring that it is fit for racing and complies with Jockey Club requirements. On the day, the Clerk of the Course is also responsible for the racing itself, under the auspices of the Stewards. After ten years of organising this superb and successful event with the help and support of her husband Brian, the year 2006 brought the retirement of Pam Tetley from this responsible position. In appreciation of their work, the Hunt presented Pam and Brian

Pam and Brian Tetley look very pleased with their presentation gift.

with a suitably inscribed bronze statue of a racehorse and jockey. Reminiscing over her association with the point-to-point, Pam recalled the time in 1985 when Fred Trinder, at the age of 65 and never having ridden as a jockey before in his life, rode her horse, Destiny, in the Members' Race. Although the pair did not win, when they came past the finishing post, Peper Harow resounded to probably the loudest bout of cheering ever heard there.

The new Clerk of the Course for the season 2006-07 will be Richard Parker, a Hunt committee member and son of a former joint-Master.

A vet has to be available at the course and in recent years it has been Ben Mays from the local veterinary practice, Mays and Scrine.

It cannot be emphasised too strongly that the race meeting is run entirely by volunteers, without whom the event could not take place. The fixture attracts a huge crowd, all of whom enjoy their picnics, the trade stands and a good day's racing. The point-to-point is a major contributor to Hunt funds.

Surrey Union owners over the past few years have included Sarah Dunsdon, Jerry Hazeltine, Kevin Tork, Rose Williams, Brian Tetley, Ray York and Ray Fielder. Local jockeys currently include David Dunsdon, Philip York, Gordon Gallagher, Daniel Hazeltine, Rose Williams and Tony Vadasz [who came second in 2006 on *Owenabue Valley* in The Rensburg Sheppards Men's Open Race].

CHAPTER 25

The Grand National and Other Racing Connections

With racecourses at Epsom, Lingfield Park, Kempton and Sandown, Surrey has had its fair share of racing yards as a consequence, particularly around Epsom itself. Not only do they produce racehorses capable of winning both "over the sticks" and on the flat, but also the jockeys that ride them. One such yard was South Hatch near Epsom, run by the Nightingall family and in the latter years of the 19th century they produced a succession of top jockeys.

Hunting was much enjoyed by the Nightingall brothers. Indeed, the eldest boy, John, rode his pony, *Punchie*, to the finish of a run on 28th February 1891 and was presented with the brush by the Master, Mr Bennett. Sadly, John was later killed when a horse bolted with him during a racing trial on Headley Heath, causing him to dash his head against a tree. He was but 14 years old.

However, his younger brother, Arthur Nightingall, went on to become one of the most famous steeplechase jockeys of his day, winning the Grand National three times – in 1890 on *Ilex*; in 1894 on *Why Not* and in 1901 on *Grudon*. He was also placed several times in the race during this period. When *Ilex* finished his racing career, his owner, George Masterman, gave the horse to Arthur, who then frequently took him out hunting. It was written of them:

Ilex, the winner of the 1890 Grand National, with Arthur Nightingall up.

"On a day there was a brilliant run with those hounds in the Chessington country, then fairly good, and foremost among the leading division was Arthur Nightingall on his 'National' champion, going great guns, or h-ll for leather, as the experts say; he looked like catching anything (particularly a fox) in a single-handed encounter. A rather swell gentleman was following him on a first-class hunter, jumping what Arthur negotiated and so on, fancying himself not a little, and seemingly intent on cutting-down tactics, until a high hedge with a stiff rail was reached. Ilex did it all right, of course, with a nice margin for contingencies; but the swell on his beautiful hunter 'took a toss'. When he got up – a fearsome object covered in ooze – a friend said to him cheerfully: 'Well, and do you know what you have been trying to beat?' 'N-no,' muttered the valiant one, now shivering. 'You have been trying,' said the other, 'to beat the winner of the Grand National and the finest cross-country jockey in the world.' 'Gracious heavens!' groaned the swell personage, 'I ought to have my head stuffed with shavings ready for Guy Fawkes' night. Trying to beat Ilex, eh? Why, in future I must be condemned to gallop after old women down a lane'".

Another racing yard with Surrey Union connections was that run by Jack O'Donoghue at The Priory Stables in Reigate. He was a great believer in the efficacy of sending horses in training out hunting and the results tend to speak for themselves. The 1951 Grand National was won by *Nickel Coin*, a mare he had trained. Her jockey in the race was ex-paratrooper, John Bullock, aged 34, and she was owned by Mr Jeffrey Royle of Jury Farm, West Horsley. Ridden by her groom and constant companion, Jo Wells, the daughter of a Merstham nurseryman, *Nickel Coin* was often seen in the mounted field of the Surrey Union during the late 1940s and early 1950s.

Nickel Coin, the winner of the 1951 Grand National, at a meet of the Surrey Union only days after her win. The mare looks totally unfazed by hounds and it seems that Jo Wells only ever rode her out hunting with a simple snaffle bridle.

Another of the horses trained by Jack O'Donoghue was *Gay Record*. When this horse first came to his stables in 1960, it was a bag of nerves. But days out hunting with the Surrey Union quietened him down and gave him confidence enough to win nine races, in addition to breaking the record for the fastest three miles at Windsor. But this horse's greatest accolade was when he became the 100th winner over jumps for Her Majesty the late Queen Mother on 20th October 1964, at a race meeting at Folkestone.

Her Majesty, the late Queen Mother's horse, *Gay Record*

The Wates family have had a strong link with the Surrey Union Hunt for many years. During the 1950s, Sir Ronald Wates was on the committee and became the hon. treasurer 1954. His passion for racing and hunting was passed down to his sons, Andrew and Paul. Living at Henfold, Mr Andrew Wates, once a successful jockey himself [including a perhaps less than memorable outing in the Grand National], is a member of our Hunt and, during the 1980s, he too was on the Hunt committee. It was from his racing yard in Beare Green that the horse, *Rough Quest*, jointly owned by Mr Wates and his late mother, Lady Wates, won the Grand National in 1996. Today, *Rough Quest* lives in retirement, but he remains very much on his toes and still makes the occasional celebrity appearance. One can gauge the temperament of this horse by Mr Wates' comment, "*If Rough Quest was a human, he would be a bouncer*"!

A more recent Surrey Union link with the Grand National is through David Dunsdon, the son of John and Sarah Dunsdon from Lukyns, near Ewhurst. In 2005, he was placed ninth on his own horse, *Joly Bey*.

Completing this series of connections is Gill Sainsbury, a new subscriber to our Hunt. She is a member of the syndicate that purchased the horse, *Inca Trail*, a full brother to Best Mate, three-time winner of the Cheltenham Gold Cup. Of the nine that finished, *Inca Trail* came home eighth in the 2006 Grand National.

Lady Wates, Andrew Wates, *Rough Quest*, Terry Casey [trainer] and Mick Fitzgerald [jockey] pose for the cameras following their triumphal return to Henfold in 1996.

CHAPTER 26

The Surrey Union Hunt and Philanthropy

Our Hunt has long had regard for its wider duty to society and for many years contributions have been made in support of a variety of worthy causes. On some occasions they have been local, sometimes almost personal charities and on others they have followed the national mood.

This first instance, taken from the Henry Goulburn archives, is a splendid Victorian example [see right] that seems to be a local initiative, but in fact has rather more history behind it than is at first apparent.

The Imperial Yeomanry had been formed in December 1899 to reinforce the beleaguered British Army in its war against the Boers in South Africa. Volunteers for enlistment needed to be between the ages of 20 and 35 and had to satisfy the authorities that they were good riders and marksmen. [So, the links with the rural community are obvious.]

Thousands of men from the Empire had left to serve in South Africa and there was much concern in Britain about their welfare. An appeal by Lady Chesham and Lady Georgiana Curzon [later Countess Howe] for funds to organise a hospital in South Africa for the Imperial Yeomanry caught the mood of the nation. Some £174,000 was raised, sufficient to equip and remunerate the personnel for four hospitals [initially only one was envisaged]; a convalescent home; a field hospital and a bearer company. So efficient was the voluntary organisation that the entire staff, with the exception of nurses, left Britain for the site of the new hospital at Deelfontein, about 30 miles south of De Aar [a strategic railway junction] in the Karoo, during February 1900. By the end of March, some 300 military casualties, including very many with dysentery and enteric fever [now known as typhoid], were being treated.

Within the Imperial Yeomanry Hospital complex, each building was named after individual donor organizations and the names of many private donors [who contributed towards china, hardware, blankets and bedding] were inscribed at the entrance to each ward. The names of the donors of beds appeared on the bedsteads themselves.

In the end, the Surrey Union Hunt bed appeal raised a total of £51-1s-6d, a very creditable sum in the economy of the day and one that reflected the feelings of members and subscribers regarding conditions on the Veldt.

More than a century on, such philanthropy is echoed in the donations that the Surrey Union Hunt continues to make to local charities. Typical of recent years are the following fund raising events:

The Sponsored Ride

Held in October, this event provides an opportunity to ride through some magnificent Surrey countryside. About 200 – 250 riders, many of whom return year after year, take part annually and follow a route of about 10 miles that incorporates bridleways, farmland and some gloriously wooded parts of the Surrey Hills. Optional jumps are included to add an extra bit of fun. It is organised by Katharine Meller and very efficient teams led by Ann Metson and Jane Williams. The start and finish is at Stilemans, near Godalming, by kind permission of Mr and Mrs G Lawson, with much of the track itself running over land belonging to the Hutley and the Anstruther families.

The charities supported by this popular autumn event have included, amongst others, Dyscover [a support group for stroke victims]; Haste [for the Stroke Unit Guildford Hospital]; Chase [a local Children's Hospice]; Cherry

January, 1900.

Dear Sir or Madam,

We the undersigned, Lily Duchess of Marlborough and Henry Goulburn, M.F.H., suggest that the Members of the Surrey Union Hunt should be asked to subscribe to give a Bed to the Imperial Yeomanry Hospital, to be called the "Surrey Union Hunt Bed."

Such a bed will, it is understood, cost about £50. Any subscription you may be kind enough to give (limited to £1) may be sent to Francis M. Rickards, Hon. Sec., S. U. Hunt, Leverton House, Leatherhead.

We are, dear Sir or Madam,

Yours faithfully,

LILY MARLBOROUGH,

HENRY GOULBURN,

FRANCIS M. RICKARDS.

An Imperial Yeomanry ambulance on the Karoo during the Boer War.

Trees [providing respite care for children]; the Mark Davies Injured Riders Fund and Headfirst [research into head injury]. This latter charity has been a particularly poignant choice as it was selected by the parents of Antonia Jones, a vivacious member of our Hunt, who was sadly killed in 2004 whilst team-chasing, aged 24.

The Point-to-Point

Each year a local charity is chosen afresh for support from our race meeting held each spring. Amongst others, donations in recent years have gone to GUTS [the Guildford Undetected Tumour Screening programme], Cheshire Homes and the Macmillan Cancer Nurses Appeal. Each year the St John Ambulance Brigade have a "blanket" collection at the car park exits and this has raised thousands of pounds for them over the years.

Midnight Steeplechase

In the 1960s, the doings at one of these occasions managed to get reported in the William Hickey column [61] of the *Daily Express*, principally because the Marchioness of Reading wore a fluffy, baby-doll, nightdress to the event – it being a general requirement that riders in the four steeplechases, run over four furlongs, should wear night-attire, albeit, perhaps, of a somewhat less exotic variety. To quote from the article: "*'Isn't it fun', cried Lady Reading, 44, whose nightdress was, as they say, a principal attraction of the evening. 'And I'm not at all cold'. Of course not. She was wearing a skirt and a thick blue sweater underneath*".
[What else did you expect? Despite the title of this book, that is as risqué as it gets!]

In its latter years, although competitors were less adventurous in their apparel, our Hunt raised a good deal of money for the rehabilitation unit at Harrowlands from this event.

As a postscript to this Chapter, it has to be said that our Hunt would have done even more philanthropic work in recent years had we not been forced by the Government and the wider 'animal rights' movement to put a great deal of our fundraising efforts into fighting our own corner against their pernicious and unprincipled attacks. That this should continue to be the case remains a constant source of sadness within our hunting community.

Notes

61 *A much-read society gossip column of the time.*

CHAPTER 27

Tales from the Hunt Poultry Fund in 1900

On the right are examples of applications for compensation from the Hunt Poultry Fund sent to Major Henry Goulburn, Master during the 1899-1900 season. Only those birds taken during the daytime or reasonably fox-proof runs during the night were usually paid for, it being considered reasonable to expect poultry owners to shut their birds up at night. Curiously, the fox only ever seemed to take the best birds!

The top letter is particularly interesting, as it is written phonetically and one can almost imagine the writer speaking the words. Indeed, the idiosyncratic grammar is still to be heard in Surrey speech, over 100 years later. Annie Bowring was a 49 year-old widow, originally from Horley, who made her living as a lodging-house keeper. Holmwood Common was much used during this period as a Cockney holiday haunt. Allied to its many natural attractions, this area of open heath land also gave the parents of town-nurtured children an opportunity to let them run free in the fresh, breezy air.

The lower letter has a more formal style and was written by Daniel Dibble, aged 24. He was employed as a publican [innkeeper], probably at the Wotton Hatch on the Dorking to Guildford road. Also resident in his household were a motor engineer brother, Percy, aged 24, and their sister, Ethel, aged 15. These siblings all originally came from Dorking.

In both instances, the fox predation probably had profound consequences for their respective domestic finances and suitable compensation from the Hunt would have been most welcome.

A TRAGEDY IN TWO ACTS

ACT 1:
THE NIGHT BEFORE: THE FOX AMONG THE FOWL

ACT 2:
THE DAY AFTER: COMPENSATION FOR LOST CHICKENS

York Cottage
Holmwood
Feb the 27 1900

Sir,

I ham sorry to tell you a fox killed one of my Geese this morning Bit its head off I would not of lost it for a sovereign as it layed & would of soon sit it is a great loss to me I hope you will see some way to make me some Recompense for it the Fox as Been seen on the Common

Sir

Yours obedet

A Bowring

Wotton Hatch
Dorking

Dear Sirs

I lost on the 15th 16 & 17th twenty young chicken and again last night eight more, would you be so good as to forward me a cheque for same as the foxes are laying around here

Yours faithfully

D Dibble

Under the watchful eye of their huntsman and 1st whipper-in, hounds are released onto a station platform from a Hunt special by the 2nd whipper-in. Previously, the Hunt horses had been unloaded from the boxes beyond the hound van. The yellow collars on the Hunt coats make the scene suggestive of Ockley, Cranleigh or Holmwood – but, alas, the true location of this photograph, found amongst Mrs Armstrong's effects, is believed to be in Northumberland.

CHAPTER 28

Hunting and the Railway

"It is still something to be a hunting man even yet, though the multiplicity of railways and the existing plethora of money has so increased the number of sportsmen, that to keep a nag or two near some well-known station, is nearly as common as to die."

The Man Who Hunts And Doesn't Like It – **Hunting Sketches**, Anthony Trollope 1865

Initially, in common with most of rural England, the hunting community in the 1820s viewed the spread of railways with disquiet. They were new, and therefore to be treated with suspicion. All that speed just was unnatural. Surely it was obvious to all that livestock would be stampeded, cows would give sour milk, hens would go out of lay and crops would be set on fire? With the free-for-all crossing of the countryside lost forever, clearly it would be the end of hunting!

But it did not take long for a less alarmist view to develop and Surtees [again] captures the mood neatly when he has John Jorrocks describing the Great Northern and the London & Birmingham Railways as being the best covert hacks in the world, taking that Cockney grocer [and others!] to the shire packs and the cream of the English hunting countries.

Similarly, the Surrey Union Hunt recognised that the railway system offered an efficient and cost-effective way of getting from the north of their country into the Weald and "below the hill". In the late 1890s and early 1900s it was common for special trains to be laid on by the London, Brighton & South Coast Railway to transport hounds, horses and Hunt members, with meet cards annotated accordingly.

To take a typical example, on Tuesday, 19th March 1907, a special train made up of passenger carriages and horseboxes was run from Epsom to Cranleigh, vîa Leatherhead, Dorking and Horsham. Drawn by a locomotive from Dorking engine-shed, it left Epsom Town at 09.05 and stopped to pick up passengers, horses and hounds at Leatherhead between 09.12 and 09.27. Dorking was passed at 09.36, and although no stop was arranged, there was a note in the Special Traffic Notice stating that the train "*May be stopped at Dorking by signal if anything to go on*". On the way, brief halts were made at Horsham [09.58-10.00], Christ's Hospital [10.04-10.05] and Baynards [10.17-10.18] for railway operating reasons. Cranleigh was reached at 10.25, where the train was unloaded. Thereafter, the carriages and horseboxes were taken back empty to Ockley station, again vîa Horsham. Arriving at Ockley at 12.15, the train was shunted into a siding and the locomotive then ran light to Epsom, probably to do some other work. It was booked to return to Ockley "*during the afternoon, time uncertain*", to work the return service from Ockley back to Epsom Town "*at an uncertain time about 4.45 pm, calling at Leatherhead*". Presumably, if anyone had been picked up at Dorking, they would have been dropped off on the return trip. The engine finally returned to Dorking "*after the service*".

But what was it really like to travel by train in this way? Happily, this account by W S Norris has survived from that time: " ... *but no matter where it was, by the time that we had given our horses gruel and hay, and ourselves hot gin and water followed by bacon and eggs and tea, there was our special train, with the boxes all assembled in the bay* [platform] *ready to collect the horses, and our comfortable coach ready for ourselves, and in no time we were homeward bound ...*". His

SURREY UNION HOUNDS

WILL MEET — AT 11 o'Clock.

Tuesday,	Dec.	13th	......	Claygate.
Thursday,	„	15th	......	Effingham.
Saturday,	„	17th	......	Cranleigh Lane End, **11-15.**
				(Special Train, Leatherhead, 9.30.)
Tuesday,	„	20th	......	Bagden Farm.
Thursday,	„	22nd	......	Forest Green.
				(Special Train, Leatherhead 9-30.)
Saturday,	„	24th	......	The Swan, Leatherhead.
Monday,	„	26th	......	Mickleham Village.
Thursday,	„	29th	......	East Clandon.
Saturday,	„	31st	......	Holmwood Station.
				(Special Train, Leatherhead, 9-30.)

☞ Special Train does not stop anywhere to pick up Boxes.

Arthur Labouchere, *Cobham.*

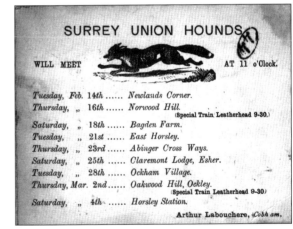

SURREY UNION HOUNDS

WILL MEET — AT 11 o'Clock.

Tuesday,	Feb.	14th	......	Newlands Corner.
Thursday,	„	16th	......	Norwood Hill.
				(Special Train Leatherhead 9-30.)
Saturday,	„	18th	......	Bagden Farm.
Tuesday,	„	21st	......	East Horsley.
Thursday,	„	23rd	......	Abinger Cross Ways.
Saturday,	„	25th	......	Claremont Lodge, Esher.
Tuesday,	„	28th	......	Ockham Village.
Thursday,	Mar.	2nd	......	Oakwood Hill, Ockley.
				(Special Train Leatherhead 9-30)
Saturday,	„	4th	......	Horsley Station.

Arthur Labouchere, *Cobham.*

[Above and overleaf] Meet cards from the season 1898-99 showing the extensive use of special trains to convey horses, hounds and personnel to railway stations serving the then more remote outposts of the Surrey Union Hunt country.

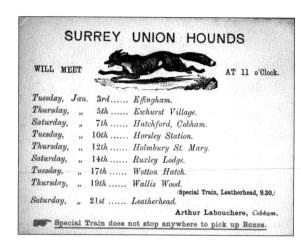

Notes

62 *As this is the season immediately before the electrification of the Dorking-Horsham railway, all payments would have been to enginemen on steam locomotives, no matter where the train was halted.*

104

only possible complaint was that, " *... sometimes, by the late afternoon, our coach had become a little chilly, because the engine was hard put to it to conserve its steam* [for heating] *... However, we bought several of the voluminous newspapers then current and wrapped the sheets round ourselves, which was most efficacious*".

As will be apparent from the accounts of runs contained elsewhere in this history, until the coming of the third rail electrification, crossing the railway line was just something that was done, irrespective of the inherent danger to horses, hounds and the rail traffic itself. Indeed, as is clear from the evidence, drivers of steam locomotives were prepared to stop their trains when practicable and might even find themselves rewarded for their trouble. [In this regard, see the *Horse & Hound* report of the 29th January 1927 run set out on page 55. There is also an entry in the Hunt accounts for 1937-38 [62], "Engine Drivers – Stopping Trains £2-0s-0d". In the previous season it seems that foxes were more risk averse, as the sum expended under this head was only 10/-.]

Mention has already been made of Mr Evelyn's representations made to the Southern Railway regarding their plans to electrify the railway line south of Dorking [see Chapter 16]. A deputation from the district met the Southern Railway General Manager in 1936 and the local disquiet was also voiced in Parliament. As human life was unlikely to be endangered and the railway company offered to erect adequate fencing along the line and cattle grids at public crossing points to protect wandering animals, the protest was effectively suppressed.

The work of installing an unprotected, live, third rail was completed on 3rd July 1938 and, when hunting started in the following autumn, the inevitable happened. A hunted fox crossed the railway at the Holmwood end of the Ockley goods yard. Although most hounds managed to negotiate the live rail safely, several came to grief. A post mortem examination showed that they had received but a slight shock initially, but it was the reflex action to bite back at their "assailant" that resulted in electrocution. Biting the third rail with 600 volts of direct current with a wet mouth was unavoidably fatal. Almost incredibly, the same thing happened again the following spring. One wonders if it was the same fox.

The third rail was clearly a continuing nuisance, causing Mr Evelyn to comment in a letter from France dated 6th December 1939 to his huntsman, Jim Goddard, "*I am also very upset about the Railway. I fear it will be the Railway that will finish hunting in Surrey quicker than anything else*". The same difficulty could also arise if a hound, having been left out, tried to make its way home across the line. Thankfully problems of this nature did not occur often, but they were regular enough for the huntsman to be issued with special gloves and boots to use on the line should the worst happen.

The railway authorities have subsequently accepted that post-and-rail or strained wire fences are not enough and that both need to be reinforced with wire mesh, as the railway fence is on the north side of the railway between Ifield Halt and Littlehaven on our southern boundary. Indeed, railway fences are currently undergoing a general renewal programme, employing wire mesh specifically to deter livestock and wildlife.

On a much happier note, in Chapter 17, there was a reference to the purchase of foxhounds from the Berwickshire. One such batch, four couple of young hounds, were put into a horsebox on Monday night, 2nd July 1951 and started their unaccompanied railway journey south. As the telephone at the Kennels had gone dead, one of the Hunt servants [probably Les Amess] had been sent to Ockley station early the next day to establish the time of their arrival. In a subsequent note to the railway authorities, Mr Sewill wrote, "*I cannot speak too highly of the courtesy and initiative of Porter Edwards of Ockley, with whose name I am to couple the Signalman, Thornton*". Following the enquiry by

Amess, these railwaymen had obligingly made several telephone calls to Redhill Control and obtained a complete picture of the movement of the horsebox and its time of arrival at Ockley station. Later that day, the hounds duly "*arrived at Ockley in first class condition and had evidently been fed and watered en route and well cared-for generally*". The letter ended with an invitation to the two Ockley railwaymen to "*come out with us on foot or on bicycles at any time hounds are in the neighbourhood and they have some spare time*".

Over fifty years earlier, a letter [on the right] records the logistical arrangements following the purchase of what seems to be a dog hound by Major Goulburn from the adjoining County.

Finally, this account by Maureen Cole [née O'Donoghue] illustrates that motor transport was not essential to enjoy Pony Club and other activities. Around 1949/50 she had been asked to participate in a show in Guildford, which involved a rail journey from Betchworth: "*We trotted from Snower Hill down to Betchworth station, where the two ponies were loaded into a rail horsebox that was waiting in a loading dock behind the station buildings. When the train arrived, it called first at the platform before drawing out of the station a short way. It then reversed into the siding and backed onto our horsebox, which was attached to the last carriage. When we started on the way to Guildford, we seemed a long way from the engine and swung about quite a bit in our position at the end of a lengthy train. At Guildford, our box was detached and shunted into a siding, where we disembarked with the ponies and went off to the show. We had a successful day and repeated the same procedure for the homeward journey, arriving at Snower Hill tired but happy, not thinking it at all unusual that we had taken our ponies to the show by train*".

STATIONS,
HAYES & BROMLEY
TELEGRAMS, KESTON

The Limes
KESTON
Kent

Aug 15th 1899
Dear Sir,
I beg to acknowledge with thanks your cheque £30.
I doubt if you will receive this before Emperor's arrival, but I shall wire you in the morning. He is being sent off by the 8.36 am train in the morning to town and then straight to Betchworth where he should arrive about 12.23. Of course, I cannot say time of his arrival for certain, as I do not know if they will put him directly onto the train for Betchworth on his arrival in London.
Trusting he will turn out entirely to your satisfaction.
Believe me,
Yours faithfully,
[Illegible]
Major Goulburn

In 1937, shortly before the installation of the electrified third rail, the mounted Field cross the railway at Arnolds, just south of Holmwood station. Hounds were running at the time.
Such farm accommodation crossings were very common until electrification caused their closure.

AFTERWORD

For over two hundred years the sight and sound of the Surrey Union Hunt has been an integral part of the rural fabric of our County, whether it be on the clay of the Weald, the wooded Greensand ridges, the chalk of the North Downs or the sandy heaths in the west. It has succeeded simply because season after season, year after year, the right people at the right time have stepped forward to shoulder the burdens that needed to be borne, whatever they may have been and whatever their cause. This poem by Will Ogilvie, a narrative poet and horseman both, expresses this theme perfectly:

THE HUNT

The dusk is down on the river meadows,
The moon is climbing above the fir,
The lane is crowded with creeping shadows,
The gorse is only a distant blur.
The last of the light is almost gone.
But hark! They're running!
 They're running on!

The count of the years is steadily growing;
The Old give way to the eager Young;
Far on the hill is the horn still blowing,
Far on the steep are the hounds still strung.
Good men follow the good men gone;
And hark! They're running!
 They're running on!

W H Ogilvie [1869-1963]

For those who were out on with us at dusk on 17th February 2005 [see Appendix: 8], the lines of this poem will always carry a particular resonance.

But let there be no mistake: we are proud of our traditions and everything we have achieved. Our foxhounds are indeed still "*running on*" and all are welcome to come and see them, be it mounted, on foot or on a bicycle.

Long may such a happy state pertain and <u>our</u> Union Hunt continue to flourish.

C'up Forrad! Forrad on ... ...

The Appendices

Appendix: 1

The expenditures of Thomas Foard [also spelt Ford], Huntsman to the Lord Bruce of Tottenham House, Wiltshire, during a sojourn in Leatherhead, Surrey, from January to March 1722:

	£	s	d
Paid at Basing Stoke [1] *for 6 horses hay @ 8* [d] *per n* [t]		4	-
Oats and Beans [2]		6	-
Meat for the Hounds and Spaniels		11	-
Paid for 10 pair of dog couples [3]		7	6
Guildford for Six horses Hay [4]		4	-
Oats and Beans		6	10
Meat for the hounds and Spaniels		13	6
Paid a Guide Sent by John Gould		9	-
Paid the Epsom Farrier [5] *Bill* [5] *as rec'd*		1	8
Paid the Tallow Chandler for Graves [6]		5	1
Butcher for sheep heads		5	4
Oatmeal maker as per Bill & Receit	13	11	4
Paid for Bavins [7] *and Straw* [8] *for y* *kennel*	3	2	-
Paid another Butcher for sheep heads		10	-
To the Leatherhead Smith for Shoeing	2	3	-
Paid to [illegible] for Earth Stopping	1	8	-
John Matthew and John Cranhams ~ ditto ~ [9]	2	10	
Thomas Lee ~ ditto ~	1	5	-
Thomas Gillett ~ ditto ~	1	-	-
Paid another ~ ditto ~		4	-
Paid for 2 pair of shoes for John Tuck [10]		6	6
Paid Shipway for Cords [11]		4	6
Paid the Dogmeat Boiler		19	-
Paid Hancock Butcher for heads		5	4
Paid for Horse Flesh and Offell	3	7	6
Antimony for the Hounds [12]		2	-
For taking up the Bitch Bonney		5	-
For odd things wanting in y *kennel*		6	-
Paid for Brooms etc		1	6
For Oyle of Turpentine & Sulpher [13]		2	-
Hoggs Lard		1	-
For five Servants Board Wages 12 weeks at 7d per week	21	-	-

1 The journey from Tottenham Park was started on 31st December. This was the first overnight stop.

2 Beans figure prominently in the provender for the horses, throughout all these accounts, presumably as a source of protein. Hence the phrase "full of beans", perhaps?

3 It seems unlikely that Foard would have set off on this trip without couples. The hounds [or the spaniels] may well have proved riotous on the first day of the journey, hence this probable extra purchase en route.

4 This was the second overnight stop.

5 This was for various "oyntments" and other items.

6 Graves [or greaves] are the sediment of melted tallow pressed into cakes for dog food.

7 Bavins are fagots of brushwood. Probably used to make the "benches" upon which, when covered with straw, hounds slept. Whereas fagots have two bindings, bavins have only one, suggesting they were also shorter.

8 The supplier was one William Sprake.

9 The normal rate was 2/6 per man, per outing. The first and last entries under this heading are untypical.

10 John Tuck was the stable boy.

11 It is not clear if this refers to bindings or measures of firewood.

12 An extremely toxic heavy metal. It was still in use as a base for preparations to treat kennel cough and distemper as late as the 1900s.

13 For treatment of colic, worms and a variety of other veterinary interventions.

Appendix: 2 – The Poor Murdered Woman

1

It was Hanky the squire, as I've heard men say,
Who rode out a-hunting on one Saturday.
They hunted all day, but nothing they found
But a poor murdered woman, laid on the cold ground.

2

About eight o'clock, boys, our dogs they throwed off
On Leatherhead Common, and that was the spot;
They tried all the bushes, but nothing they found
But a poor murdered woman, laid on the cold ground.

3

They whipped their dogs off, and they kept them away,
For I do think it's proper that she should have fair play;
They tried all the bushes, but nothing they found
But a poor murdered woman laid on the cold ground.

4

They mounted their horses, and they rode off the ground,
They rode to the village, and alarmed it all round;
"It is late in the evening, I'm sorry to say,
She cannot be removed until the next day."

5

The next Sunday morning, about eight o'clock,
Some hundreds of people to the spot they did flock;
For to see the poor creature your heart would have bled,
Some cold-hearted violence had come her head.

6

She was took off the Common, and down to some inn,
And the man that has kept it, his name is John Simm.
The coroner was sent for, the jury they joined,
And soon they concluded, and settled their mind.

7

Her coffin was brought; in it she was laid,
And took to the churchyard that was called Leatherhead;
No father, no mother, nor no friend, I'm told,
Came to see that poor creature put under the mould.

8

So now I'll conclude, and I'll finish my song,
For those that have done it shall find themselves wrong;
For on the last day of Judgement a trumpet shall sound,
And their souls in heaven, I'm afraid, won't be found.

This ballad, which is surprisingly faithful to the contemporary account in *The Times* newspaper, was collected from a Mr Foster in Surrey by Lucy Broadwood and published in *English Traditional Songs and Carols* in 1909. It has subsequently been recorded, in various forms, by Shirley Collins and the Albion Country Band on '*No Roses*' [1971] and also by Martin Carthy and Dave Swarbrick on '*But Two Came By*' [1969].

Appendix: 3

A VISIT TO THE SURREY UNION HUNT KENNELS by "H.H."
4th January 1870

"On Tuesday last I found myself jogging over the heavy roads between Guildford and the kennels at Burnt Common, behind the worst and slowest it was ever my fate to hire. Drearily the poor brute crawled up the hills and shuffled down, until a time that should have compassed at least double the distance had been got through; and when we stopped at the turnpike gate, the poor wretch's roaring was something fearful to hear. He is a melancholy-looking, long-tailed black, and I advise all visitors to Guildford to religiously eschew him, though his driver is a civil, well-conducted man.

Arrived at the kennels, I found George Summers, whom I remember when he first took to the pigskin under his father with the Hursley, walking out the dog pack; and we were very soon on the flags and passing some of their best under review."

[2007 Editor's Note: For the sake of clarity, Surrey Union hounds are shown thus: **Sportsman** (dogs) and *Susan* (bitches). Other hounds, the hunt that entered them given first, are shown thus: *Berkeley Festival*]

"The first to make his appearance was the rich Belvoir tan **Rutland**, *by the Berkeley Prodigal, out of their Ruby. This is an exceedingly nice hound in appearance, with a well-formed head and neck, good legs and feet, and altogether a very smart, taking appearance. He quite inherits the famous Berkeley nose, and is particularly good on a road or ride. The New Forest used him last year, and intend sending bitches to him this.* **Sportsman**, *a dark tan of the same age, by the Cotswold* **Sportsman**, *out of the Berkeley* **Festival**, *is considered by Summers quite the best hound in the pack. He has a fine nose, and is very resolute in the chase, allowing no fence or stuff, however strong, to stop him for a moment. In this particular his stock, fortunately, turn after him. He is a close, useful hound, with good bone, and has qualities about him that are of far more importance than good looks.* **Denmark**, *a stylish, hare tanned hound, is a very hard runner, and not quite so good in his constitution as he should be, consequently he shows a want of muscle. He is by Mr Garth's Proctor out of Mr Greaves's Dairymaid, and is now in his seventh season.* **Comrade**, *by the Grove Barrister out of Lord Fitzhardinge's Curious is a very strong dog, with immense bone, but not quite straight; he is capable in work, and has been used for the sake of his undeniable blood, which runs back to the Belvoir Chorister.* **Romulus** *comes from Lord Leconfield's, and is by his Romulus out of his Lofty. He is a plain but very good hound, quick as thought, and so true that, in all his three seasons, he has never been known to speak to a hare but once.* **Wrangler**, *black and white, has all the characteristics of the Berkeley kennel as I remember them a few years ago – wheel-backed, close and powerful - is straight, and has good bone; he is by the Berkeley Reveller, whom Harry Ayris swore by as almost a second Cromwell, and declared it was difficult to tell which really was the better of the two. His dam was the Berkeley Whimsey* [sic]. **Trouncer**, *from Mr Garth's, by his Traveller out of Famous, is a neat hound with a peculiarly small short head. These are all that have been used. Amongst the younger ones,* **Sampson** *and* **Saladin**, *by* **Sportsman** *out of* **Susan**, *are both doing very well in their work, and are nice hounds with good forehands.* **Saladin** *has got himself somewhat light from hard work.* **Regulus**, **Roderick**, *and* **Rifleman** *came from the South Berks, where they work nothing but bitches, and are got by Mr Garth's Rasselas out of their Watchful. They are very useful hounds, and pleased Mr Garth so much when he saw them that he said he should use their sire in his own kennel. One curious thing about them is their colour, a very faint tan, and where hounds are usually black, a dull slate colour. All the litter are like it, but turn after neither sire nor dam, as both were different. They most probably strain back a generation or two in this respect.* **Vanguard**, *a Berkeley-bred one, by Byron out of Volatile, showed badly from shyness, but is, I hear, very good in work.* **Whipster** *and* **Wildair**, *by the Berkeley Commodore from their Wrathful, are both useful, and* **Whipster**, *a badger-pied one, is a remarkably nice young hound.* **Alfred** *is a low hound, very strong and with great quarters, and* **Banker** *has about the biggest ribs I ever saw in a foxhound. He is by the Berkeley Anglesea from their Betsy, and is a useful dog, straight, and with great bone, although he stands rather too high (over 24 in.).* **Actor**, *a neat little Belvoir tan dog, of Lord Macclesfield's and Lord Poltimore's blood, goes with the small pack, and is wonderfully quick; and* **Saracen** *is more for his blood than good looks, being by the Grove Smuggler out of the Berkeley Delicate. The first Belgravian* mother we saw was the smart* **Susan**, *by Lord H. Bentinck's Stormer out of his Lavender, a useful bitch on good legs and feet. The grey* **Countess** *was bred here; and has been a wonder; although in her sixth season, she can go as fast as most of them now, and in her prime was almost too fast. Her parents hail from the Puckeridge, Mr Parry's Comrade being her sire, and Honesty her dam. There is nothing grander in the kennel than* **Rapture**, *by Mr Parry's Random out of his Watchful, although I believe she was bred here; and when Summers drew* **Rubicon**, **Resolute**, **Roebuck** *and* **Ruby** *(four two*

* In this context, Belgravian seems to mean either aristocratic or extremely fashionable.

season hunters), out of her, the old bitch stood up like a queen amongst them still. **Rubicon** *is a very handsome dog, straight and good, and would credit to any kennel, either in the field or on the flags.* **Resolute** *is a fine hound, but not so straight and good; and though* **Roebuck** *and* **Ruby** *are nice bitches, they cannot compare with their dam, who runs well up now. The old lady, I am pleased to hear, has another good litter at walk; so also has* **Wishful**, *a neat one-eyed bitch, who looks as quick as thought. She is a York and Ainsty bred one, by their Villager out of their Wisdom.* **Cautious**, *by Berkeley Comus from their Benefit, another rare, useful matron, is a granddaughter of old Cromwell.* **Diomed, Destiny, Didymus** *and* **Dreadnaught** *were introduced with her and their sire,* **Denmark**, *and formed as clever a three couple of hare tans as one need wish to see, though here again, I must say, I think the "old 'uns" had the best of it.* **Nosegay** *claims the Tedworth Nathan as her sire, and is out of the Berkeley Frantic. Her nose is so good that Summers says if there is any scent at all a fox must, bar accidents, die when she is out. She has a good litter now at walk.* **Ring** *is another very useful one, by the Berkeley Reveller out of their Relish; and* **Sempstress** *[sic], sister to* **Sportsman**, *is another that never loses a chance of accounting for her fox. In the young bitches, of which this year's entry is rather short,* **Songstress** *is one of the best – a rare hard one, and never tired – and her sister* **Sportley** *[sic], is very useful, and especially good through the heart; they are of the same litter as* **Saladin** *and* **Sampson**, *already mentioned.* **Tasty**, *by the Berkeley Pomfret from their Truelove, is, I hear, doing very well. These comprise, I believe, the cracks of the kennel; and amongst them are to found, not only good-bred hounds and good workers, but some really good-looking ones, although of course, here, as in other packs where they are principally dependant on drafts, appearance must not be studied if a hound is good in the field, and where both cannot be obtained straightness and symmetry must be sacrificed to nose and dash.*

The new kennels are without show, and are the simple adaptation of farm buildings and cottages to the purpose of stabling, kennel, and all its convenience. The arrangements are tolerably complete. The simple contrivance of zinc sides and covering render mouse-proof the granary and meal room; from the latter the meal is shot down into the boiling house by a tube. The two coppers are heated by one furnace, the flues heating one or both by dampers, the furnace being outside – an arrangement conducive to coolness, cleanliness and economy, and not applied, so far as I know, to any other kennel. The same fire also heats a third copper, constantly supplied with water, and furnishes the stables adjoining with the hot water they require. The kennels have a good slope, a good exposure, and are very healthy, and there is an abundant supply of water."

Although one rather gets the impression that the writer was being paid by the line to write this piece, there is much useful information that can be drawn from the information supplied. Perhaps the most obvious is the extensive reliance on drafts to make up the pack. From this, it may be supposed that a specific Surrey Union hound-breeding policy was not in place, either by accident or design, and that this may have been the case for several seasons previously. However, with the apparent ready availability of drafts of reasonable quality, albeit at a financial cost presumably, such a position is perhaps understandable.

The reference to the boilers confirms that hounds were being fed in the traditional manner on oatmeal 'porridge' and the failure to mention a flesh-house implies that this almost certainly formed their main diet. The quantity of coal consumed by the furnace and other grates in the establishment must have been considerable and, with the nearest coal staithes at either Woking or Guildford railway stations, cartage costs must have added to the Master's burden. [The railway line *vîa* Clandon was not opened until 1885.]

Appendix: 4 – The Surrey Union Hounds Season 1888-89

THE SURREY UNION HOUNDS SEASON 1888-89

By "Plantagenet"

"*Whiten is a huntsman worthy to wear the mantle of George Summers, under whom he had five years of excellent training after being educated being educated in a totally different school with George Castleman, of the Atherstone. It would be difficult to mention a combination more likely to develop the qualities that constitute an expert in woodcraft than this grafting of the science as practised in woodland counties like Hampshire and Surrey, on the more dashing methods pursued in the midland shires, and Whiten has proved himself an apt student of the best characteristics of both. It was natural that the old love should influence him somewhat in his system of breeding, but that has not blinded him to the merits of a stock on which his predecessor had set the stamp by long descent. The Atherstone blood was freely used, with good results; but old characteristics specially suited to the Surrey Union country still survive. On point lost sight of by so many huntsmen, but carefully kept in view by Whiten is the harm done by retaining old hounds beyond their working days simply out of affection. More packs than one would care to remember have been spoilt by this amiable weakness. The veterans of the Surrey Union were entered only six seasons ago and, though there are six couples of them, not one shows signs of being worn out or shirking work.*

[2007 Editor's Note: For the sake of clarity, Surrey Union hounds are shown thus: **Pembroke** (dogs) and *Cobweb* (bitches). Other hounds, the hunt that entered them given first, are shown thus: *Burton Duster*]

First on the list is **Boaster***, by Burton Duster, out of East Sussex Boundless. Next among the dog hounds is* **Pembroke***, whose pedigree seems to have been unrecorded; but his qualities are not likely to be forgotten, for there are five couples of young ones in this year's entry by him.* **Roman** *and* **Rambler** *were the first of the Atherstone draft, by their Regent – Novelty. Another of the same draft is* **Transit***, a very comely daughter of the well-known Traitor and Annie.* **Warrior***,* **Whalebone** *and* **Vengeance** *are by Belvoir Weathergage – Brocklesby Lightening, a combination of good strains the value of which Whiten has not been slow to recognise, and it appears to have nicked very well with the* **Pembroke** *blood.* **Cottager** *and* **Cobweb** *are the only five-year-old hounds now in the pack. They are by Crawley & Horsham [C&H] Chieftain - Violet, who was descended from a sire in which Summers placed great faith. Among those now in their fourth season,* **Bluebell***, by Goodwood Chaser – East Sussex Blameless;* **Hastings, Hermit, Hopeful, Hotspur** *and* **Housemaid***, by Tedworth Hastings – Brocklesby Wanton; and* **Rarity***, by Lord Leconfield's Rayman – Chiddingfold Buxom, show most quality, and the blood of which they are representatives comes out again in a younger generation, though not through them in all cases.* **Ladybird** *and* **Lavender***, in their third season, are the only remaining couple of a very comely litter by Brocklesby Leveller – Chiddingfold Rival, but* **Raglan, Rover, Refuge** *and* **Rantipole***, of the same season's entry, also sustain the reputation of the Chiddingfold Kennels, where their sire, Rambler, was much prized. With the exception of a couple and a half, all entered last year were drafts, the best of them coming from the Bicester, and having a strong infusion of Belvoir blood. These are* **Challenger** *and* **Chainer***, by Bicester Rover – Belvoir Cautious;* **Gamble** *and* **Gainer***, by the great Belvoir Gambler – Bicester Anxious;* **Sampson, Stentor, Scum** *[sic !!] and* **Spangle***, by Bicester Settler – Old Berkshire Hunt [O.B.H.] Beatrice, who strains back to the same illustrious country.* **Forester***, Fancy and Sprightly, who came in a draft from the Old Surrey, are also of Belvoir descent, through their sire, Sampson. It is a long time since the Surrey Union had a better entry than Whiten is able to put forward for the coming season, and their names are, therefore, worthy of being recorded:-*

SURREY UNION HUNT ENTRY

Names	Sire	Dam	Names	Sire	Dam
Cossack			Harbinger	**Latimer**	*Healthy*
Cromwell			Rector	**Lifeguard**	*Redwing*
Commodore					
Collier	**Pembroke**	*Cobweb*	Rocket	**General**	*Roguish*
Cruel			Roman		
Countess					
Caroline			Galliard	**General**	*Lively*
Courtly			Gaylad		
Prodigal	**Pembroke**	*Vengeance*	Lawyer	**Lifeguard**	*Gamesome*
Prompter			Franklin	**Latimer**	*Frailty*
			Creditor	*C&H Chieftain*	*Their Cowslip*
Tomboy			Marksman	*O.B.H. Hero*	*Goodwood Mystery*
Traveller	*Mr Hargreaves's* Tomboy	*Bluebell*	Stockwell	*Sir W.W. Wynn's Steamer*	*Goodwood Riot*
Tuneful			Warrior	*Goodwood Worcester*	*Their Truelass*
Telltale			*Skilful**	*Goodwood Saladin*	*Their Daisy*
			*Captive**	*Lord Leconfield's Splendour*	*Goodwood Caroline*

* Bitches?

*The young ones by **Pembroke** – **Cobweb** to whom reference has already been made, are a litter full of good qualities, and are also twins [?], half brothers from **Vengeance**, daughter of Belvoir Weathergage. Mr Hargreaves's Tomboy, is a sire of celebrity, whose characteristics are strongly marked in the two couples out of **Bluebell** who was by Goodwood Chaser. No more judicious course could have been taken than that indicated by an importation of stout Goodwood blood which is represented by drafts, but of all the young ones, none are more shapely or show more quality than those of home breeding, and Whiten may well be proud of the success, thus far obtained."*

As with the 1870 kennel visit, the writer seems to be intent on getting words onto the page rather than aiming for precision. It is unfortunate that no clear distinction between dogs and bitches has been made throughout the piece and, in the modern attempt to inject lucidity, it may be that there have been misidentifications of gender. Once again, one is struck by the extensive reliance on drafts to make up the pack, although it is clear that an emergent Surrey Union hound-breeding policy is starting to be developed by the new Master.

From a pack of 24 couple inherited from Colonel Pilkington Blake in May 1886, Mr Bennett had increased its size to some 45 couple by May 1889, by the adoption of an extensive breeding programme as described above and the continuing purchase of drafts from other Hunts.

Appendix: 5 – Press Report of the Surrey Union General Meeting 23rd April 1898

THE SURREY UNION HUNT

INTERESTING PRESENTATIONS

There was a large gathering of sporting gentlemen at the Swan Hotel, Leatherhead, on Saturday afternoon, on the occasion of a meeting of the Surrey Union Hunt. Mr J B Hankey presided, and those also present were Lord Foley, Messrs F Hue Williams, A W Aston, H J Adkins, H J Wood, A Seth Smith, W Noakes, T Land, T Lowe, Vacher, O Price, J Cropley, S J Hack, D Campbell, W S Le Grand, S Dale, C A Madge, G Dodge, A T Miller, W Weller, A Labouchere and A H Tritton (hon. Secretary).

Mr Tritton said that the first business was to elect a new secretary. It was with very much regret that he had vacated the position, but it had become such a heavy tie upon him that he felt bound to place his resignation in the hands of the committee. -The chairman said the difficulty was to find another gentleman to fill the vacancy.

Mr Aston said he thought that an opportune moment for them to give expression to their sense of deep regret at the loss of Mr Tritton's services. He felt he should be expressing not only his own feelings but those of every other gentleman present when he said the Surrey Union Hunt had rarely, if ever, seen such a splendid secretary as they had in Mr Tritton during the past seven years (applause). In the discharge of his duties, Mr Tritton had been most agreeable to everyone, and the efficiency with which the secretarial work had been carried out would, he felt, make it all the more difficult for the man who was chosen to succeed him. They all greatly appreciated the good work he had done, and when the idea was mooted of presenting him with a testimonial as some slight recognition of his services, every member of the hunt was ready to subscribe to it. The total number of subscribers was 114, the amount being limited to half-a-sovereign. On behalf of the hunt, he had the greatest possible pleasure in asking Mr Tritton's acceptance of a loving cup and fruit dishes, and he hoped and trusted that he might be spared for very many years in the enjoyment of the best of health and every happiness (applause).

The cup bore the inscription: "Presented to Arthur H Tritton Esq, by the members of the Surrey Union Hunt as a slight recognition of his many services as honorary secretary" and the fruit dishes were inscribed "A H T from the S U H, 1898".

Mr Tritton said that words failed him to express his gratitude for the most kind expressions of feeling they had tendered to him through Mr Aston, and for the most beautiful present they had been good enough to give him. He should always value it immensely, not so much for its intrinsic value, but in the knowledge that his services as secretary of the hunt had been appreciated. He thanked them one and all most heartily, and although he should no longer fill an official positioning the hunt, he hoped to have many happy and jolly days with them all for many years to come (applause). He wished also to take that opportunity of thanking them most sincerely for the kind and courteous way they had always treated him during the seven years of his secretaryship, and also as his last year as master. He felt sure that that kindness and forbearance would be extended to his successor, Mr Labouchere, whom he wished to introduce to them.

Mr Labouchere, who was cordially welcomed, said that was the first time he had had the opportunity of meeting the members of the hunt, and he desired to thank them for the honour they had done him in electing him as master. He could assure them that he should do his best to show them all the sport he possibly could. With regard to the vacancy, he regretted as much as anybody that it had been brought about by an unfortunate illness. Their late master was a man so deservedly popular, and did his work so thoroughly well, that doubtless he would find it a difficult matter to follow him. Misfortune seldom came singly, and by the resignation of Mr Tritton, they had another cause for deep regret. A man who had acted as secretary in the manner that Mr Tritton has done during the past seven years deserved well of those around him, and he was pleased to notice that his services had been recognised so handsomely. He already knew a great many farmers in the neighbourhood, and he hoped before very long to make the acquaintance of the whole of them. Having been a farmer himself he knew the unpleasantness they had to put up with, but farmers as a rule, and especially those in Surrey, were a long-suffering, good-natured race, and he had no doubt he should be able to get on with them (applause). Keepers he had always found to be a class of straight-forward sensible men, and he had always been able to get on with them very well. In conclusion he could assure them that he would use his best endeavours to show them all the sport he could, and study the interests of the landowners, farmers, keepers, and every individual member of the Surrey Union Hunt (applause).

Mr Tritton said a very pleasant task now fell to his lot, namely to hand a testimonial to one who had been of the greatest service to the hunt. He referred, as they all knew, to William Holdaway, who had been their huntsman for ten years. During the whole of that time he had been most courteous and polite to everyone, and had done all he could to give the best possible sport. He had the greatest pleasure in handing him a cheque for £100 and he desired at the same time to thank him for the help he had rendered him in the discharge of his duties as secretary.*

Mr Holdaway said he was deeply grateful to the members of the hunt for their handsome gift. He had tried to do the best he could, and he hoped he had succeeded. Sport during the past year, however, had been out of the question. There had been no scent whatever, and everything from the commencement of the year had gone against them. He hoped that next season things would improve, and that under the new master he might get on as well as he had done in the past.

Mr Tritton mentioned that up to the present time the hunt had been out 59 times, and had accounted for 17 brace of foxes. They had been stopped by frost twice, and had two blank days-a thing that had not occurred for eleven years. Once they were stopped by fog.

Mr Aston suggested that the appointment of a successor to Mr Tritton should stand over for a month. Mr Hue Williams said that he had a gentleman to propose, but he was willing to fall in with the wishes of the meeting.

Mr Aston said it was Mr Labouchere's first appearance amongst them that day, and possibly he might need a little breathing time. He suggested that the selection of a new secretary be left to the committee and Mr Labouchere. This was agreed to, and the meeting terminated with a vote of thanks to the chairman, proposed by Mr Hue Williams.

* On the original cutting, the last two words have been struck through and replaced by *during his Mastership*, in manuscript.

There is a lot going on in this report! The meeting started at 5 o'clock on Saturday 23rd April 1898 and its main purposes are plain. The congratulatory back-slapping is palpable, and doubtless well deserved, but the statements by William Holdaway are curious. To what is he alluding? Is it an example of none but a huntsman knows a huntsman's woes, or is there something deeper? In marked contrast to his comments, the statistics given by the outgoing acting-Master look encouraging and seem not to indicate a disappointing season at all. It is all very intriguing!

Appendix: 6 – The Surrey Union in the early 1900s – A Hunt Servant's Perspective

There are few opportunities to gain an appreciation of the thoughts and aspirations of those in Hunt service during this period, so it is particularly valuable that Jack Molyneux, the second whipper-in under Mr Longman, should have recorded some Surrey Union memories in his book "*Thirty Years a Hunt Servant*", published in 1935. These extracts from this work show life as it was really lived, warts and all:

"On May 1st 1901, when sixteen years old, I went as second whipper-in to the Surrey Union Foxhounds. I had to work in kennel in summer, and in the stables in winter. Altogether it was a rough job. The kennels were near Cobham, quite the roughest I have ever seen. They were built of wood and infested with rats; in fact, the place was simply swarming with them. The explanation was that the kennels were near a big farm owned by Mr T H Bennett, who had been Joint-Master of the Surrey Union with Mr G H Longman for a season. The hounds were never walked out, but were turned into a grass yard, which must have been very bad for them. Mr G H Longman was sole Master from 1900 to 1904 and hunted hounds alternate days with the huntsman, Will Kennett. Kennett and Jim Hackett, the first whipper-in, were two of the queerest characters I have ever come across. At the same time, they were good at their work. They both used to get up on their horses to go hunting with a little clay pipe, well alight, in their mouths, and as soon as the day's hunting was over, on would go their little pipes again. On more than one occasion they left me outside one of their "call houses" with hounds and horses, whilst they played "rings" or darts. It was all right for them, but when I arrived back I had my horse to do as soon as I got in, and then had to get my own dinner ready. I lived by myself in a two-roomed hut at the kennels, and no one else lived on the place. Thus it was a pretty hard school for a youngster who had so looked forward to his promotion from harriers to foxhounds. Nevertheless, one has to take the rough with the smooth in hunt service. Kennett was the best man on a horn I have ever heard, and my father always said the same. He blew a "Littleworth" horn, and I always used the same make, having found them the best-toned horns procurable.

Mr Longman, the Master, lived at Epsom, and we could drive to Epsom races in the kennel-cart. The first year I saw the Derby was in 1901, when it was won by *Volodyovski*. We used to draw a covert in those days by Tattenham Corner, and Colonel Gordon Colman, who was Master of the Surrey Union from 1904 to 1910, and is the present Master of the Belvoir, lived at Nork Park, Epsom, which was one of our meets. We used to hunt three and four days a week, and I had four horses to ride. Their names were *Oxford*, *Emperor* and *Khaki*, and later I had a horse named *Ginger*. They were useful hunters, but I had to do them all myself.

The first season I was there we were stopped by frost just before Christmas, and the day before Christmas Eve Kennett decided to take hounds on a long exercise. He told me over-night to get a good breakfast, and it was well I did so, for we started off and called at one place, then another, they taking the Christmas cheer offered to them, and how ready people seem to bring out glasses for hunt servants although it means the undoing of many of them! Late in the afternoon we called at a house in Abinger Hatch, at which they were given a bumper of old cider to drink. There is cider and cider, and this absolutely bowled them over. It was now quite dark, and we were many miles from home. Going up a long drive by Lord Ashcombe's place, Kennett stopped to light his pipe, and hounds went after a rabbit. I followed to stop them, but he said: "It's all right, John, leave 'em alone, they won't hurt." The next minute they were disappearing up a hill in the dark into a big wood — the whole pack of 40 odd couple! It was now pitch dark, and Kennett blew for them, but as we could not tell in the dark how many we had, we were 12½ couple short when we arrived home. A thaw had set in, and a wire from the Master giving orders to hunt next day was waiting for Kennett when we arrived. This pulled us all up sharp. Well, we hunted next day with Mr. Longman's pack, but what Kennett told him about the lost hounds I never knew. It was not really fit to hunt that day, but we had a go, with the frost coming out of the ground, which was just like a skating rink. We found a fox at a covert called High Ridges. The Master jumped a biggish fence out of the covert. I attempted to follow, but the slippery ground brought my horse down, and he finished up in the ditch. We had to get a cart-horse to pull him out. The Master then thought it was time to go home. My horse having been upside down in a dirty ditch, the saddle was in an awful mess, but I had to ride him home, and do him and his tack when I got there.

A message had arrived informing us that our lost hounds were shut up at the Rectory on Ranmore Common, and next morning (which was Christmas Day) I had to ride our old trap-horse over to fetch them - a matter of about ten miles, with ice and snow on the road. When I got to the Rectory the parson was at church, and I had to wait, as he had the key of the coach-house, in which they were locked. When I reached kennels I had to get my Christmas dinner ready, and do my tack, etc., for next day's hunting, which, taken altogether, made anything but a merry Christmas for me.

Another story comes into my mind about being stopped by frost, This morning the ground was as hard as iron after a very sharp frost, and Kennett decided off his own bat it was not fit to hunt, instead of getting in touch with the Master. So we started off on one of our exercise-cum-calling-for-hospitality jaunts. We must have looked pretty beauties, for Kennett had on a scarlet coat which was almost black, dirty old breeches and jack-boots. Jim Hackett wore a pair of rough kennel-boots and leggings, a dirty coat and an old hat, whilst I was dressed in an old pair of breeches and a pair of jack-boots somebody had given me, and hat and coat to match the others. Well, when we had got a few miles from home, in the direction the meet should have been, we met a man ploughing. Old Kennett stopped suddenly, and said: "James, it looks like hunting!" and we pushed on. A few miles farther on who should come to meet us but my father, who was then huntsman to the Burstow, our meet being on their side. He first stared in astonishment, and then roared with laughter at our rig-out, and told us a big field was waiting for us, which was quite correct. It was a 'lawn meet', which made it worse. However, we hunted and had quite a good day, Kennett smashing his old bowler hat and vowing he would charge the Master for a new one.

In my second season new kennels were built near Great Bookham, with Leatherhead our nearest station. They were put up by Boulton and Paul, and were very nice, and, at any rate, we were free of rats, which was a great blessing.

Of course, we did have some good hunts, and certain parts of the Surrey Union country are quite good. One day in particular, I recall was December 23rd, 1902, when my brother Ted was second whipper-in to my father, and was having a day with us on their side of the country. We met at Stanhill Court, Charlwood. The first fox found was quickly and killed, but we soon found again, and, to quote the entry in my diary: "We had the best run I was ever in, and over the best country, with jumping enough to suit anyone. We found at 1.30, and hounds were still running at dark, about 4.20". My brother Ted was fifteen years old, whilst I was seventeen, and we had a great ride together. Another outstanding day was March 18th, the same season. We found at Wonersh, near Guildford, and ran an eleven-mile point into the Chiddingfold country, only Mr Longman, Jim Hackett and myself getting to the finish. If you made a wrong turn in this country you would sometimes have a difficult job to find hounds.

The whippers-in with the Surrey Union used to ride in the point-to-point races in those days, and Jim Hackett, the first whipper-in, as a rule rode a winner or two. I never succeeded in doing so, although I always had a good ride.

My two seasons as second whipper-in with the Surrey Union were hard and rough, but I would advise any young whipper-in to start in such a country. It teaches a man to be quick, knocks the conceit out of him, gives him wide experience in many directions, and makes him appreciate a good country later on. When I was twenty-two years of age, and first whipper-in at the Quorn, I was offered the huntsman's place at the Surrey Union, and if I had never whipped in there I might have gone; but as it was I thought it wise to carry on in good countries whipping-in."

Appendix: 7 – Foxhound Packs at the Reigate Hound Show 1913

Name of Pack	Master
Beaufort's, The Duke of	Duke of Beaufort
Berks, South	Mr H W Boileau
Blackmore Vale	Mr F J Wingfield Digby
Burstow	Mr C Selby Lownes
Cattistock	The Rev. E A Milne
Chiddingfold	Admiral Sir G Atkinson Willes
Craven	Messrs W J Yorke Scarlett & J A Fairhurst
Dorset, South	Mr J A Radcliffe
Essex	Capt. S F Gosling
Essex Union	Capt. G Haseltine
Grafton	Mr H Hawkins
Hambledon	Capt. Standish
Hurts', Mr	Mr F C A Hurts
Kent, East	Mr H W Selby Lowndes
Kent, West	Mr A Havelock-Allen
Leconfield's, Lord	Lord Leconfield
Ledbury	Sir G Bullough
Oakley	Mr E Arkwright
Southdown	Mr C B Kidd
Surrey, Old	Mr C Leveson-Gower
Surrey Union	Mr A H Tritton
Tickham	Lord Harris & Mr W C Dawes

This table shows how popular the Reigate Hound Show was in the years leading up to the Great War and quite how far Masters were prepared to travel in order to attend. Those coming from any distance at all would have travelled by train.

Appendix: 8 – Horse & Hound report 10th March '05

Surrey Union

There has been a curious paradox about this season: seemingly there may not have been many days to write home about and scent has been notoriously fickle, yet our tally of 54 brace from 28 days' autumn hunting and 40 days from the opening meet to 17 February was more than set to exceed [before the politicians intervened] last season's total - and that was reckoned to be the best in living memory! Of the current tally, 31½ brace (60%) were killed on top, which is very pleasing, given the type of country that we hunt.

Of course there were some notable days – four brace on top at Ifield Wood during autumn hunting; hounds hunting just about all day at Coldharbour on 7 February and 2½ brace at Newdigate on 10 February. Indeed, from the end of January, our hardworking Huntsman, Ian Shakespeare, ably assisted by first whipper-in, Nicholas Prior, has pulled out all the stops to provide three or four days hunting a week.

So was there a singular lasting memory? For this correspondent indeed there was, although it came at the absolute end on 17th February. The mist had been closing in throughout the late afternoon and the light was rapidly fading as the sun went down. Suddenly, in the thickets below Exfold Farm, a hound spoke. This challenge was rapidly confirmed and the volume of music rose to an echoing crescendo, as each of the pack owned the line. Ian Shakespeare doubled his horn encouragingly and away down the hedgerows they went. A distant tally-ho over indicated that the fox had crossed the Horsham road and was making for Frenches Copse. Breasting the rise, the field loomed out of the gloaming and, with our horses' breath turning to vapour, we all realised that the very essence of the hunting that we know and love was encapsulated in those few short moments.

But, of course, it was too dark and dangerous to hunt on. The heart-breakingly hard decision finally had to be made and home was blown. Standing in the pitch dark of the yard at Honeybush Farm, I could hear our huntsman whistling to his hounds in the depths of the wood and eventually their spectral shapes turned into solid form. As Ian rode by he raised his cap and said "Goodnight, Sir." "Goodnight, Ian", I replied, raising my hat in salute. A string of goodnights followed as the Joint-Masters and the rest of the field clattered by. As they faded from sight, I felt sure that it was the mistiness and the moonless night that caused the blurred vision – not the tear in my eye.

Yet, fear not, the fight-back has already begun! The turnout at the meet on 19 February at Stilemans was nothing short of phenomenal. With at least 200 horses in the mounted field and some 3000* supporters on foot, this Hunt is far from down and out.

We demonstrated that we could still hunt and kill a fox [within the new law] and, as required, intend to do so again. Just as importantly, in addition to this continuing fox management, we will still provide a fallen stock service to our farmers. Let there be no misunderstanding, we can, and will, survive to hunt another day.

Covertcoat, *Horse & Hound*, March 10th 2005

* a later police figure gave 5000

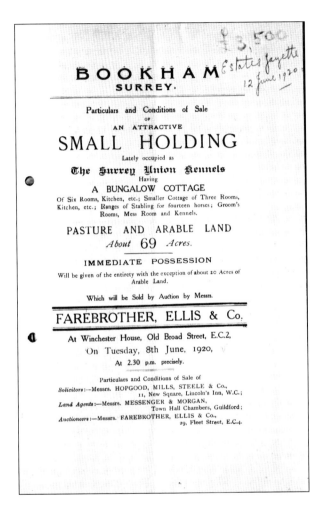

BOOKHAM
SURREY.

Particulars and Conditions of Sale
OF
AN ATTRACTIVE

SMALL HOLDING

Lately occupied as
The Surrey Union Kennels
Having
A BUNGALOW COTTAGE
Of Six Rooms, Kitchen, etc.; Smaller Cottage of Three Rooms, Kitchen, etc.; Ranges of Stabling for fourteen horses; Groom's Rooms, Mess Room and Kennels.

PASTURE AND ARABLE LAND
About 69 *Acres.*

IMMEDIATE POSSESSION
Will be given of the entirety with the exception of about 20 Acres of Arable Land.

Which will be Sold by Auction by Messrs.

FAREBROTHER, ELLIS & Co.

At Winchester House, Old Broad Street, E.C.2,
On Tuesday, 8th June, 1920,
At 2.30 p.m. precisely.

Particulars and Conditions of Sale of
Solicitors:—Messrs. HOPGOOD, MILLS, STEELE & Co.,
11, New Square, Lincoln's Inn, W.C.;
Land Agents:—Messrs. MESSENGER & MORGAN,
Town Hall Chambers, Guildford;
Auctioneers:—Messrs. FAREBROTHER, ELLIS & Co.,
29, Fleet Street, E.C.4.

(handwritten: £3,500 Estates Gazette 12 June 1920)

Two Bed Rooms; Sitting Room; Kitchen, with range; Scullery, with copper and sink; W.C.

Gas and Water both laid on.

The Extensive Stabling

comprising accommodation for fourteen horses, is built of corrugated iron, all match-lined, on dwarf brick walls, with capital cement-paved floors, and is capable of

Easy Conversion into Farm Buildings

It is erected on four sides with large gravelled Yard in centre and cement-paved walks at the side; thus:—Ten Boxes, three Stalls and a single Box, Hay Store, Corn Store, Saddle Room with large copper, Inner Saddle Room, Gig House, and man's accommodation of two single Bed Rooms and one large Room with range, Men's Mess Room, and W.C. *Gas and Water laid on.*

At the Back are

The Kennels

of similar construction and capable of useful conversion for Stores, etc., thus:—Range of four Kennels, Feeding or Mixing Room, Boiling House, with engine and two steamers; Small Kennel in Yard; Meal House; Another Range of four Breeding Kennels and a Young Hound Kennel; Detached Slaughter House.

The Land

which has several commanding positions, with some grand views, comprises some

45 Acres Excellent Pasture

and about

20 Acres Productive Arable Land

as set out in the following Schedule:—

No. on Plan		Description		Area
Pt. 236	...	Arable	...	2·625
237b	...	Grass	...	1·293
237c	...	Kennels & Cottages		2·508
237d	...	Grass	...	2·414
237e	...	Spinney		·509
237f	...	Pasture	...	15·218
237g	...	Spinney		·322
237h	...	Pasture	...	26·765
Pt. 238	...	Wood Fringe		·897
Pt. 239	...	Arable	...	17·197
		Total Area		A. 69·748

The Arable Land and Wood Fringe are in the farming occupation of Mr. D. W. Macfarlane, of Phœnice Farm, Great Bookham (with other land of the Vendor not included in this sale) on a lease dated 2nd September, 1913, expiring 29th September, 1925, at a rent apportioned for the purposes of sale of £11 10s. per annum. **Early Possession can be had by giving Mr. Macfarlane three months' notice at any time and paying him compensation for his crops and unexhausted interest in the land.**

Possession of the remainder of the Property which was used by the Hunt will be given on Completion of the Purchase.

The Purchaser shall take over and pay for, by valuation, all unexhausted manures, acts of husbandry, and growing crops upon the land in hand, and shall in the conveyance to him covenant to erect and for ever maintain along the south-eastern boundary of the land where marked T on plan a wire fence similar in all respects to the existing wire fence on the other boundaries of the property.

Land Tax, *nil.*   Apportioned Tithe, £18.

Appendix: 10 – Point-to-Point Press Report 1921

SURREY UNION HUNT

_____

POINT-TO-POINT RACES AT LEIGH

The revival of the Surrey Union Hunt point-to-point races at Shellwood Manor, Leigh, by kind permission of Mr F L Crow, on Saturday was greatly appreciated, judging from the large attendance of farmers and others interested in sport. The event clashed with the Eridge meeting, with the result that the Burstow Hunt was not so well represented as in pre-war years. The meeting, however, was not overlooked by pencillers, who were there in good numbers, and punters who followed favourites must have had a good day. The course was over three miles of meadow and plough land of typical hunting country. The jumps were not too difficult, and although several horses refused some of the fences, there were very few spills and no one was injured. The Reigate Borough Motor Ambulance, in charge of Inspector Hood, was in attendance in case first aid was required. Inspector Bensted, of the County Police, and a number of men were in evidence, but their duties were comparatively light.

The racing was keen and exciting. Certainly one event had to be cancelled owing to the coal strike, the race being one which was confined to officers who had been officers of the Woolwich Garrison. The services of these gentlemen were required elsewhere, hence the abandonment. Mr B B Lemon's *Patsy* repeated his Edenbridge success, and won the nomination race by half a length. Mr H C Lee-Steere, the Master of the Hunt, and Mr Malcolm B Bovill, the hon. secretary, are to be congratulated upon the whole of the arrangements, which were carried out to the satisfaction of all. The principal officials were: Judge, Mr A H Tritton; clerk of the scales, Mr W Dawtry; Clerk of the Course, Mr A G Williams; starter, Mr I H Ward.

There were eight entries in the Heavy-weight race, but owing to accidents during the week several horses were scratched, and Mr A G Williams' *Dorking* (Mr H Etherington) had a walk-over.

Six turned out in the Light-weight race, and Captain B M Hudson's *War Bonus* was installed favourite. Passing the judges' wagon for the first time *War Bonus* was leading, and was well ahead of the field in the open country. Half a mile from home Mr E W R Ritchie's *Robert Hallidan* (Mr E Pinker) challenged, and it was a neck and neck race for the last fence. Coming up the straight *Robert Hallidan* got in front and won by half a length. Mr A E *Berry's Follow Me II* (Mr N C P Howard) was third, a distance in the rear.

Unattributed Local Press Cutting

Notes:

- *War Bonus* was ridden by her owner, Captain Hudson.

- There is no mention of the Ladies' Race on the race card. Perhaps this was a late substitution for the abandoned race for the Woolwich Garrison Cup?

- Mr J C Calvert came fourth in the lightweight race, riding his gelding, *Delight*.

Appendix: 11 – Extracts from the Diary of J C "Jack" Calvert

The background to the Captain Hudson episode [see Chapter 15], as perceived by a subscriber:

Saturday 31st December 1921: The Kennels

". . . I rode Delight in a snaffle today again, he jumps much better in it. It does not seem to be much good riding for a start with these hounds, as they never seem to get well away, but one always hopes that they will settle down and run."

Saturday 7th January 1922: Leigh

"We met at the Rinkers' place at Bury's Court. Dancing at Dorking the night before, only had 2 hrs in bed so was not feeling too fit . . .

. . . I was larking Delight about a lot, he is jumping very well just now & people are talking about him. I want to sell him as he is getting on in years & has seen his best days I fancy."

Saturday 21st January: Clarke's Green

". . . They ran quite fast, but more like a pack of drag hounds than foxhounds, no dash in them at all."

Saturday 28th January: Bagden Farm

"With 12 couple of hounds down with distemper in the kennels, only 9 couple came to the meet & they were a very sorry looking lot. We never looked like having sport & we never got it . . . "

Saturday 18th February: Northlands

"This was a real bad day spent in the woods. Apparently no scent & the hounds terribly slack . . . "

Saturday 4th March: Ellen's Green

". . . This was the best bit of work these hounds have done. They never ran fast, lacked drive, but stuck to their fox and gave tongue to a certain extent . . .

. . . There is a lot of grumbling going on about the Master, but it is said he will kill foxes if turned out!!"

Saturday 18th March: Norwood Hill

"A rotten day with no scent spent round about Henfold & the Hammonds. Plenty of foxes. We hear today that Mr Heath has written to Mr Steere saying that as they have shown no sport, he thinks they better retire. We shall certainly get no sport till the former [sic] does."

Saturday 25th March: Four Wents Pond

"There has been so much grumbling lately on the part of the field that they decided to hold a Committee Meeting before hunting today. This was brought about by a letter Capt. Hudson wrote to the secretary saying he no longer thought it worth his while to walk puppies. This letter was read out at the meeting. Mr Heath then got up and made a very nice speech saying he would resign, but continue to help the hounds in every way he could. Mr Steere then also resigned (with a very bad grace). This was exactly what we wanted. However Heaton, who never hunts himself, then got up & said this would be a great calamity & would they not reconsider their decision. Father then proposed that a general meeting should be held next Sat. where, the Masters being absent, everyone could freely express their opinions. This course was adopted.

The hunting was quite unworthy of record. We found foxes on Holmwood Common, but could not do anything with them. Found close to Beare Gill & ran up the hill."

Saturday 1st April: Northlands Corner

"I went to the general hunt meeting last night. They appointed a fresh committee independent of the Masters & passed a resolution asking the Masters to carry on. Previously, however, during the week certain matters had been settled.

1) A new huntsman.
2) Two whips
3) Country S & E to be more hunted
4) Independent committee to retire yearly.

Mr Steere agreed to the above & has certainly seemed anxious to please lately. But it is not likely to last long & one fails to see how these matters will give us a pack of hounds to hunt.

From Northlands they marked a fox to ground in the Duchesses but did not find again."

Summary of Season 1921-22

This has undoubtedly the worst season hunting I have ever had. On not one occasion have we had a real good hunt. When these hounds have run, it has been more like a drag hunt with the hounds following, no dash or drive in them that distinguish the foxhound.

We have also had bad luck, no cubbing on account of the lack of rain. Just as hounds were getting fit, Jim Dawson has his accident. White came in, a gallant old man to ride, but a bad huntsman & with apparently wrong ideas on kennel management. All the hounds went down with some skin disease & came to the meets a sorry looking lot of wrecks. They never recovered from this & when Jim came back it was seen that he could no longer do the work.

There was also trouble with the Masters.

However we are to start next season with a clean slate, money has been forthcoming for new hounds, renovating the kennels (in a most deplorable condition, with no ventilation) & a new huntsman & whip.

We feel convinced that no sport will be shown until there is a new Master, but everyone says that is impossible till the present one is dead. An absurd predicament!

As for horses we have Delight, Agra, Tim, Grey Friar, the four year old Nigger for next season.

Appendix: 12 – The Surrey Union Hunt Masters, Office Holders and Subscribers Season 2006-07

President:	Corinna, Lady Hamilton of Dalzell DL
Chairman:	Ian Agnew
Joint-Masters:	Mark Sprake MFH, Ian Gilchrist MFH, Katharine Meller MFH, Edmund O'Reilly-Hyland MFH & Jeremy Gumbley MFH
Treasurer:	Nigel Morland
Hunt Secretaries:	Rachel Brooker, Judeth Chamberlain, Penny Wilson, Jane Williams & Geraldine Firth [co-opted]
Point-to-Point Secretary:	Andrew Ayres
The Hunt Committee:	Tom Dale, Daniel Davies, Sarah Godley, Colin Marsh, Catherine McIlwraith, Richard Parker, David Radcliffe & Julian Womersley

Subscribers to the Surrey Union Hunt

Agnew, Ian & Mandy
The Albury Estate (The Duke of Northumberland)
Ayres, Andrew
Bankfield, Sophie E
Barford, Benedict
Barnes, David & Julia
Barnes, Philippa
Bennett, Patricia
Bennett, Richard
Bovill, Chris
Brooker, Rachel
Bryan, Suzie
Buckley, Cami
Bull, Lindsay
Calvert, Lizzie
Cannon, Tom
Chamberlain, Judeth
Chapman, Denise
Clarke, Helen
Clarke, Jane
Clarke, Jonathan
Cole-Fontayn, Anne Marie
Cole-Fontayn, Florice
Crate, George
Crate, Peter

Davies, Danny
Dunsdon, Alice
Edge, Julian
Edmondson, Peter
Finegan, Conor
Firth, Geraldine
Fisher, Alyce
Ford, Freddie
Forde, Doreen
George, Eric
Godley, Sarah
Godwin, Emma
Goodchild, Prue
Grassly, Richard
Harris, Rachel
Harvie, Becca
Harvie, Rupert
Hawes, Mark
Hawkes, Annette
Hazeltine, Jerry
Heilbron, Catherine
Ingram, Russell
Ivey, Claire
Jackson, Holly
Loates-Taylor, Michael

Lockyer-Nibbs, John
Lynch, Carole
de Mallet-Morgan, Edward
Marsh, Colin
Metson, Ann
Miller, Vikki
Morland, Angela
Morland, Nigel
Mulnier, Henrietta
Norton, Fraser
Norton, Lynne
O'Reilly Hyland, Edmund
O'Reilly Hyland, Susanna
Pain, Jean
Piper, Zoe
Potts, Elizabeth
Radcliffe, David
Rand, Graham
Regester, Shelagh
Sasserath, Jacqui
Saxton, Gretta
Scott, Sue
Skinner, Peter
Sprake, James
Sprake, Louise

Tetley, Mr & Mrs Brian
Thomas, Martin
Tork, Kevin
Trinder, Fred
Tyrrell, Kate
Wallace, Glenn
Welch, Mark
Westaway, Julian
Williams, Jane
Williams, Rose
Wilson, Penny
Winch, Andrew
Winser, Charlotte
Womersley, Jenny
Womersley, Julian
Yeomans, Bonnie
York, Maureen

DONATIONS ALSO RECEIVED FROM:
Davey, June
Fisk, Yvonne
Knight, David
Lady Prideaux
Thomas, Martin
Wates, Andrew

Surrey Union Hunt Supporters' Club

Chairwoman:	Sharan Braham
Vice-Chairwoman:	Bonnie Yeomans
Treasurer:	Fraser Norton
Secretary:	Jane Robinson
Committee:	Fund Raiser: Simon Autie
	Catering: Sue Porter

Merchandise: Becky Seviour
Terrier Show: Keith Nickolson [co-opted]

Marquee: Tricia Bicknell
ex officio Mastership Representative: Jeremy Gumbley MFH

Appendix: 13 – List of Masters Surrey Union Hunt to date

Year	Master	Kennels	Remarks
Before 1798	Mr Leech's Hounds	Lea Park, near Godalming	A private pack of foxhounds.
	Mr Godschall's Hounds	Dogkennel Lane, Albury	A private pack of foxhounds.
1798	Mr Godschall		Amalgamation of Mr Leech's and Mr Godschall's packs to form the Union Hunt.
1802-12	The Rev. Hugh Onslow	East Clandon	Kennels provided by Colonel Sumner MP
1812-?	Captain Boulton		
?-1815	John Barnard Hankey 'The Squire'	East Clandon & Fetcham Park	New kennels at Fetcham Park built in 1814
1815-22	Mr Thomas Seawell		
1822-31	Captain Richard Boulton		Perhaps the same Capt Boulton as 1812?
1831-42	John Barnard Hankey		'The Squire'
1842-58	Colonel Holme Sumner	Fetcham Park	Colonel Sumner - son-in-law to Mr Hankey
1858-66	Capt. Francis Barnard Hankey RN		Colonel Sumner & Francis Hankey were brothers-in-law
1866-76	The Hon. Francis Scott	Send	
1876-82	Mr John Barnard Hankey	Fetcham Park	
1882-84	Mr W Farnell Watson		
1884-86	Colonel Pilkington Blake	Worcester Park	
1886-97	Mr Thomas H Bennett	Cobham Court	
1897-98	Mr A H Tritton		
1898-99	Mr A Labouchère		
1899-00	Major Henry Goulburn		
1900	Messrs T H Bennett and G H Longman		Mr Bennett died before the opening meet in 1900
1900-04	Mr George H Longman	Bookham	New kennels leased from Lord Ashcombe in 1902
1904-07	Mr F G D Colman		
1907-08	Messrs F G D Colman & E Murray		Mr Colman was abroad, hence the appointment of a joint-Master
1908-10	Mr F G D Colman		
1910-13	Mr E Murray		
1913-18	Mr A H Tritton		
1918-19	Mr H C Lee-Steere		
1919-27	Messrs H C Lee-Steere & C E Heath OBE	Oakwood Hill	These kennels formerly occupied by Mr Lee–Steere's hounds
1927-30	Major F C G Naumann MC & Mr C E Heath		

Year	Master		Remarks
1919-27	Messrs H C Lee-Steere & C E Heath		
1927-30	Major F C G Naumann MC & Mr C E Heath		
1930-36	Major H D Roberts & Mr C E Heath		
1936-37	Major H D Roberts, Mr C E Heath & Major P G Evelyn		
1937-39	Major P G Evelyn & Mr C E Heath		Mr Heath died 1939. Mr Evelyn hunted hounds on bye days
1939-40	Colonel Bridges & Mrs Evelyn		Hunt establishment put on austerity regime after this season
1940-45	Major & Mrs Roberts	Kennels at Oakwood Hill	Acting Masters for the remainder of the war period.
1945-50	Messrs N C Tritton & Roger W Sewill		
1950-55	Messrs R W Sewill & H M Gordon Clark		
1955-58	Messrs R W Sewill & R Dutton-Forshaw		
1958-60	Messrs R Dutton-Forshaw & Mrs M Stuart-Hunt		Mrs Stuart-Hunt was the first lady joint-Master and then in 1960, the first, sole, lady Master.
1960-66	Mrs M Stuart-Hunt		
1966-67	Mrs M Stuart-Hunt & Miss J Biggs		
1967-69	Mrs M Stuart-Hunt & Mrs J Bolton [née Biggs]		Mrs Bolton died in 1969
1969-71	Mrs Elizabeth Armstrong		
1971-76	Mrs E Armstrong & Mr P W W Parker		
1977-80	Messrs P W W Parker, M G M Taylor & R Davidson		
1980-81	Messrs P W W Parker & M G M Taylor		
1981-84	Messrs P W W Parker, M G M Taylor & Mrs R Peters		
1984-87	Mr M G M Taylor & Mrs R Peters		
1987-90	Mr M G M Taylor, Mrs R Peters & Mr N Fawcett		
1990-91	Messrs A Drysdale & R C A Hammond, Mrs P Goodchild & Mr J Funnell		Mr Funnell hunted hounds
1991-92	Messrs A Drysdale & R C A Hammond, Mrs P Goodchild, Messrs J Funnell & M G Sprake		
1992-93	Mr R C A Hammond, Mrs P Goodchild, Messrs J Funnell & M G Sprake		
1993-96	Mr R C A Hammond, Mrs P Goodchild, Messrs M G Sprake & I R Gilchrist		Mr Sprake hunted hounds until the end of season 1997-98
1996-98	Messrs R C A Hammond, M G Sprake, I R Gilchrist & Mrs K Meller		
1998-02	Messrs R C A Hammond, M G Sprake, I R Gilchrist, Mrs K Meller & Mr J Ford		
2002 to date	Messrs M G Sprake, I R Gilchrist, Mrs K Meller & Messrs E O'Reilly-Hyland & J Gumbley		

Acknowledgements

This work is founded on the first serious history of the Surrey Union Hunt produced in 1957 by the late Ruth Sewill, who has proved to be a meticulous and accurate chronicler. Without her pioneering efforts, this book simply would not have been possible.

A further debt is owed to all those people, both living and dead, who bothered to keep a record or make a note of contemporary events. Just as vital, arguably, are their successors who decided to keep such ephemera intact. Without those papers and manuscripts, there would be no authentic material worthy of research and recovery.

A great many people have contributed time, effort and memories during the compilation of the manuscript and I am most grateful to each and every one of them. My questions have frequently been at odd hours and often impertinent. In this regard, the equanimity shown by Ricky Bennett when quizzed about his antecedents at 5.30 am on a hunting morning in August 2006 was particularly memorable.

My special appreciation goes to: Ian & Mandy Agnew; Luiz Ataide; the staff of the British Library Newspaper Reading Room at Colindale, especially Nasia Ruhomutally, who rescued me from folly with photocopy machines; Sian Woodward at the British Postal Museum & Archive; Lizzie Calvert; Yolanda Carslaw; Maureen Cole [née O'Donoghue]; Anne Marie Cole-Fontayn; John Coussmaker; Dorking Museum and the Dorking Local History Group, especially Mary Turner and Alan Jackson, an expert on Surrey railways; Veronica Toner at East Surrey & Sussex Newspapers; William and Pippa Funnell; Jean Hazeltine; Diana Hewitt [née Goddard]; the editor of *Horse & Hound*, Lucy Higginson, for her gracious support and to her PA, the ever cheerful Jenny Sims; Ian Gilchrist MFH and the staff at Hartley Fowler; Sarah Godley; Janice Gumbley; Ron Hancock; the late James, Lord Hamilton of Dalzell; Leatherhead Museum and the Leatherhead History Society, especially John Morris, Alan Pooley and Ed Tims; Katharine Meller MFH; the National Library of Scotland, Edinburgh; the National Portrait Gallery, London, in particular Helen Trompeteler; Rosemary Peters; Steve Porter; Tessa Radcliffe, for her inspired thoughts that led to the title; Brendon Sewill; Mark Sprake MFH; the Mervyn H. Sterne Library, Birmingham, Alabama USA; the Surrey History Service, especially Julian Pooley, Duncan Mirylees and the staff at Surrey History Centre, Woking; the Surrey Library Service, especially all those patient ladies in Redhill; Elizabeth Vandeleur-Boorer [née Coussmaker]; the Wiltshire & Swindon Record Office, in particular Martyn Henderson.

A specific acknowledgement is made to David Radcliffe, who first suggested the project and undertook much initial research. The fruits of his labour are to be found in several chapters. He also obtained the necessary venture capital from the generous sponsors and kindly arranged an introduction to the occupants of Cobbett's Farm.

Finally, three people need to be singled out for their particular help and generosity. The first is Jane '*but I don't do history*' Williams, who has gone on to demonstrate time and again not only that she does, but is also tenacious as a terrier when it comes to research. Her work on postal marks during the reigns of George IV and William IV was breathtaking. She is an ace photographer, too. The second is Nick Onslow. He is, in addition to being a lover of books and hunting, just brilliant at design, layout and all that sort of malarkey. His contribution to this project has been immeasurable and I shall miss our clandestine meetings in motorway service areas. Last, but by no means least, is my wife, Lindsay. She has had to put up with tales of yesteryear [and, it seems, not all of them were interesting] for far too long, whilst our home slowly crumbles around us.

The errors, misunderstandings and omissions are all my own, as are the various opinions expressed in the text.

J.S.W.

Acknowledgement is also made to the following photographers or keepers of collections for the use of their illustrations: David Bebber [38]; Jonathan Clarke [(iv)]; Maureen Cole [95,97(lower),98(top)]; the Covertcoat collection [1,6,7 (lower),9,14(lower),35,66]; Dorking Local History Group [30,36,56, 63,64]; Dale Durfee [39,40-41,42(top left, mid lower),43(top left), 44,86(top left, right),87(top),91(lower)]; Sarah Godley [43(right),83]; Horse & Hound [(v)]; Leatherhead History Society [16(right),45]; Valerie Martin [16(left & mid)]; The National Library of Australia [99(lower)]; The National Portrait Gallery [4]; Keith Nickolson [78(right)];Céline Philibert of Céline Photography [(iii),42(mid top),86(mid lower) 91(top)]; Brendon Sewill [57,58,105(lower)]; Dudley Styles ARPS Dorking [62,65]; Surrey History Service [2,7(top),10,11,14(top),18,19,28(top),31,32,34,103,104,105(top),119]; Rodney West [71,78(lower left)]; Jane Williams [(viii),13,37,42(lower left, right),43(lower left, middle),76,86(left lower, mid top),87(lower),88, 90,91(top),96].

Bibliography

Apsley MFH, the Lady Viola, *The Fox-Hunter's Bedside Book* - Eyre & Spottiswoode London 1949

Arigho, Bernie [editor], *Twentieth Century Holmwood* - Holmwood Village Produce Association 2000

Biographical Press, The [publishers], *British Hunts and Huntsmen in four volumes: The South-East, East, and Eastern Midlands of England* - London 1909

Bradley, Cuthbert, *The Foxhound of the Twentieth Century* - George Routledge & Sons Ltd, London 1914

Bray, William, *The Diaries of William Bray, Esq* 1760-1800

British Railways, *British Railways Magazine Southern Region: Vol. 2.9* page 164, September 1951

Brock MFH, David W E, *The Foxhunter's Week-End Book* - Seeley Service, various editions, esp. 1939 - [In my opinion, the most informative and enjoyable book on foxhunting ever written - JSW]

Brown, Thomas, *The Complete Modern Farrier* - John Grant Edinburgh [31st Edition] 1900

Chambers Ltd, W & R [publishers], *Chambers Twentieth Century Dictionary of the English Language* - London 1905

Clarke, John, *The Life and Times of George III* - Weidenfeld & Nicolson Ltd London 1972

Cobbett, William, *Rural Rides* - various editions, especially Everyman's Library J M Dent & Sons London 1966

Dickens, Charles [Jnr], *Dickens's Dictionary of London* - [pub. unknown] 1879

Dorking Local History Group , *Dorking History - No. 13 1995* - Dorking Museum 1995

Dorking History - The Journal of the Dorking Local History Group 1999 - Dorking Museum 1999: *The Journal of the Dorking Local History Group 2000* - Dorking Museum 2000

Harding, Keith, *Dorking and District in Old Photographs* - Alan Sutton Publishing Ltd Stroud Gloucestershire
Betchworth Within Living Memory - Goodness Gracious Surrey 2001

Harrod, John, *'Up The Dorking' - Southern Notebook 88*, page 227. Winter 1986, Southern Railway Group

Janaway, John, *Surrey: A Photographic Record 1850-1920* - Countryside Books Newbury Berkshire 1984

Hunter, A B de M., *Gentlemen of Merstham and Gatton* - The Book Guild, Lewes, Sussex 1993

Jennings, A; Robson, J & Weller, L. , *300 Years of Hunting in Surrey and Sussex* - [pub. unknown] 1991

Kelly, Ian, *Beau Brummell -The Ultimate Dandy* - Hodder & Stoughton Ltd, London 2005

London, Brighton & South Coast Railway, *Special Traffic Notice 36*, for the week ending 23rd March 1907

Maldon, H E [Editor], *The Victoria History of the County of Surrey* - Archibald Constable & Co Westminster 1902

Marsh, Sam, *Hunting, Showing and 'Chasing* - Jarrolds Publishers London Ltd 1939 [?]

Menzies, Mrs Stuart, *Lord William Beresford - Some Memories of a Famous Sportsman, Soldier and Wit* - Herbert Jenkins Ltd London 1917

Mitchell, Vic & Smith, Keith, *Branch Lines to Horsham* - Middleton Press Midhurst West Sussex 1982

Molyneaux, Jack, *Thirty Years a Hunt Servant* - Hutchinson & Co London 1935

Nightingall, Arthur, *My Racing Adventures* - T. Werner Laurie, Clifford's Inn London 1934 [?]

Norris, W S., *'Steam Days in Southern England'* - Trains Annual 1954 Ian Allen Ltd 1954

Osmer, William -, *A Dissertation on Horses* - T Waller, London 1756

Pye-Smith, Charlie, *Rural Rights - Hunting and the Politics of Prejudice* - All Party Parliamentary Middle Way Group 2006

Ray, Cyril [editor], *Robert Smith Surtees - Scenes and Characters* - The Falcon Press London 1948

Rowe, John [publisher], *Hand-Book of Dorking* (2nd Edition) Dorking 1858

Sassoon, Siegfried, *Memoirs of a Fox-hunting Man* - Faber & Faber Ltd London 1928

Sewill, Ruth, *Surrey Union Hunt* - [pub. unknown] 1957

Sewill, Ruth & Lane, Elisabeth, *The Freemen of Charlwood* - Rose Garland Press 1951

Smith MFH, Thomas, *Extracts from the Diary of a Huntsman* - [pub. unknown] 1838

"Sontech", *Surrey Union Hunt* - various editions, Chase and Hunting Association Pyramid Press, early 1950s

Sporting Magazine, The: A Monthly Calendar of the Transactions of the Turf, the Chase and every other Diversion Interesting to the Man of Pleasure, Enterprise and Spirit - various, but particularly Volumes for the years 1796-1803 & 1830-31. [There is more research to be done here.]

Surrey Local History Council, *Surrey History Vol. IV, No.4* - Phillimore & Co Chichester 1992

Surtees, Robert Smith, *Jorrocks's Jaunts and Jollities* - 1838
Handley Cross - 1843
Analysis of the Hunting Field - 1846

Trollope, Anthony, *Hunting Sketches* - 1865 various editions, esp. Hutchinson & Co London with The Golden Head USA 1934

Watson, J P N, *Victorian and Edwardian Field Sports From Old Photographs* - B T Batsford Ltd London 1978

Watt, S A, *'Deelfontein - A hospital in the Karoo during the Anglo-Boer War, a cemetery today'* Military History Journal Vol. 7:4 December 1987 - The South African Military History Society [Die Suid-Afrikaanse Krygshistoriese Vereniging]

Welcome, John, *The Sporting World of R S Surtees* - Oxford University Press 1982

Welsh, Robert [editor], *Galloping Through Punch* - David & Charles Newton Abbot 1976

Wisden [The Cricketers' Almanack] - various editions, esp. 1877, 1885, 1916, 1918, 1964 & 1977

LIST OF SUBSCRIBERS TO THE FIRST EDITION

—◆—

Ian & Mandy Agnew
Imogen Alland
Andrew C. Ayres
David Barnes
Mr & Mrs Richard Barnes
Clare Blomeley
Hugh, Jan, Charlie, Daniel & Bart Burkitt
Mrs. Belinda Burt
Jill Burt
Jane & Jonathan Clarke
Daniel Davies
Mr. Geoff Dorsett
Arthur & Trisha Eales
Richard & Anne Eschelby
Richard Gan
Ian Gilchrist MFH
Richard Grassly
Jeremy Gumbley MFH

Mrs. V. Harrison
Rebecca Harvie
Wim Hautekiet
Jean Hazeltine
Norman Heriz-Jones
Lady Elizabeth Huntly
Graham Jackman
David Knight
Gordon Lee-Steere
Nancy & Michael Loates-Taylor
Mr. J. B. Lockyer-Nibbs
Sebastian Madden
Tommy de Mallet Morgan
Mrs. K. Meller MFH
Mrs. J. Miller
Nigel Morland
Danny Murphy
David & Maria Noel Ogilvie-Kee

Edmund O'Reilly Hyland MFH
Susanna O'Reilly Hyland
Tessa Radcliffe
Mrs. Sue Raymond
Jacqui Sasserath
Sue Scott
Mark Sprake MFH
Louise Sprake
Pam Tetley
Elaine Thompson
Patrick Thompson
Mr. F. C. Trinder MM
Sally Waller
Mrs. Sue Ward
Andrew Wates
The late George Whittick
Penny Wilson
Lindsay, Jenny & James Womersley

—◆—

Together with the very generous help from The Surrey Union Hunt Supporters' Club, without which publication of this book would not have been possible.

The Surrey Union Hunt
Going strong since 1798